SOCIAL PROBLEMS AND THE SOCIOLOGICAL IMAGINATION

A PARADIGM FOR ANALYSIS

David R. Simon

Professor of Sociology
and Criminal Justice Administration
San Diego State University

Research Associate
University of California, Berkeley

D0061207

McGRAW-HILL, INC.

New York   St. Louis   San Francisco   Auckland   Bogotá
Caracas   Lisbon   London   Madrid   Mexico City   Milan
Montreal   New Delhi   San Juan   Singapore   Sydney   Tokyo   Toronto

To My Father, Lewis Morris Simon,
who died as this book was being written.
I miss you, Dad.

This book was set in Times Roman by ComCom, Inc.
The editors were Jill S. Gordon, Katherine Blake, and Elaine Rosenberg;
the production supervisor was Paula Keller.
The cover was designed by Larry Didona.
The photo editor was Anne Manning.
R. R. Donnelley & Sons Company was printer and binder.

SOCIAL PROBLEMS AND THE SOCIOLOGICAL IMAGINATION

A Paradigm for Analysis

This book is printed on recycled, acid-free paper containing 10% postconsumer waste.

2 3 4 5 6 7 8 9 0 DOC DOC 9 0 9 8 7 6 5 4

ISBN 0-07-057623-8

Library of Congress Cataloging-in-Publication Data

Simon, David R., (date).
    Social problems and the sociological imagination: a paradigm for
analysis / David R. Simon.
      p.   cm.
    Includes bibliographical references (p.   ) and index.
    ISBN 0-07-057623-8
    1. Sociology.   2. Social problems—United States.   3. Mills, C.
Wright (Charles Wright), 1916–1962. The sociological imagination.
   I. Title.
HM51.S538   1995
301—dc20   94-30656

THE AUTHOR'S SINCERE GRATITUDE IS EXPRESSED TO THE FOLLOWING SOURCES FOR PERMISSION TO REPRINT MATERIAL REPRODUCED IN THIS BOOK:

Allyn & Bacon, Figure 2-1 in Chapter 2, and textual material from David R. Simon and D. Stanley Eitzen, *Elite Deviance,* fourth edition, 1993 © Allyn & Bacon.

Dr. Inge P. Bell, material from pages 135–36, 140–41, and 154–55, *This Book Is Not Required* (Fort Bragg, California: The Small Press) © 1985, 1991 by Inge P. Bell.

The Hellen Dwight Reed Educational Foundation, portions of my article "Ideology Awareness Project," *Teaching Political Science,* July 1981, pages 458–62.

McGraw-Hill, material from pages 18–23 of Warren Farrell's *Why Men Are the Way They Are* © 1986 by Warren Farrell.

ABOUT THE AUTHOR

DAVID R. SIMON is Professor of Criminal Justice Administration and Sociology at San Diego State University and Research Associate in Sociology at the University of California, Berkeley. Dr. Simon has authored dozens of articles in a wide variety of academic journals and is also author of *Ideology and Sociology, Crimes of the Criminal Justice System* (with Joel Henderson), and *Elite Deviance,* 5th edition, 1995, in press. Dr. Simon received his doctorate in sociology in 1975 from Rutgers University and was National Institute of Alcohol Abuse and Alcoholism Postdoctoral Fellow in 1983–84 at the University of California, Berkeley School of Public Health's Alcohol Research Group.

CONTENTS

PREFACE

Almost every student who takes an introductory course in sociology learns about C. Wright Mills and *The Sociological Imagination*. Sadly, this initial experience with Mills seldom goes any further. It has always puzzled me that Mills's paradigm is celebrated as the essence of the sociological worldview when so few sociologists have ever used it. Mills's work is only slightly dated in this post–Cold War world. He remains in many ways a voice in the wilderness.

One of Mills's great contributions to sociology is his synthesis of what he termed the classic tradition. Mills emphasized that all the classical sociologists investigated social structure, history's "main drift," and the varieties of men and women society was producing. The classic tradition provided a beginning to sociological inquiry. What Max Weber, Emile Durkheim, Karl Marx, and others provided were models from which theories and hypotheses could be derived. The models did not need to be "correct." They could and should, Mills thought, be subjected to continual reinterpretation.

The classic tradition was, for Mills, the beginning of an inquiry into the relationship between private troubles and public issues. What Mills provided American sociologists was important answers to questions about structure, history, and biography. His concepts of the power elite and mass society, the postmodern era, and the cheerful robot were ahead of their time. Today Mills is remembered largely for pointing out that the military-industrial complex made the "big" decisions in American life. Postmodern culture is being thoroughly examined by a host of disciplines, but only rarely is Mills mentioned as its pioneer investigator.

What is most unappreciated, perhaps, is that Mills's paradigm represents a viable model for the analysis of social problems. To paraphrase one of the early reviewers of this manuscript, it's surprising that no one has thought of using it in this way before. This use of the sociological imagination requires students to be well grounded in Mills's sociology. I have attempted to provide such a grounding in this book. Each chapter centers on one of the basic concepts of the paradigm (structure, biography and alienation, historical main drift, ideology, social change).

I have also provided two exercises at the end of each chapter. The first exercise is brief, designed for classes in which multiple exercises can be used. The second exercise is appropriate for classes in which term projects are assigned. Most of the latter exercises involve content analysis and study of the mass media. I believe that content analysis is an ideal method for undergraduates. A representative sample of materials can be gathered and analyzed without the need for a research grant, time-consuming interviews or observations, or costly research assistants. I have designed exercises that my students have told me were fun and interesting, a welcome relief from the traditional research paper.

I have spent considerable space in this book analyzing social character (biography) and alienation. These two concepts rarely figure in analyses of social problems, yet Mills considered them essential to an understanding of the relationship between private troubles and social problems. The idea of social character is like an iceberg: it comes up above the intellectual surface every few years, only to sink into obscurity until the next Christopher Lasch or Robert Bellah redeems it. Social character and the alienation that characterizes it are much too important to the study of social problems to be left to fads of social criticism. As Chapters 3, 4, and 6 make clear, an understanding of social character is an important element in both self-help and societal analysis.

The sociological imagination, at its heart, is about the interrelationships of the individual, the immediate milieu, and the macro environments that compose social life. Too many students, including sociology majors, have difficulty grasping the sociological. This is another reason why the idea of social character is so crucial. Once the sociological nature of individualism and the social problems caused by it are understood, an appreciation of the sociological is possible. Until this appreciation is achieved, sociology often remains mysterious in this, the most ideologically individualistic of societies. Thus much of what I have to say in the chapters ahead is about American individualism as myth and as a cause of social ills.

Employing Mills's categories in the way I have done here has made me painfully aware that Mills explored some subjects much more deeply than others. Mills spends less than a paragraph in *The Sociological Imagination* on what causes social problems. Thus in some places I have had to fill in gaps with contemporary analysis that complements Mills's central ideas. I have found that the idea of social problems as social harms is useful. Certainly harms are what Mills had in mind when he spoke of genuine crises, as opposed to phony manipulations.

This book is informed by my earlier work in the tradition of C. Wright Mills, especially *Elite Deviance,* which I cite and borrow freely from throughout. This was essential in explaining the macro-micro links in social problem analysis.

Finally, I believe, as Judith Richman pointed out in her analysis of this manuscript, that students understand social problems best when they can relate those problems to their personal experiences. I have attempted to merge self-help and social change into one interrelated discussion. In Chapter 6, which constitutes my effort at a sociology of self-help, I analyze two topics central to the lives of most students: love and career. Here I have had the pleasure of using the ideas of Inge Bell, whose *This Book Is Not Required* I cite throughout.

This book is written in a spirit of optimism and exploration. It approaches the study of social problems as an adventure in exploration of both self and society. It is also written in the confidence that the great crises of our age are resolvable.

ACKNOWLEDGMENTS

Aside from C. Wright Mills, to whom I owe a great intellectual debt, many people have offered encouragement and stimulating ideas that have aided me immensely in writing this book. Joel Henderson, my co-author of *Crimes of the Criminal Justice System,* helped write Chapters 4, 5, and 6 of this book and played devil's advocate throughout.

A number of my sociological and criminological colleagues deserve my heartfelt thanks, especially Abraham Blumberg. Abe's constant assurance that "C. Wright got it right" has never left my thoughts. Abe and Ron Boostrom read early drafts of this work and were generous in their praise. I also sincerely thank John Wozniak, Frank Cullen, David Fredericks, Marty Schwartz, and Jim Messerschmidt for their valuable advice. In addition, special thanks is due Judith Richman for her excellent suggestions and kind encouragement.

A special word of appreciation is due the members of the Department of Sociology at the University of California, Berkeley. This department has generously provided use of its facilities, and many of its faculty have discussed this project with me. Special thanks are extended to Marty Sanchez-Jankowsky, William Kornhauser, and Troy Duster. I am also grateful for the advice and friendship of Berkeley alumnus Bob Dunn at Cal State Hayward.

My sincere thanks to the staff at McGraw-Hill. My editors, Phil Butcher and Jill Gordon, have been supportive and encouraging throughout. Linda Gal has kindly tolerated my questions and unusual notions. All deserve appreciation for their willingness to gamble on this venture.

I would also like to express my appreciation to Editing Supervisor Elaine Rosenberg and my copy editor Barbara Salazar for a masterful job (and their great patience) in assisting me in this unique venture.

The following reviewers offered many helpful comments and suggestions: Susan Chambre, CUNY–Baruch College; Cheryl Gray Kimberling, Tarrant County Junior College; Janet Hope, Eastern Illinois University; Frances Reader, Arizona State University; Judith Richman, University of Illinois at Chicago; Dean G. Rojek, University of Georgia; Ellen Rosengarten, Sinclair Community College; Edward Silva, El Paso Community College; and Joan Cook Zimmern, College of Saint Mary.

Most important, I am grateful for the love and support of my patiently impatient wife, Carol. She has labored mightily to provide an atmosphere of calm encouragement within which this project could reach fruition. My children, Molly, Danny, and Joshua Simon, all listened to my agonies and ecstasies as this work progressed. My love to you all.

David R. Simon

1

SOCIAL PROBLEMS AND THE SOCIOLOGICAL IMAGINATION

AMERICA'S PROBLEMS: TROUBLES OR CRISES?

There are times in the life of every civilization when it must either honestly confront the realities or face its decline (Phillips, 1990, 1993; Ehrenreich, 1990:196–207). During such moments:

- Myths created by the mass media must be separated from realities.
- Political rhetoric must be divorced from forthright evaluation of the political process.
- Myths about family, education, religion, and community must be distinguished from the actual events occurring in those institutions.

These times also require that the origins of the crises of personal life be properly related to the social problems from which they stem. We live in an era of crises and confusion.

America's "main drift" (master trend) today is toward economic, political, social, and ethical crisis, and the nation is "declining at an alarming rate" (Schaef, 1988:3). This decline is the subject of daily headlines. Consider what now occurs on an average day among American youth.[1]

- 2738 unmarried teenagers bear children.
- 2000 teens attempt suicide.

[1]The following lists are base on information in *Scandal Annual* (1989).

- 4.4 million youths consume illegal drugs or alcohol.
- 5200 children aged 10 to 17 are arrested.
- 5500 adolescents run away from home, and 14,000 drop out of school.
- Children 13 and under collectively watch 192 million hours of TV, yet the average mother spends eleven minutes per day with her offspring, the average father eight minutes per day with his.
- 800,000 high school seniors are unable to read.

Consider the dimensions of an average day's crime and drug problem:

- Employees steal $34 million from employers.
- Organized crime reaps nearly $250 million.
- Arsonists torch 225 buildings.
- Street criminals steal nearly $11 million from victims while engaging in about 82,000 criminal acts against property.
- Criminals assault 12,000 people and rape 2430 women.
- Americans smoke 87,000 bales of marijuana, snort 380 pounds of cocaine, and pay drug dealers $123 million.
- More than 1,000 Americans die from the effects of cigarette smoking, *the single most preventable cause of death in America.*

Meanwhile, at the highest strata of society:

- Corporations illegally take in $550 million.
- Individual white-collar criminals steal $110 million.
- Prosecutors indict five public officials on corruption charges.
- Industry produces 15 billion pounds of hazardous waste.
- Over 2500 people lose their jobs.

Finally, episodes of wrongdoing spread cynicism and pessimism throughout the land (Kanter & Mirvis, 1989; Goldfarb, 1991; Garment, 1991):

- Hate crimes make headlines almost daily. Among the latest incidents are the murders of foreign tourists in Florida. Arsonists set off firestorms in southern California, forcing the rich and famous to evacuate or risk death. Teens in San Francisco set a sleeping homeless man afire for fun.
- U.S. officials indict the Panamanian dictator for taking drug smugglers' payoffs while in the employ of the CIA.
- The State Department dismisses an employee for searching the passport file of the mother of a presidential candidate.
- The savings and loan scandal is the largest financial crisis in the nation's history, with costs estimated to run as high as $1 trillion. About 40 percent of the savings and loan failures were due to fraud and corruption.
- The nation is experiencing its longest economic slump since the Great Depression while American corporations export jobs to Third World nations.

Meanwhile, American executives are paid almost 300 times more than the average worker.

• In 1992, Oliver Stone's movie *JFK* sparks renewed interest in the 1963 assassination of President Kennedy. A poll taken at the time of the movie's release indicates that nearly 70 percent of the public believes that either the Central Intelligence Agency or the American military, or both, murdered their own commander in chief (*Time,* January 13, 1992, p. 56). The willingness of the public to doubt the government's version of events underscores the increasing loss of the government's legitimacy in the eyes of its citizens. Many Americans doubt that even the release of all classified files in the case will reveal the truth behind the crime.

One could easily expand this list of crises into a catalog of social problems. Yet merely extending a laundry list of crises both societal and personal would

President John Kennedy and Mrs. Kennedy arriving in Dallas on November 22, 1963. President Kennedy may have been the last president most living Americans truly admired. Issues concerning who fired the shots that killed him that day have been debated for over 30 years. About 90 percent of Americans feel that his assassination involved a conspiracy, and nearly 75 percent think government agencies were part of that conspiracy. The manner in which the government-appointed Warren Commission handled the investigation into President Kennedy's murder was so controversial that it contributed to doubts about the official findings. (UPI/Bettmann)

not help us understand the origins and possible solutions of social issues. What are the public attitudes regarding the causes and solutions of such conditions? What, in this nation that considers itself the greatest experiment in democracy in world history, are the people's reactions to these multiple crises? What impact have these conditions had on the public mind?

PUBLIC RESPONSES TO THE CRISES OF OUR AGE

In late 1990, two advertising researchers asked a representative sample of 2000 American adults 1800 questions regarding what they really believed about their lives. James Patterson and Peter Kim (1991) asked people about a wide range of individual beliefs and behaviors, as well as about leading economic, political, and social problems. The results were so startling that they made headlines in newspapers across the nation. The findings reveal that the majority of Americans suffer a crisis of belief.

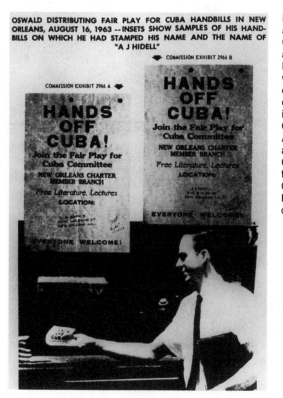

OSWALD DISTRIBUTING FAIR PLAY FOR CUBA HANDBILLS IN NEW ORLEANS, AUGUST 16, 1963 -- INSETS SHOW SAMPLES OF HIS HAND-BILLS ON WHICH HE HAD STAMPED HIS NAME AND THE NAME OF "A J HIDELL"

COMMISSION EXHIBIT 2966 A

COMMISSION EXHIBIT 2966 B

Lee Harvey Oswald was accused by the Warren Commission of being the lone assassin who killed President Kennedy. However, Oswald was no loner. He had extensive ties to New Orleans organized crime figures, who included his own uncle. Oswald also had ties to American intelligence agencies and to anti-Castro Cubans who were being funded and trained by the Central Intelligence Agency. His real motives remain hotly debated. (UPI/Bettmann)

A Crisis of Morality   Few, if any, stable values exist on which to base decisions about daily life or social issues. Only 13 percent of Americans believe in all of the Ten Commandments. People now choose which rules they will obey.

There is no longer a moral consensus in the United States, as there was in the 1950s, and "there is very little respect for any rule of law" (Patterson & Kim, 1991:6). Many of the results of their survey support this notion:

• The official crime statistics are off by at least 200 percent. Sixty percent of Americans report being crime victims; over half of those 60 percent report being victimized twice.

• One-fourth of Americans say they would abandon their families for $10 million.

• Two-thirds believe there is nothing wrong with lying, and lie regularly.

• 30 percent of employees have personally witnessed violations of crimi-

Jack Ruby walked into the Dallas police headquarters building 36 hours after Oswald's arrest and shot Oswald (who was surrounded by about 200 armed guards) on national television. Ruby had been a member of organized crime for decades, but his Mafia ties were virtually ignored by the Warren Commission's investigation. (UPI/Bettmann)

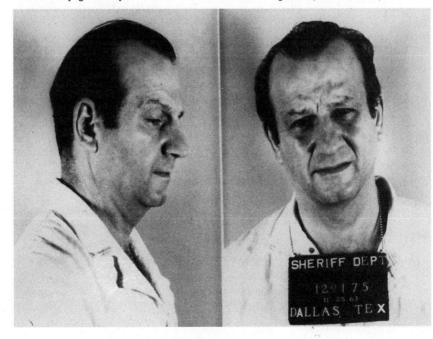

nal or ethical codes by their bosses, and 43 percent say they cannot trust their co-workers.

• 80 percent of Americans want morals and ethics taught in public schools, and a majority believe that the leading cause of America's economic decline is "unethical behavior by [business] executives" (Patterson & Kim, 1991:237).

A Crisis of Confidence in Authority   Public confidence in America's institutions is at an all-time low, and 80 percent of Americans say there are no living heroes. Among the lowest-rated occupations for honesty and integrity are congressional representative and local politician; lawyer; TV evangelist; stockbroker; executives in oil, network television, and labor unions; and car and insurance salespeople.

Item: Studies in 1987 and 1991 detailed what Americans feel about their political system. Americans are deeply alienated from the political life of their nation. When the pollster Lou Harris asked a national sample in 1987 if their interests were represented by politicians, 60 percent said they were not—the highest percentage since Harris first asked the question in 1966 (Harris, 1987:35–37). A 1991 Kettering Foundation study found that most Americans believe there is no point to voting and that money has overwhelming influence in political campaigns, with millions being spent to secure jobs paying $100,000 a year. This sample of respondents believed that media coverage of campaigns alienates voters, partly because of reliance on "sound bites"—politicians' practice of reducing complex public problems to empty slogans (*Seattle Post Intelligencer,* June 11, 1991, p. A-3). Polls taken in 1992 and 1993 reveal that the average American believes that the federal government wastes 48 cents of every dollar, and only 20 percent of the public trust Washington to do the right thing most of the time (down from 76 percent in 1963) (Gore, 1993:1).

Pessimism about the Future of the Nation   Americans feel their nation has become "colder, greedier, meaner, more selfish, and less caring" (Patterson & Kim, 1991:213) and they are markedly pessimistic about the future. How do Americans picture their world in the year 2000?

• 52 percent believe that Japan will be the world's economic world leader.
• 77 percent believe the rich will be richer and the poor, poorer.
• 72 percent believe that crime rates will have risen and 71 percent believe there will be more violence in the streets.
• 62 percent believe the homeless rate will have risen.
• 60 percent feel AIDS will have become epidemic, and 60 percent believe that no cure will have been found.

President Richard Nixon resigning in 1974 as a result of the Watergate scandal. Watergate was really a series of scandals that involved violations of civil rights, illegal electioneering, and acts of personal enrichment. Watergate not only brought down Richard Nixon, it was also a major cause of declining public confidence in government that continues to this day. (UPI/Bettmann)

- 58 percent feel drug and alcohol abuse will have worsened.
- 62 percent see pollution as worse, and 43 percent believe it will be so bad that life will become unbearable.

Item: A majority believe that such social problems as poverty and racism will outlast their children's lifetimes.

Contradictory Beliefs about Individualism and Community   Although most Americans believe that social problems will worsen, they think their private lives will get better. This means that they have become increasingly alienated from what happens to other people and the nation—yet they believe they are patriotic. People believe they are "little islands, that they don't really belong to any larger unit" (Patterson & Kim, 1991:217). They have withdrawn from public issues. Thus from 1965 to 1990, the percentage of Americans who read a daily newspaper fell from 67 percent to 30 percent, and the percentage of people who watched television news fell from 52 percent to 41 percent.

General Richard Secord (upper left), Admiral John Poindexter (upper right), and Lieutenant Colonel Oliver North (lower left) created their own intelligence agency, with its own army, navy, and air force in order to smuggle arms to the Nicaraguan Contras in the 1980s. Much of the money made from the selling of arms to Iran never reached the Contras. The final report on Iran-Contra claimed that key Reagan administration officials, including former President George Bush, lied about their knowledge of this scandal. Iran-Contra was one of many scandals during the Reagan-Bush years. Over 120 elected and appointed members of these administrations resigned under ethical clouds. (Upper left and right: J. L. Atlan/Sygma; lower left: Arnie Sachs/Sygma)

A Crisis of Ideology   A major reason for these pessimistic attitudes is that Americans have little confidence in either the political parties or the dominant schools of ideological thought.

• More Americans now identify themselves as environmentalists (39 percent) than as either Democrats (31 percent) or Republicans (20 percent).

• Only 27 percent of Americans describe themselves as ideologically conservative.

• A mere 9 percent of Americans identify themselves as liberals. Even the 1992 nominee of the Democratic party claimed he was a "centrist."

Yet Americans want to do the right thing to resolve the crises of our age. Half say they would volunteer to help prevent child abuse. Forty-one percent say they would volunteer to help others learn to read. Twenty-nine percent say they would volunteer to clean up the environment, and 66 percent say they would pay more taxes to do so.

Clearly, Americans are troubled and confused about their own values and about the future of the nation. This confusion was recently depicted in a Broadway play that aroused considerable attention, *Twilight of the Golds*. The play is about a couple who, through a recent technological advance, find out the baby they are expecting will probably be born homosexual. (Shortly after the play opened, scientists announced that they had found such a genetic link.) Mrs. Gold makes a speech to the audience about her confusion. Every Sunday, she says, she sits down with the week's issues of the *New York Times* and spends all day reading them. When she finishes, she feels overwhelmed by all the information she has absorbed; she has no way to sort out what it all means. She feels that Americans are so overwhelmed by facts that continually keeping up with the news is of questionable value.

Like Mrs. Gold, people want to help resolve social problems but feel confused about what to do. They feel the leading schools of thought on social problems have failed the nation. We do not need to stop learning about social issues, but we do need a way to analyze and assess them and their impact on our daily lives.

The sociologist C. Wright Mills described the nature of Mrs. Gold's confusion decades before the play was written. Mills once remarked that ours is an era of uneasiness and indifference, a time when people experience their personal lives as a series of traps (Mills, 1959:3). In the 1950s and 1960s Mills warned against the dangers inherent in celebrity worship and mass media addiction, militarism and criminal and unethical behaviors among the nation's leaders, conformity, status seeking, bureaucracy, and alienation. (Mills's work is profiled in Box 1.1.)

Mills believed that ordinary people lack a sociological imagination—an ability (quality of mind) to see the interrelationship of their own lives and the historical period and institutional arrangements (society) in which they live. A sociological imagination allows one to conceive of the relationship between seemingly private troubles and social problems. It encourages its possessor to resolve both personal problems and societal crises. One goal of this book is to stimulate a sociological imagination that can serve as a tool for help with personal problems and for an analysis of societal ills. *The sociological imagination is a mode of critical thinking that will help you to understand how social problems affect you personally.*

The sociological imagination is a paradigm—an orientation for looking at reality. It is also much more. Virtually all schools of thought advocate policies for the resolution of social problems. The sociological imagination is no

BOX 1-1

C. WRIGHT MILLS: PERSPECTIVE AND PARADIGM

C. Wright Mills (1917–1962) was a professor of sociology at Columbia University. In a series of influential books in the 1950s and early 1960s he openly criticized American society, its foreign policy, and many of his fellow sociologists. Yet some people consider Mills "the greatest sociologist the United States has ever produced" (Horowitz, 1963: 20). In *Character and Social Structure* (1953), written with Hans Gerth, Mills developed the sociological model he used to analyze postmodern America. Gerth and Mills argued that institutions select and shape social character (Eldridge, 1983:14; Scimecca, 1977:37).

Mills applied the model in *White Collar* (1951), where he examined the character of white-collar workers and their social structure (the organizations that employed them). The white-collar employees of impersonal business and government bureaucracies, Mills found, were bored at work and lacked satisfying leisure activities.

White Collar is a portrait of the worker as victim. Controlled by bosses, white-collar workers are "cheerful robots." Outwardly they are pleasant, courteous, and helpful to customers and bosses. Psychologically, they suffer self-alienation because their resentment and anger remain hidden. Politicians fail to keep their promises and regularly lie to them, and they are at the mercy of advertisers' appeals. White-collar workers are unaware of their membership in a distinctive class (a potential interest group) and lack an understanding of the larger economic and political institutions that shape their lives.

In *The Power Elite* (1956), a best-seller, Mills gave Americans a horrifying view of America's dominant institutions. Corporations and communications media, portions of the federal government, and the military are interlocked in a "military-industrial complex." The power elites who head these key institutions undemocratically make decisions about war and peace, where to locate factories, how many people to hire for what jobs. Collectively, these elites lack morals. Scandals (flouting of antitrust laws, political corruption) are commonplace. In *The Causes of World War III* (1958) Mills warned of the power elite's preparation for war and their "crackpot realism" (a nuclear war, they determined, was "winnable"). Mills also preached a "pagan sermon" to the clergy, urging them to protest the preparation for a war that could end civilization.

In *The Sociological Imagination* (1959) Mills noted that sociologists (wrongly) attributed social problems to individual deviance. Mills argued that social problems are caused by institutional contradictions, not by deviant individuals.

Mills criticized sociologists' fascination with "grand theories" that are politically conservative and scientifically untestable. He also objected to sociologists' obsession with methodology and measurement, and their neglect of moral issues.

All of Mills's concepts are explored in this book. I hope this discussion will motivate you to read these and other works by Mills.

exception, and its relation to solutions to social problems is discussed in this book's last chapter.

Like any paradigm, the sociological imagination defines "what should be studied, what questions should be asked, and what rules should be followed in interpreting the answers obtained" (Ritzer, 1980:7). At its heart, a paradigm is "a fundamental model that organizes our view" (Babbie, 1989:47) of issues related to the sociological analysis of social problems. These key issues include:

1 A critique (deconstruction) of other paradigms or ideologies, especially their contradictions (Rosenau, 1992:xi).
2 The relationship between personal troubles and social problems.
3 A model for analyzing the relationships between (a) the structure of society, (b) the historical epoch (period) in which that society is located, and (c) the social character (human nature) being produced.
4 A model for the analysis of social problems.

MILLS'S CRITIQUE OF SOCIOLOGY

In the 1940s, when Mills was a college student, both conservative and liberal scholars concerned with social problems unquestioningly accepted the prevailing structure of private property (capitalism) and the American political system as normal and untroubled.

Conservatives of Mills's day were "straightforward moralists, staunch supporters of the virtues of thrift, hard work, sexual purity, and personal discipline" (Skolnick & Currie, 1991:2). Since long before Mills's day, conservative social scientists had concentrated on the "social pathology" of the lower ("dangerous") classes, whose *personal* defects, either biological or moral, caused their poverty, sexual deviance, drug and alcohol abuse, crime, delinquency, mental illness, and suicide. Their analysis focused on nonwhite, non-Protestant, newly arrived immigrant groups from Southern Europe. The conservatives' view of these "nuts, sluts, and 'preverts' " (Liazos, 1993) was colored by the fear that lower-class deviance and crime might throw society into total chaos (anarchy). In fact, many people feared that if newly arrived immigrant factory workers were allowed to congregate in saloons, they would soon be plotting revolution.

Conservatives advocated strict social control of these individuals: harsh prison sentences, incarceration in mental hospitals, the death penalty for serious felons, and (in the 1920s and 1930s) sexual sterilization for everything from stealing chickens to insanity (Simon, 1977, 1981).

A second group of scholars, the liberal reformers, believed that *everyday environments,* especially dysfunctional families and socially disorganized (pathological) neighborhoods, caused social problems (Horton, 1968). Like conservatives, liberals defined social problems as deviations from the rules of "society" (Mills, 1963). Liberals took pity on the lower classes, however, and advocated a series of social welfare measures. These measures included counseling and the joining of various neighborhood groups dedicated to clean living, such as the Boy Scouts and the Girl Scouts (Mills, 1963). The goal of these reforms was to adjust the lower classes to middle-class norms.

In *The Sociological Imagination* Mills recognized three basic units of analysis in sociological research: (1) the conservative focus on individual personalities, (2) the liberal focus on immediate environments, and (3) a larger (macro) sociological environment, which included both cultural values and larger sociological units such as the nation-state, the political economy, and groups of nations. Much of what passed for a "sociological" analysis of social problems, Mills argued, was merely the study of individual personalities, or an analysis of the immediate environment of the family or neighborhood. A study conducted more than thirty years later (Gregg et al., 1980) confirmed that Mills's critique was still valid. Theodor Gregg and his colleagues examined about 500 articles in social problems journals published in 1936, 1956, and 1976 and recorded the unit of analysis used in each study. They found that 60 percent of the studies used the individual as the unit of analysis, 30 percent focused on the immediate environment, and only 10 percent involved macro-level variables.

A genuine sociological analysis of social problems is one that appreciates and interrelates all levels of analysis. A key reason for the lack of sociological imagination can be found in Americans' belief in individualism (Bellah et al., 1986: 10). Our notions of sin, of legal responsibility, and of rights focus on individuals. In a less complex era, perhaps, these ideas seemed progressive. Today these beliefs function largely to mask the workings of a society that is primarily corporate and bureaucratic. The lone individual is somewhat at the mercy of these organizational forces. One reason for this state of affairs is that organizations (the mass media are the prime example) try to define reality for mass audiences. Official views of reality often mystify the causes and solutions of social problems.

MYSTIFICATION

Contradictions are often hidden from public view because the actual values, processes, and goals of organizations are discussed behind closed doors and in classified documents. These actualities are submerged beneath the ideologies of free enterprise, democracy, community, and traditional values. Organizations mystify contradictions and the social problems they engender by denying the structural causes of public issues. Thus layoffs are blamed on greedy workers who refuse to take pay cuts. Massive government indebtedness results not from huge increases in defense spending but from the greedy demands of recipients of "entitlement" programs (which never include the large corporations that receive government subsidies). Mystification is thus often cloaked in an ideology of personal responsibility.

A sociological imagination sometimes invites the charge that one has lost sight of individual responsibility. The responsibility that needs to be emphasized is not the individual's but the organization's and the elite's (a distinction we shall explore in depth later). The power elite's National Advertising Council, for example, used to produce public service messages starring the cartoon character Woodsy Owl. Woodsy informed Americans of a "great" pollution problem. Picnickers were failing to dispose of their litter in garbage cans. Woodsy never bothered to inform us, though, that American corporations generate half of the world's industrial pollution. Polluting firms are a major cause of our fouled waters, dirty air, threatened water supplies, and toxic waste crisis. The environmental crisis is difficult for Americans to confront precisely because their culture lacks a notion of organizational wrongdoing and has created no institutions to counter organizational propaganda concerning the cause of this and numerous other problems.

The National Advertising Council has done its best to convince the public that pollution is the fault of irresponsible picnickers who fail to dispose of their litter properly. A focus on individuals serves to mask the underlying causes of many social problems. Moreover, many individuals suffering from problems that spring from their society remain convinced that their troubles are strictly personal. The relationship between seemingly personal troubles and social problems is a key aspect of the sociological imagination.

PERSONAL TROUBLES AND SOCIAL ENVIRONMENTS: SOCIAL PROBLEMS AS SOCIALLY PATTERNED HARMS

Mills argued that people's personal troubles, their feelings of being trapped and manipulated, their marital and career fortunes, and their goals and ways of achieving those goals are sociological in both origin and consequences. To use the sociological imagination we must be able to interrelate the structural causes of social problems, major trends, private troubles, and social (public) issues that occupy our everyday existence. Such relationships involve:

1 *Personal troubles*—troubles that "occur within the character of the individual and within the range of . . . immediate relations with others; they have to do with [the] self and with those limited areas of social life of which [one] is directly and personally aware" (Mills, 1959:8). Perceptions of and solutions to personal troubles lie within one's immediate environment, one's family, workplace, school, religious organization, or neighborhood. Thus if two college roommates quarrel and decide they no longer wish to room together, each can resolve the problem by finding a more compatible partner, and most college campuses have a place to post "seeking roommate" notices. Thus the problem is resolvable within the immediate environment of the college campus. Social problems, on the other hand, are of a dramatically different nature.

2 *Public issues (social problems)*—issues that transcend the local environments of work, family, and community. Social problems involve a genuine crisis in institutional arrangements. Crises are genuine only when they demand that choices be made about situations that confront a society. Troubles become issues when they become widespread.

Consider unemployment. If, in a society of over 100 million workers, the only people who are unemployed are those who refuse to work, that is a personal trouble. The cause is within the characters of individuals who are either mentally incapacitated or morally wanting. If, however, that society suffers massive layoffs as businesses "downsize" and move factories overseas in search of cheap labor and other financial advantages, sociological forces are clearly at work. No amount of counseling or punishment of errant workers will resolve a crisis of permanent recession.

Consider education. If a few hundred high school students of various backgrounds drop out annually, one can point to various personal deficiencies that inhibit learning. However, when almost 30 percent of the nation's secondary students withdraw before graduation and another 700,000 graduate despite their inability to read and write, then clearly some institutional factors are at work. Insufficient educational achievement is a great financial harm because high school and college graduates' earnings greatly exceed those of high school dropouts.

Consider marriage and the family, those venerable institutions our politicians never tire of telling us are the backbone of American life. If only a few thousand divorces and cases of abuse took place annually, one could conclude that a few dysfunctional personalities needed therapy. However, when half of first-time marriages end in divorce and 4000 spouses and significant others murder each other every year, something is clearly wrong with the institutions of courtship and the family.

Consider street crime. If only a hundred or so murders took place annually, the problem would obviously be a matter of violence-prone individuals. Unfortunately, the United States' homicide rate is ten times higher than that of the entire continent of Europe. Clearly, patterned violence is at work.

Consider corruption. If a few ward politicians in a few cities were on the take, their corruption could be attributed to a deficiency in personal integrity. But what if prosecutors indict five public officials each day, and the nation regularly experiences scandal after scandal? The resolution of recurrent scandal lies within the political process and within the institutions in and outside of government that influence that process.

Finally, consider the seemingly most individualistic of problems, mental illness. If a minute proportion of the population exhibited neurotic symptoms or psychotic episodes, then hormonal imbalances or childhood traumas would be the relevant issues. But when one in five persons is mentally impaired, societal stresses and cultural strains merit examination.

Mills believed that many social problems indicate a "crisis in institutional arrangements" (Mills, 1959:9). Such crises involve what sociologists term macro social problems. Macro-level problems involve "certain economic, political, social, and technological arrangements that have come to prevail [and] are problematic because these arrangements harm millions of people" (Neubeck, 1991:12). Such problems include the maldistribution of global and national resources, global and national environmental pollution, economic inequalities and poverty, political corruption, business fraud, war, unequal access to health care and the justice system, and such constant economic harms as unemployment, inflation, and indebtedness. Another set of macro problems consists of the exploitation of groups of people on the basis of sex, age, race, gender, or handicap.

Micro social problems, in contrast, consist of "the troublesome and troubled behavior of individual societal members" (Neubeck, 1991:13)—such behaviors as drug and alcohol abuse, suicide, mental illness, street crime (including violent crimes inside and outside families), and sexual deviance (child pornography, child molestation, incest).

An essential aspect of both macro and micro social problems is that they are harmful. Social problems are *objectively* harmful conditions. In other words, the harms involved can be measured or counted. These measurable harms are of three types (Schrager & Short, 1978):

1. *Physical harms:* physical injury, illness, death.

2. *Financial harms:* robbery, fraud, and various scams that are not legally defined as fraud but that nevertheless cause consumers and investors to be deprived of their funds without receiving the goods or services for which they contracted.

3. *Moral harm:* deviant behavior by elites (people who head governmental and corporate institutions) that encourages deviance, distrust, cynicism, or alienation among the rest of the population.

Before Richard Nixon resigned from the presidency in 1974, for example, his administration had been involved in a broad range of deviant acts: burglarizing of the headquarters of the Democratic National Committee, attempts to rig elections, lying to Congress and the American people about the secret illegal bombing of Cambodia, bribery, and tax evasion (Simon, 1992; Simon & Eitzen, 1993). After the Watergate scandal and Nixon's resignation, confidence in government fell dramatically, and it has never recovered (Simon & Eitzen, 1993: 3–7).

Not all harmful conditions are social problems. Harms become social problems only if they are socially patterned. Socially patterned harms are traits, characteristics, or behaviors exhibited by groups of people or institutions. Emile Durkheim described one such pattern when he studied suicide in European countries. He found the highest suicide rates among people of certain characteristics: unmarried civilian Protestant males with a high level of education who lived in cities. Durkheim also found that the suicide rate rose in times of economic recession and during times of dramatically increasing prosperity (Durkheim, 1951; Walton, 1993:68–69).

If harms are suffered at high rates with regularity by groups of people with certain characteristics and in specific historical circumstances, they may be said to be socially patterned. If harms are socially patterned, they must, it follows, be caused by social conditions. A recognition of such conditions is a key element of the sociological imagination.

The idea that social problems are conditions that are measurably harmful is not shared by all schools of sociological thought. The notion that social problems are value-relative social constructions is popular among contemporary liberals. In this view, social problems are "real" only if they are publicly recognized as problems (Thio, 1988; Manis, 1974; Gusfield, 1984, 1989). The problem with this approach is that harm often exists whether a problem is acknowledged or not.

Before President John F. Kennedy won election in 1960, for example, poverty was not publicly defined as a social problem, but many poor people were hidden in America's rural areas and urban ghettos. Once Kennedy drew attention to the issue, congressional hearings were held and legislation was passed as part of a "war" on poverty. By 1980, concern over poverty and the expectation that government could solve the problem had drastically waned. Yet there were more poor people in the United States in the 1980s than there had been in the 1960s.

This is why it is important to view social problems as harms that exist regardless of public recognition. Social problems have "careers" (Blumer, 1971; Spector & Kitsuse, 1973), over the course of which public concern about them and the resources devoted to their resolution wax and wane. If left unresolved, the social problems merely reappear later, and when they do, they tend to worsen.

THE INTERDEPENDENCE OF SOCIAL PROBLEMS

Modern society is, in part, a series of interconnections. We depend on supermarkets for food, on letter carriers to deliver mail, on lawyers, doctors, dentists, and countless others to provide us with the goods and services necessary for our well-being. These people in turn are dependent on us to buy their products and services so that they, too, may buy what they need.

Given societal interdependence, it is understandable that social problems are interrelated as well. Harvey Brenner (1977) did a unique study of what takes place when unemployment increases for a time. He discovered that for every 1.4 percent rise in the unemployment rate that lasts for 18 months or longer, numerous social problems become worse. The rates of homicide and property crime, of deaths from alcoholism and suicide, of deaths from cardio-vascular and kidney disease, of new cases of mental illness—all increase. So do rates of admission to state mental hospitals and prisons. What is true of un-employment is true of virtually all types of social harms. There are often vital and unrecognized interrelations between various social problems.

In this regard, consider the nation's crime and drug problems. The United States' crime problem resembles a factory in which a different type of crime is manufactured on each floor. The floors in the factory are connected by dis-tribution systems of money and drugs. The first floor of the factory is inhab-ited by street criminals—the robbers and burglars. They commit the vast ma-jority of their crimes to obtain money to support their drug addiction. Drug-related crime accounts for over half of urban homicides. It is also asso-ciated with prostitution, shoplifting, arson, and vehicle theft.

The second floor of the plant is inhabited by criminal gangs, such as the Bloods and Crips of Los Angeles. These gangs now flourish in virtually every state, selling drugs to the criminal addicts. The gangs are largely the retailers of the drug trade. Their suppliers and processors are located on the third floor of the factory. The suppliers are people of various nations who have orga-nized criminal syndicates to engage in international drug trafficking: the American and Sicilian Mafia and criminal syndicates in Latin America, the Far East, and various Caribbean nations. Each syndicate is involved in a dif-ferent trade route by which drugs are imported into the United States.

The next floor of the factory belongs to money handlers. The world's drug traffickers launder $750 billion to $1 trillion a year (Mills, 1986). The gangs and syndicates deal strictly for cash. Banks, investment firms, jewelry and gold exchanges, and check-cashing services launder (disguise) this money. Large sums of cash are deposited in accounts and then electronically trans-ferred to secret bank accounts in Switzerland and other banking havens. These transactions are made in exchange for a commission (about 2 percent of the amount deposited). In this way, corporate crime is related to both orga-nized crime and street crime.

Finally, the top floor of the crime factory is occupied by representatives of the political system, including the criminal justice system. The illegal drug trade is an important source of bribes for police and judicial and correctional personnel. Organized criminal syndicates also bribe politicians in various na-tions around the world. In some countries, such as Haiti, political and military leaders are deeply involved in drug trafficking as suppliers. U.S. intelligence organizations, especially the Central Intelligence Agency, have helped originate narcotics syndicates for the last forty years (Simon & Eitzen, 1993: 82; Henderson & Simon, 1994:17–18) as part of their anticommunist covert operations. (The details are spelled out in Box 1-2.)

BOX 1-2

THE CIA AND NARCOTICS TRAFFICKING

When most people think about drug abuse, images of the needles that transmit AIDS and vials of crack cocaine come to mind. The idea that the Central Intelligence Agency (CIA) has been a major force in international drug trafficking is difficult to believe, yet the evidence to support this claim is overwhelming.

Item: In France in 1950 the CIA recruited Corsican gangsters, the Ferri-Pisani family, to break a strike by dockworkers. The workers had refused to ship arms to Vietnam (where France was then at war). Corsican gangsters assaulted picket lines of communist union members and harassed union officials. In return for stopping the strike, the Ferri-Pisani family was allowed to use Marseilles as a shipping center for heroin (Simon & Eitzen, 1993:82).

Item: For over thirty years the U.S. government supported opium production in Southeast Asia's Golden Triangle by providing arms, military support, and protection to corrupt officials—all in the name of anticommunism, of course. This relationship began in the 1950s, after the Chinese Communists defeated Chiang Kai-shek's Nationalist Chinese army (the Kuomintang) in 1949. The CIA helped the Kuomintang regroup and settle in Burma's Shan states, bordering on China. The Shan area is a rich source of opium poppies. The CIA even helped smuggle the heroin out of Laos on its own air line, Air America. The CIA was aided in this project by American Mafia members whose lucrative Cuban market had dried up after Fidel Castro ousted the corrupt dictator Fulgencio Batista (Simon & Eitzen, 1993:82). The story of Air America was made into a movie starring Mel Gibson in the 1980s.

In the 1970s the Kuomintang's Cholon triad (Chinese Mafia) began producing injectable heroin and importing it into Vietnam. It has been estimated that 100,000 American soldiers in Vietnam had become addicted to heroin by 1974 (Posner, 1988:69–70).

Item: The CIA also aided its Southeast Asian drug producers by establishing money-laundering facilities for them in Australia. The Nugen Hand bank was established by a number of ex-CIA agents and U.S. military officers. William Colby, former director of central intelligence, was hired as the bank's lawyer. The bank was involved in a host of illegal activities, including a scheme to defraud U.S. oil workers in Saudi Arabia of their wages (Henderson & Simon, 1994:18; Kwitney, 1987).

Item: Other incidents link U.S. government agencies to drug trafficking by the Nicaraguan Contras in the 1980s. The Medellín cocaine cartel paid the Contras $10 million to allow its agents safe passage through Contra-held territory, with the full knowledge of the CIA. The Enterprise operation established by Lieutenant Colonel Oliver North and Admiral John Poindexter provided airplanes to the Medellín cartel in 1984–85. The cartel paid the Enterprise for use of planes, landing strips, and labor to load drug shipments. The proceeds were allegedly used to buy arms for the Contras (Simon & Eitzen, 1993:320).

Item: In 1985, the CIA supplied arms to the Afghans under General Hekmatyar. The CIA aided the mujahedin (holy war fighters) after the Soviet army invaded Afghanistan to prop up the Communist regime it had installed there. Hekmatyar and his army promptly went into the heroin business, and by 1988 they had 100 to 200 heroin refineries just across the border in Pakistan. By the late 1980s, heroin from these Southwest Asian nations accounted for about 50 percent of the European and American heroin supplies (McCoy, 1991a, 1991b:12).

The "CIA connection" demonstrates how different social problems (here governmental crime and street crime) are interconnected. To develop a sociological imagination one must examine not just the causes of social problems but the linkages between them as well.

The link with other social problems does not stop here. Drug addiction itself is related to a host of additional harms. Drug addicts are the source of one-third of all AIDS cases. They account for over a million visits to hospital emergency rooms each year. The public cost of treating the gunshot wounds resulting from street and gang crime is currently estimated at $13 billion annually (*Los Angeles Times,* November 11, 1993, p. A-1). The drug problem in the nation's schools has prompted the hiring of numerous security guards and the installation of metal detectors, thereby eating into already strained public school budgets. Drug-related crime cases have clogged the nation's court dockets and overcrowded the prisons of more than thirty states, thereby increasing the indebtedness of state and local governments. All social problems, both domestic and international, are interrelated.

ANALYZING THE CAUSES OF SOCIAL PROBLEMS

Which social conditions cause social problems? Mills believed that social problems were caused by *contradictions (antagonisms)* within the structure of society. Structural contradictions are conflicts that are virtually built into societal institutions (Worsley, 1982:28). One contradiction within the economic institution concerns workers' demands for increased wages versus owners' need to hold down labor costs. The two sides react to this contradiction in many ways: unions and management engage in collective bargaining, management relocates factories in places where labor is cheaper, workers purchase their companies, and so forth. Still, the conflict between business and labor over wages goes on.

A basic assumption of the sociological imagination is that much human history is about the conflict between the few who have control over scarce resources and the many who do not. These resources include *wealth* (property), *income* (wages and salaries), *power* (the ability to make economic and political decisions that affect the entire society), and *cultural values* (standards of right and wrong, beautiful and ugly).

Where do such contradictions originate? Mills believed that the way to locate contradictions was to begin by asking key questions. These questions, which form the elements of the sociological imagination paradigm, are listed in Table 1-1. Central to these questions are three issues:

1 Social structure.

2 The master trend ("main drift") of the current historical period.

3 Biography, or social character, and the degree of alienation it exhibits (Mills, 1959:7, 171).

TABLE 1-1
THE SOCIOLOGICAL IMAGINATION: THE KEY QUESTIONS

Structure   What is the particular structure of the entire society and what are its essential component parts? How do the parts relate to one another? How does this society differ from others?

The Historical era's main drift   Where does the society stand in history—is it on the ascendant or in decline? How does social change happen? What are the essential features of the historical epoch? How is history made? What master trends (main drift) of the current era will soon cause contradictions and social problems?

Biography (social character)   Mills believed it is important to answer the following questions about social character:

• What kinds of men and women characterize the society?
• What kinds of "human nature" are evolving?
• In what ways are social characteristics shaped?
• Which characteristics are encouraged and which are repressed?
• What types of "human nature" are revealed in the character we observe in the society in this period?
• How is human nature shaped by the society's dominant institutions?

For Mills a feature of social character that must be addressed is *alienation.*

• What are the institutional conditions responsible for feelings of alienation and low self-esteem in individuals?
• How are these alienating conditions within institutions related to various macro and micro social problems?
• What can be done to overcome alienating conditions and the feelings they engender in individuals?
• Why are people confused about (mystified by) the causes of their alienation?
Mills's questions concerning structure, history, and biography provide a road map with which sociological inquiry can be undertaken.

The Social Structure

The social structure is an interrelated set of societal institutions. *Institutions* are collections of social roles, norms, and social organizations that are organized to meet some societal need (Messner & Rosenfeld, 1994: 72). Among these institutions are:

1 The economy, which produces and distributes goods and services.

2 The polity (political system), which functions to resolve conflict and protect society from internal and external threats to stability.

3 The family, which functions to regulate the sex drive, produce and rear children, and serve as the emotional center of people's private lives.

4 Education, which imparts skills necessary for playing roles in the economy and other institutions, and socializes the young to accept the values of the society.

5 Religion, which functions to meet spiritual needs and provide answers to life's fundamental questions: What is life's purpose? How did we get here? Why do we die? Why do some people escape punishment for evil acts? Why do the innocent often suffer victimization?

6 The aesthetic institution, which functions to produce and distribute works in the arts and humanities (art, music, literature, opera, plays, movies, television shows).

The Main Drift

The master trend, or the main drift, consists of the means by which social change takes place within the social structure. Almost all the founders of sociology—those who wrote in what Mills termed "the classic tradition" (Mills, 1960)—assessed modern society for its main drift.

Karl Marx: Class Struggle and Alienation   Karl Marx (1818–83) viewed the main drift of industrial capitalism as another chapter in the history of conflict. This conflict took place between the class that owned the society's economic base (the mode of production) and the class that toiled for the owners (the proletariat). For Marx, since the coming of modern society the working class had engaged in joyless, alienating work. Factory jobs reduced work to meaningless monotony and separated (alienated) workers from the products they produced, from the process of work, from other workers (all of whom constituted a potential revolutionary class), and from the workers' own (human) nature, which Marx viewed as free and creative (Roberts, 1978:85–86).

Further, Marx saw the owning class (the bourgeoisie) as controlling the government, religion, and education as well as all dominant ideas (values, ideologies, ethics, and laws) by which society was ruled. However, Marx was an optimist. He believed the workers would in time realize that their labor was exploited, used only to profit the owners, while they themselves barely survived economically (Worsley, 1982:90). Marx believed that social change would be accomplished by a revolution in which the workers would seize the economic base of society from the owners.

Emile Durkheim: Mechanical Solidarity and Anomie   Emile Durkheim (1858–1917), a leading French sociologist, focused on the social bonds (emotional and moral) that held societies together. In more traditional societies these ties were formed by strong traditions based on customs, ceremonies (weddings, for example), religious beliefs, and values. These bonds made for what he called *organic solidarity.* The coming of modern society, Durkheim argued, had resulted in a marked decline in these traditional ties. Whatever societal glue was left seemed to make for *mechanical solidarity,* a functional set of social relationships based on a specialized division of labor (different jobs or careers). Thus people in modern societies use the money they earn to purchase goods and services from various others who occupy specialized posts in the economic order.

Durkheim lamented the passing of traditional norms (accepted rules of right and wrong) and expressed fear that the result would be a form of institutionalized moral chaos that he termed *anomie.* Anomie (literally lawlessness) is a structural alienation that occurs when rapid social change causes large numbers of people to recognize no rules to guide their behavior. They lose faith in both major social institutions and the rules they seek to enforce. The result is a high rate of crime and deviant behavior (such as suicide), which in turn further weakens people's belief in the legitimacy of major institutions and laws. Durkheim believed that social change could come about when people formed institutions (such as workers' cooperatives) that would lead to the establishment of moral and emotional bonds.

Max Weber: Iron Cages and Disenchantment   Max Weber (1864–1920), a leading German sociologist, wrote on an incredible number of topics. Some of Weber's most influential writings concern the coming of bureaucracy and what he termed the rationalization of the world. Weber described the great shift from a society in which people looked to the traditions of their ancestors to guide their decision making to a mass society in which decision making was based on impersonal rules that had been codified into laws. This rationalization of the world takes many forms, among them the rise of science and dependence on experts in various fields; modern democratic government, with its rights and laws as the bases for the conduct of both organizations and citizens; and the modern corporation, with its focus on efficiency and the bottom line.

Weber deeply lamented the expansion of bureaucracy into every area of social life. He feared that the oppression of serfdom would be replaced by new "iron cages" in which all forms of value-oriented social conduct (feelings and creativity) would be suffocated by bureaucratic organizations and their rational laws and regulations. The result would be a generalized malaise in which individuals would suffer disenchantment with "official tasks" that excluded love, hate, and virtually all other human feelings (Josephson & Josephson, 1962:23). Weber believed that the only alternative to increasing regulation by bureaucracies was the emergence of charismatic individuals. A charismatic leader is one to whom followers have a strong emotional attachment. When such individuals manage to exert control over systems of bureaucratic administration, they inspire their followers and society in general to grow and develop (Denhardt, 1984:31–32).

Social Character

Biography, or social character, consists of personality traits and behaviors that are widely shared by members of a culture. Social character stems from the values that are widely shared within a culture. The concept of social character is central to both the sociological imagination paradigm and our study of social problems. Objectively, there is no innate "human nature": there is no evidence to suggest that any specific character trait, such as greed, aggression, or "sin," is inborn in humans. Social character consists of widely shared cultural values, beliefs, goals, attitudes, and norms. This is what Mills refers to when he asks in what ways men and women are "formed, liberated, and repressed, made sensitive and blunted" (1959:7).

Social character, then, consists of those character traits that are widely "shared among significant social groups and which . . . [are] product[s] of the experience of those groups" (Riesman, 1950:3–4). Social character can be thought of as the parts of our personalities we have in common with most other members of our society. In a nation as diverse and multicultural as the United States, there are also social characters specific to genders (also known as gender roles), ethnic groups, regional groups (such as southerners), ethnic groups (Italians, Irish, Swedes, etc.), and members of other influential groups (such as Republicans and Democrats).

Within this view two components of character are crucial. Various types of social characters may be classified by (1) the structure of selfhood in question and (2) the nature of the value system embraced by a given social character. It is within the realms of self and values that social character interrelates with social problems. The notion of selfhood is difficult to grasp because it is so taken for granted. If I asked you what is your "self," you would probably say, "Well, myself is me. It's who I am." In the psychological sense, this is true. Sociologically, however, selves are more complex. What you are telling me by noting that your self is you is that you possess what is termed an individualized sense of selfhood. That is, you are aware of your individuality; you realize you are psychologically and physically separate from others. Moreover, you probably think that all people conceive of themselves in the same way, but they do not.

Many cultures in the world exhibit what is called a collectivized sense of self. People in these societies conceive of themselves as part of a group—their family (including their ancestors), a clan, tribe, or nation. People in such cultures see themselves as both psychologically and physically connected to other people (Guttman & Wrong, 1968). If someone is hospitalized in Japan, for example, a nurse stays in the patient's room twenty-four hours a day. Workers in Japan go to their bosses for personal advice. Some bosses even set their workers up with Geisha girls as dates. These practices exist because of a collectivized sense of selfhood. People have different obligations to one another in collectivized cultures than in individualized cultures. Indeed, in some African nations a person whose life is saved by another person becomes that person's slave for life.

In the United States, few subjects are more written about then the self. Go into any bookstore and you will find an entire section titled "Self-Help," literally help for the self. The vast majority of these books are written by psychologists and other members of the so-called helping professions. Why do so many American selves need help? The issue is alienation.

No sociological understanding of social character is complete without an analysis of alienation. Alienation involves such feelings as powerlessness, meaninglessness, loneliness, isolation, normlessness, and estrangement from oneself, from other people, and from society at large.

Alienation has a sociological and an individual (emotional) component. That is, *alienating social conditions* cause *feelings of alienation in individuals.* Alienation also involves a lack of self-esteem. When feelings of alienation and low self-esteem are widespread, macro and micro social problems ensue.

ANSWERS TO THE QUESTIONS POSED BY THE SOCIOLOGICAL IMAGINATION

One purpose of this book is to answer questions regarding structure and historical drift, social character and alienation. As you explore these answers, please keep in mind that structure, history, and biography constantly intersect and affect one another. Take Weber's view of bureaucracy as the main drift of modern society, for example. Bureaucracy is as much a structure (a form of social organization) as it is a trend. Bureaucratic organizations are constantly shaping the social characters of the people they employ and the publics they supposedly serve. Thus one cannot point to a simplistic cause-and-effect relationship here.

Second, the answers to the questions posed by the sociological imagination are not eternal. Social structures, historical drift, and social character vary with the society and period of history under study. The America of the 1990s is not the America of the 1790s. The America of the 2290s will not be the America of the 1990s. The questions that make up the sociological imagination are constant, but the answers are always evolving.

What is the social structure of the United States today? What is its main drift? What sort of social character does it have?

The Structure of American Society

The *structure* of American society is that of a mass society. A *mass society* is characterized by:

1 A capitalistic economy dominated by huge multinational corporations. Corporate elites (owners and managers) frequently take temporary positions in government and its military establishment.

2 A centralized government that has the power to make the big decisions about war and peace, inflation and unemployment, and the production of cultural values. There is increased coordination and cooperation between large corporations and the federal government on matters of domestic and foreign policy that affect large corporations. (These policies are discussed in Chapter 2.) The power structure of mass society is not monolithic. There are influences that compete with the elite for dominance. Among them are competitive interest groups and middle-class voters. Important decisions, however, are increasingly made in secret by such organizations as the Central Intelligence Agency, which are not effectively regulated by democratic forces.

3 Mass media owned by corporate institutions and influenced by government. The danger is that the media can manipulate the masses of people who lack such power. Such manipulation takes the forms of advertising, public relations, government propaganda, and other media fare (Kornhauser, 1968).

4 A highly mobile population of nonelites.

A mass society is one in which small, intimate (primary) groups, such as extended families and communities, have lost their substance. People still spend time with their friends and family members, but interaction in the social world is impersonal. People interact impersonally with bureaucratic organizations (large corporations, political parties, government bureaus, television networks, universities) and have superficial (secondary) contacts with clerks and auto mechanics—people with whom they have no real friendship (Mills, 1951:161–286).

Families no longer grow their own food, make their own clothing, or construct their own shelter, so people in mass societies are increasingly dependent on one another for goods and services. Likewise, there is great emphasis on expertise in such fields as medicine, law, journalism, dentistry, tax preparation, show business and sports, and religion. These and many other fields have become the monopolies of various professionals, on whom nonprofessionals depend for help. As a result, much of life in mass society revolves around the various organizations and institutions that have taken over functions that in earlier eras were performed by families and communities—care of the sick and the elderly, child welfare, criminal justice, mental health. Consequently, the family, religion, the schools, and the local community have lost importance as sources of morality and relationships. People in mass societies move in and out of communities at will. They marry, divorce, and remarry with bewildering speed, and switch religions as if they were test-driving cars.

These changes generate numerous contradictions and resultant social problems. People are crowded close together in cities and suburbs, yet are largely strangers to one another. Millions of people have migrated to cities only to experience endless traffic snarls, delinquent gangs and high crime rates, AIDS, environmental pollution, and unaffordable housing.

A central vulnerability in mass societies is manipulation of masses of people "from above," by a bureaucratic elite. Entire populations are presented with the same products, "news," candidates, sports, and popular culture idols. People select between carefully structured alternatives: the next president will be either a Republican or a Democrat. What is "right" or "good" becomes what sells, wins elections, or becomes popular. This state of affairs gives mass societies a strange form of egalitarianism, in which all consumers or voters are equally valued as objects of manipulation. This manipulation makes for a major form of societal alienation.

Mass societies are also prone to spontaneous behavior "from below." Such collective behaviors as riots, protests, and labor strikes threaten to disrupt society. Mass societies are economically and politically linked, so disruptions in one area of life, such as the rail system, can adversely affect all economic activity. Mass behavior at its extreme—rioting, looting, burning—poses the threat of chaos or anarchy. When such behavior occurred in Los Angeles in 1992, more than fifty people were killed and $1 billion in damage was done.

People who engage in mass behavior are usually among the least rooted in their communities and least incorporated in workplace organizations. This is especially the case among the younger and poorer members of society. The vulnerabilities of mass societies have been viewed from a variety of vantage points (Kornhauser, 1959, 1968: 62–65), as Box 1-3 makes clear.

To summarize, a mass society is a modern society that is characterized to various degrees by:

BOX 1-3

MASS SOCIETY THEORY AND ITS ORIGINS

Mass society theory consists of four distinct yet interrelated views on the meaning of modern life. Mass theory has been referred to as the "kitchen sink" because new ideas continue to be added to the theory and nothing is ever removed. Postmodern theory is a continuation of mass society theory.

The aristocratic conservative view

Aristocratic conservative theorists worry about the decline of morality, authority, and order in modern society. They also decry the decline of cultural standards in art, music, literature, and entertainment. The original aristocratic writers were Catholic conservatives who feared the rise of mass rule with the French Revolution of 1789. To conservative critics, the masses (not usually specifically defined by these writers) are morally, intellectually, emotionally, and culturally inferior to the elites. The elites are people who occupy social roles as the heads of such wealthy, powerful, and culturally influential institutions as corporations, government agencies, and the communications media.

Today this view of the masses continues in the writings of Thomas Dye and Harmon Zeigler (1990:14–16). In their eyes,

the irony of democracy in America is that elites, not masses, are committed to democratic values. Despite a superficial commitment to the symbols of democracy, the American people have a surprisingly weak commitment to individual liberty, toleration of diversity, and freedom of expression. . . . Democratic values have survived because elites, not masses govern. . . . Unchecked mass influence could threaten democratic values. . . . Occasionally the masses mobilize, and their activism is extremist, unstable, and unpredictable . . . is usually an expression of resentment against the established order, and . . . usually occurs in times of crisis when a "counterelite" (demagogue) emerges from the masses. . . . Democracies can survive only if the masses are absorbed in the problems of everyday life, and are involved in groups that distract their attention from mass politics. . . . The masses define politics in simplistic terms. They want simple answers to society's problems, regardless of how complex those problems may be.

The democratic view

Democratic critics of mass society worry about the domination of the masses by elites, and view elites as the real threat to democracy (Mills, 1956). As Daniel Hellinger and Dennis Judd (1991:v, 5–7) argue,

America's elites have evinced chronic anxiety about their position. . . . They have employed a panoply of strategies to manipulate democratic processes . . . controlled the compositions of the electorate and restricted political discourse, with the consequences that elections concern "safe" political issues and voters are able to decide only between candidates who represent elite preferences. . . . In the past decades they have taken decisive steps to insulate government policy making from elections altogether. . . . The elites that have governed in America have shown little attachment to democracy except as a device to legitimate their political control. . . . From time to time they have resorted to [violent] repression . . . and elites have made much more liberal use of it . . . than the mainstream textbooks will ever reveal.

The ultimate fear of democratic critics is the imposition of a totalitarian state on the masses, as in Germany under the Nazis and in Russia under the Soviet regime.

Mass psychology

Many writings about mass collective behavior are elitist in tone. Such early theorists as Sigmund Freud and Gustav Le Bon viewed the masses as highly sug-gestible and easily manipulated, especially when they are together in crowds. Crowd behavior is viewed as unrestrained by conscious thought. Crowds are dangerous because they are suggestible. They can be manipulated by unscrupulous demagogues at public rallies.

The rural-urban continua

Virtually all the founders of sociology agonized over the consequences of the transition from a close-knit rural society to an impersonal urban one. Each of them analyzed a different aspect of the decline of social attachment and the rise of the alienation, loneliness, impersonality, and disenchantment that characterize the mass society.

1 Centralized power in the hands of bureaucratic elites.

2 Manipulation of the masses by elites in undemocratic ways by such means as mass culture and government propaganda.

3 The creation of alienated masses, groups of people who no longer feel attachment to their community or to society.

4 Disruptive mass behavior.

Overall, the mass society is one in which the many without power are vulnerable to manipulation and control by the elites, and the elites are vulnerable to disruptive behavior by the powerless masses.

The Main Drift of the Postmodern Era

Our postmodern era is characterized by two sets of tendencies. First, the international social structure that has emerged since World War II makes for worldwide political and social instability. This structure consists of groups of nations whose wealth and power are grossly unequal. The end of the Cold War and the collapse of the Soviet empire have ensured the ascendancy of the richest capitalist countries—the United States, Canada, Japan, and the leading democracies of Western Europe. Most of the so-called Third World nations of Asia, Africa, and Latin America (accounting for 60 percent of the world's population) are very poor. This great inequality of wealth and power is a major cause of the world's social problems—its political instability and wars, its environmental pollution, its terrorism, even its uncontrolled population growth. The Third World has experienced either a war or a revolution every month since the postmodern world system emerged in 1945. The nations of the former Soviet empire also face a future clouded by the threat of civil wars, economic collapse, and massive scandals involving elite corruption.

The postmodern era is also characterized by a popular culture that is spread throughout the world by television, movies, advertising, popular music, plays, newspapers and magazines, and consumer goods. Postmodern culture contains some disturbing tendencies that are making many social problems worse:

1 Preoccupation with sex and the separation of sex and love.

2 Increasing reliance on violence as a solution to conflict.

3 Commodification—that is, the turning of virtually every human impulse, moral principle, and sacred belief into a commodity.

4 Endless advertising of commodities and the cultivation of conspicuous consumption.

5 Lifestyles of mass consumption centering on the fast-food restaurant, the theme park, the shopping mall, and the mass media, which together promote a confusing culture that lacks stable values and makes it difficult to separate fantasy from reality.

6 A disbelief in old political ideologies (Denzin, 1991:1–20).

The Social Character of the Postmodern Era

The postmodern era is characterized by the antisocial character. The antisocial character is typified by:

1 A "cheerful robot" mentality at work and in private life (Mills, 1959:171; 1951:182–88): people display a false pleasantness to customers, co-workers, and bosses for purposes of personal gain. In private life, they often manipulate personal relationships to gain sexual favors.

2 An unhealthy self-centeredness, or narcissism, which makes one unable to empathize with other people or to form emotional or moral bonds with them.

3 A disturbing tendency toward "wilding" (Derber, 1992:29–32), the commission of deviant or criminal activity without guilt or concern for its effects on others. A well-publicized case of wilding occurred on August 20, 1989, when Lyle and Erik Menendez killed their father, the multimillionaire head of the company that produced the movie *Rambo II,* and their mother. José Menendez had wanted his sons to become successful and rich, as he had done. After they received the first shares of their inheritance, the boys went on a spending spree. One bought a new Porsche, a Rolex watch, and expensive clothes. Lyle Menendez had told a friend that he did not want to struggle for success the way his father had had to do. He wanted things quick and easy, and he had a better way in mind. His "better way" turned out to be the murder of his parents (Derber, 1992:31–37).

Underlying the antisocial character are two forms of alienation: inauthenticity and dehumanization.

Inauthenticity   Inauthenticity is characterized by the presence of *positive overt appearances* coupled with *negative underlying (hidden) realities* (Simon & Eitzen, 1993:340ff).

Inauthenticity can be seen in advertisements for cigarettes, liquor, cosmetics, cars, deodorants, clothing—products of every sort. Nearly all of these so-called lifestyle ads (those picturing people) have a common theme in the form of *implied promises.* The implied promise in each ad constitutes the positive overt appearance that is a hallmark of inauthenticity. We are promised that if we drink the whiskey or smoke the cigarettes, we will find sex, romance, or love; we will become successful or powerful (note that all such ads picture the trappings of affluence); and we will be popular and have friends.

What are the consequences of smoking and drinking? These two drugs combined kill about 500,000 Americans each year. They cause a variety of diseases and cost billions of dollars in medical bills and lost workdays. These harms—death, disease, and financial loss—are the negative underlying realities of lifestyles based on the consumption of alcohol and tobacco.

In our personal lives, too, we are subjected to the inauthenticity of lies and manipulation as people put on a false front for financial or sexual purposes.

Dehumanization   Dehumanization takes two interrelated forms, object-directed and self-directed. *Object-directed dehumanization* occurs when people are labeled less than human for purposes of profit, exploitation, and manipulation. We see this form of dehumanization in mass-media stereotypes (the dumb blonde, for example). Racial, gender, ethnic, and age stereotypes are common in corporate and governmental institutions, too. Bureaucracies tend to treat people as undifferentiated items in nonhuman categories. Employees once valued become "labor costs" when the time comes to "restructure" and "downsize" the "organization." Thus real people suffering the pain and trauma of job loss are no longer involved, only "units" in organizations. (By the way, I am not a human being, according to my university. As a member of the faculty, I am a "Unit 3 element.")

Self-directed dehumanization is a symptom of self-alienation. One turns oneself into a "cog in a wheel," a dehumanized machine. The workaholic is subject to such stress-related diseases as ulcers and heart attacks and to job burnout (feelings of intense dislike of one's job).

The natures of mass society, the postmodern era, and the antisocial character are explored in depth throughout this book.

LOOKING AHEAD

The remainder of this book provides an in-depth view of social problems
though the eyes of the sociological imagination.

Chapter 2 focuses on social structures and contradictions in the world system of nation-states and in the dominant corporate, government, and media
institutions in the United States.

Chapter 3 examines the relationship between alienating conditions inherent in a mass-media society and individual feelings of alienation. The discussion centers on deception and fraud, violence, sexual deviance, and mental illness.

Chapter 4 deals with master trends, structural conditions in American society and the global economic system that are likely to cause future social problems. Master trends—the main drifts, in Mills's language—are an important
yet unappreciated aspect of the sociological imagination (Simon, 1977, 1981).

Chapter 5 explores the theory and method of the sociological imagination.
You will learn how to ask research questions suggested by the discussions of
structure, social character and alienation, and master trends. You will also
learn how to analyze various schools of thought regarding social problems.
The chapter also contains suggestions concerning ways to cultivate useful intellectual skills (Mills, 1959:Appendix).

Finally, Chapter 6 offers some suggestions for self-help in love relationships and at work, and for getting involved in changing your society for the
better. It stresses self-help, constructive social change through active participation, and learning to view the world from a sociological perspective.

A final word: many students who study social problems find the experience grounds for cynicism and doubt. The sociological imagination focuses
on the idea of social harm precisely because such harms must be ended. To
acquire a sociological imagination is also to acquire a set of beliefs about:

- The dignity and worth of all human beings.
- The promise of genuine democracy.
- The ability to think critically and independently of dominant ideologies
and forms of mystification.

This book is written in hope, not despair.

REFERENCES

Babbie, Earl. 1989. *The Practice of Social Research.* 7th ed. Belmont, Calif.:
   Wadsworth.
Bellah, Robert et al. 1986. *Habits of the Heart.* New York: Harper & Row.

Blumer, Herbert. 1971. "Social Problems as Collective Behavior." *Social Problems* 18 (Winter): 298–306.

Brenner, Harvey. 1977. "Estimating the Social Costs of National Economic Policy." Paper no. 5, Joint Economic Committee, U.S. Congress (26 October).

Denhardt, Robert. 1984. *Theories of Public Organization.* Belmont, Calif.: Brooks/Cole.

Denzin, Norman. 1991. *Images of Postmodern Society: Social Theory and Contemporary Cinema.* Newbury Park, Calif.: Sage.

Derber, Charles. 1992. *Money, Murder, and the American Dream: Wilding from Wall Street to Main Street.* Boston: Faber & Faber.

Durkheim, Emile. 1951. *Suicide.* New York: Free Press.

Dye, Thomas, and Harmon Zeigler. 1990. *The Irony of Democracy: An Uncommon Introduction to American Government.* 8th ed. Pacific Grove, Calif.: Brooks/Cole.

Ehrenreich, Barbara. 1990. *The Worst Years of Our Lives.* New York: Harper/Collins.

Eldridge, John. 1983. *C. Wright Mills.* London: Tavistock.

Garment, Susanne. 1991. *Scandal.* New York: Anchor.

Gerth, Hans, and C. Wright Mills. 1953. *Character and Social Structure.* New York: Harcourt, Brace & World.

Goldfarb, Jeffery. 1991. *The Cynical Society.* Chicago: University of Chicago Press.

Gore, Al. 1993. *Creating a Government that Works Better and Costs Less.* Washington, D.C.: U.S. Government Printing Office.

Gregg, Theodor, et al. 1980. "The Caravan Rolls On." *Knowledge* 1 (Autumn): 31–61.

Gusfield, Joseph. 1984. "On the Side: Practical Action and Social Constructionism in Social Problems Theory." In *Studies in the Sociology of Social Problems,* eds. J. Kitsuse and J.W. Schneider. (New Jersey: Ablex): 31–51.

———. 1989. "Constructing the Ownership of Social Problems." *Social Problems* 36 (December): 431–42.

Guttman, Robert, and Dennis Wrong. 1968. "Riesman's Concept of Character." In *Culture and Social Character: The Work of David Riesman Reviewed,* ed. Seymour Martin Lipset and Leo Lowenthal. New York: Free Press.

Harris, Louis. 1987. *Inside America.* New York: Vintage.

Hellinger, Daniel, and Dennis Judd. 1991. *The Democratic Facade.* Pacific Grove, Calif.: Brooks/Cole.

Henderson, Joel H., and David R. Simon. 1994. *Crimes of the Criminal Justice System.* Cincinnati: Anderson.

Horowitz, Irving Louis. 1963. "An Introduction to C. Wright Mills." In *Power, Politics, and People: The Collected Essays of C. Wright Mills,* ed. Irving Louis Horowitz, pp. 1–20. New York: Ballantine.

Horton, John. 1968. "Order and Conflict Theories of Social Problems." In Radical Perspectives on Social Problems, ed. Frank Lidenfield, pp. 590–602. New York: Free Press.

Josephson, Eric, and Marie Josephson. Eds. 1962. *Man Alone: Alienation in Modern Society.* New York: Dell.

Kanter, Donald L., and Philip H. Mirvis. 1989. *The Cynical Americans.* San Francisco: Jossey-Bass.

Kornhauser, William. 1968. "Mass Society." In *International Encyclopedia of the Social Sciences,* ed. D. Sills, pp. 58–64. New York: Free Press.

Kovic, Ron. 1976. *Born on the Fourth of July.* New York: McGraw-Hill.

Kwitney, Jonnathan. 1987. "Crimes of Patriots." *Mother Jones* 6 (August/September): 15–23.

Liazos, Alex. 1993. "Nuts, Sluts, and 'Preverts': The Poverty of the Sociology of Deviance." In *Social Deviance: Readings in Theory and Research,* ed. H. Pontell, pp. 164–79. Englewood Cliffs, N.J.: Prentice-Hall.

Manis, Jerome. 1974. "Assessing the Seriousness of Social Problems." *Social Problems* 22 (Fall): 1–15.

McCoy, Alfred. 1991a. "The CIA Connection." *The Progressive,* July, pp. 20–26.

———. 1991b. "The Afghanistan Drug Lords." *Convergence,* Fall, pp. 11–12, 14.

Messner, Steven, and Richard Rosenfeld. 1994. *Crime and the American Dream.* Belmont, Calif.: Wadsworth.

Mills, C. Wright. 1951. *White Collar.* New York: Oxford University Press.

———. 1956. *The Power Elite.* New York: Oxford University Press.

———. 1958. *The Causes of World War III.* New York: Simon & Schuster.

———. 1959. *The Sociological Imagination.* (New York: Oxford University Press).

———. 1963. "IBM Plus Humanism = Sociology." In *Power, Politics, and People: The Collected Essays of C. Wright Mills,* ed. Irving Louis Horowitz, pp. 568–76. New York: Ballantine.

———, ed. 1960. *Images of Man: The Classic Tradition in Sociological Theory.* New York: Braziller.

Mills, James. 1986. *The Underground Empire.* New York: Dell.

Neubeck, Kenneth. 1991. *Social Problems: A Critical Approach.* 3d ed. New York: McGraw-Hill.

Patterson, James, and Peter Kim. 1991. *The Day Americans Told the Truth.* Englewood Cliffs, N.J.: Prentice-Hall.

Phillips, Kevin. 1990. *The Politics of Rich and Poor.* New York: Random House.

———. 1993. *Boiling Point: Democrats, Republicans, and the Decline of Middle-Class Prosperity.* New York: Random House.

Posner, Gerald. 1988. *Warlords of Crime, Chinese Secret Societies: The New Mafia.* New York: Penguin.

Ritzer, George. 1980. *Sociology: A Multiple Paradigm Science.* Boston: Allyn & Bacon.

Roberts, Ron. 1978. *Social Problems: Human Possibilities.* St. Louis: Mosby.

Rosenau, P. M. 1992. *Postmodernism and the Social Sciences: Insights, Inroads, and Intrusions.* Princeton: Princeton University Press.

Schaef, Ann W. 1988. *When Society Becomes an Addict.* New York: Harper/Collins.

Schrager, Laura, and James F. Short. 1978. "Towards a Sociology of Organizational Crime." *Social Problems* 25 (February): 407–19.

Scimecca, Joseph. 1977. *The Sociological Theory of C. Wright Mills.* Port Washington, N.Y.: Kennikat Press.

Simon, David R. 1977. *Ideology and Sociology: Perspectives on Contemporary Social Criticism.* Washington, D.C.: University Press of America.

———. 1981. "Ideology Awareness Project: An Exercise in Item Unit Content Analysis." *Teaching Political Science* 8 (July): 487–92.

———. 1992. "Watergate and the Nixon Presidency." In *Watergate and Afterward: The Legacy of Richard M. Nixon,* eds. Leon Friedman and William Levantrosser, pp. 5–22. Westport, CT: Greenwood.

Simon, David R., and D. Stanley Eitzen. 1993. *Elite Deviance.* 4th ed. Needham Heights, Mass: Allyn & Bacon.

Skolnick, Jerome, and Elliott Currie. 1991. *Crisis in American Institutions.* 8th ed. New York: Harper/Collins.

Spector, Malcolm, and John Kitsuse. 1973. "Social Problems: A Reformulation." *Social Problems* 21 (Fall): 145–59.

Thio, Alex. 1988. *Deviant Behavior: An Integrated Approach.* 3d ed. New York: Harper & Row.

Walton, John. 1993. *Sociology and Critical Inquiry,* 3d ed. Belmont, Calif.: Wadsworth.

Worsley, Peter. 1982. *Marx and Marxism.* London: Tavistock.

EXERCISE 1-1. RELATING PERSONAL TROUBLES AND SOCIAL PROBLEMS

Write a short paper (three to five pages, double spaced) stating your opinion in response to the following questions. *Be sure to make a copy of your paper. What's important now is your impressions of the issues raised here.*

1 *Social problem*   Select a magazine or newspaper article about a topic currently in the news—a murder in a high school, say, or an indictment of a politician on corruption charges, a kidnapping, a terrorist bombing incident, or a shootout between rival drug gangs. Does the article's topic indicate a more widespread problem in America? What types of harm result from this socially patterned problem?

Consider the following dimensions of the sociological imagination.

2 *Contradiction*   What are the institutional contradictions surrounding the problem? For example, do some institutions in American society approve of drug use, either legal or illegal, while other institutions condemn it? What contradictions are inherent in American institutions that may cause the problem you selected?

3 *Historical epoch*   What events in the recent past have raised concern about this problem?

4 *Immediate milieu*   To what extent is this problem a part of your immediate environment? For example, do you know other students who abuse alcohol or illegal drugs? Has someone ever attempted to sell you illegal drugs? Have you experienced any direct contact with the problem you chose to analyze?

5 *Personal troubles*   Have you or members of your family experienced problems with the issue you chose? Are any of your friends experiencing problems with it? If so, what sorts of trauma have you experienced because of this social problem? Is the problem resolvable within your immediate environment, or do you believe that some larger effort is necessary—perhaps a private effort in your local community, or governmental legislation, or public service education by the mass media? If so, what kinds of efforts do you believe are necessary to rid your everyday life of this problem?

EXERCISE 2-2. PERSONAL TROUBLES AND SOCIAL ISSUES

Ron Kovic and Vietnam

The United States' involvement in Vietnam from 1964 to 1975 became a social issue when the public perceived that the government was lying about many aspects of the conflict. Critics argued that the war was not a crusade against communism but a longstanding civil conflict between factions of the Vietnamese. It was also perceived that the government was lying about the competence of the South

Vietnamese government to fight the war, about the ability of the United States to "win" the war, about the numbers of enemy troops that were overrunning South Vietnam. Some important institutional contradictions were also involved. The U.S. government accused communists of using chemical weapons, yet the United States had embarked on a massive defoliation campaign with Agent Orange. The South Vietnamese were officially praised as democratic allies, yet their government violated human rights by imprisoning enemy soldiers in tiger cages, and many South Vietnamese officials engaged in corruption on a wide scale.

America's military behaved in a contradictory fashion. While the Pentagon charged that the enemy did not value human life, U.S. soldiers were raping, torturing, and massacring innocent civilians. The army professed high morale, yet a disturbing number of American soldiers either returned home as drug addicts or deserted the military altogether.

The Historical Epoch

Once these realities reached public awareness, the war's continuation became a social issue. Antiwar demonstrators and their critics clashed in public demonstrations. The public's opposition to the war after 1968 clearly challenged the ability of the military to motivate troops. Social change was being attempted from below as hundreds of thousands of people confronted their government in massive street demonstrations.

Personal Troubles and the Immediate Milieu

Ron Kovic was a young man from Long Island, New York, who graduated from high school just as a large troop buildup was taking place in Vietnam. Kovic had been socialized to believe in the necessity and rightness of fighting for one's country. His childhood movie idols were such stars as Audie Murphy and John Wayne, who played brave war heroes. His family and school stressed participation in sports, which reinforced the importance of winning. His toys were guns, and he and his friends regularly played at war. He joined the Cub Scouts and marched in Memorial Day parades. Since 1957, when the Soviet Union launched the first space satellite, Ron had been taught the importance of beating the Soviets at everything. Ron wanted to be a hero, and this very shy guy also dreamed of having a girlfriend. Everything in his immediate environment led him to join the Marines and go to Vietnam.

Once he was in Vietnam, Ron's striving for heroism resulted in his being seriously wounded and paralyzed. This trauma, along with others from his Vietnam tour, led to a great personal change. The social and personal contradictions he experienced resulted in a profound personal transformation. He became enraged over the lies the government was telling the public about the war, and about the bad treatment he received at the Veterans Administration hospital where he recovered from his wounds. Rats gnawed on his bedding, and machines vital to his treatment were not kept in proper repair.

For the first time, Ron challenged the basic values of blind patriotism, obedience to authority, and the rightness of American foreign and defense policy. He turned against the war and became active in the antiwar movement. The contradiction between the government's proclaimed reason for pursuing the war (communism) and the reason Ron perceived (protection of multinational corporations and the military-industrial complex) was glaring. Another contradiction lay in the demeaning treatment of veterans by a nation that professed to care about them.

Ron Kovic's experiences show clearly how institutional contradictions can result in both social problems and personal troubles. The contradictions surrounding our involvement in Vietnam divided the nation politically, plunged many families into crisis as the war separated them both physically and emotionally, and brought severe personal trauma to returning veterans.

A film based on Ron Kovic's book about his experiences, *Born on the Fourth of July* (1976), was nominated for an Oscar. It has been released on videotape. See the film, then collect a sample of reviews of it published in various newspapers and national magazines. Analyze the reviews by answering the following questions:

1 Did the critics point out any contradictions relating to Vietnam or Kovic's experiences, such as maltreatment of veterans by the Veterans Administration?

2 Did reviewers notice any symptoms of inauthenticity or dehumanization, such as perceptions of the enemy as barbarians?

3 Did reviewers mention any mystification of social problems, such as deliberate lying by the government to the American people about the war?

SUGGESTED READINGS: A BRIEF BIBLIOGRAPHIC ESSAY

The works of C. Wright Mills are the most important source of knowledge about the sociological imagination. The best survey of Mills's works is *Power, Politics, and People: The Collected Essays of C. Wright Mills,* edited by Irving Louis Horowitz (New York: Ballantine, 1962). Horowitz also edited a book of essays in Mills's honor titled *The New Sociology* (New York: Oxford University Press, 1964). The most important of Mills's works are *The Sociological Imagination* (1959), *The Power Elite* (1956), and *White Collar* (1951), all published by Oxford University Press. Mills also wrote *Character and Social Structure* (with Hans Gerth) (New York: Harcourt, Brace & World, 1953), an important source of the model that would become the sociological imagination. Mills also wrote an interesting book on Marxism, *The Marxists* (1962), published by Dell Books. Finally, Mills's anthology in sociological theory, *Images of Man: The Classic Tradition in Sociological Theory* (New York: Braziller, 1960), is a magnificent collection of works on the classic tradition.

There are also some interesting works about Mills's thought and life. Joseph Scimecca's *Sociological Theory of C. Wright Mills* (Port Washington, N.Y.: Kennikat Press, 1978) is an excellent survey of Mills's thought. A good brief introduction to Mills is John Eldridge's *C. Wright Mills* (London: Tavistock, 1983).

Works in the Tradition of C. Wright Mills

Two works inspired by Mills's view of power and crime are David R. Simon, *Elite Deviance,* 5th ed. (Needham Heights, Mass.: Allyn & Bacon, forthcoming), and Joel H. Henderson and David R. Simon, *Crimes of the Criminal Justice System* (Cincinnati: Anderson, 1994). A fine study influenced by Mills's view of white-collar workers is Arlie Hochschild, *The Managed Heart* (Berkeley: University of California Press, 1984).

Finally, the most important works inspired by Mills's political sociology are those by G. William Domhoff: *Who Rules America?* (Englewood Cliffs, N.J.: Prentice-Hall, 1967); *The Higher Circles* (New York: Random House, 1970); *Fat Cats and Democrats* (Englewood Cliffs, N.J.: Prentice-Hall, 1972); *The Bohemian Grove and Other Retreats* (New York: Harper & Row, 1974); *The Powers That Be* (New York: Random House, 1979); *Who Rules America Now?* (Englewood Cliffs, N.J.: Prentice-Hall, 1983); and *The Power Elite and the State: How Policy Is Made in America* (New York: De-Gruyter, 1990).

2

STRUCTURE AND CONTRADICTION IN MASS SOCIETY

GENERAL ELECTRIC: A SYMBOLIC CASE STUDY

General Electric (GE) is a massive multinational conglomerate with 107 factories in the United States and 103 plants in twenty-three foreign nations. It employs 243,000 American workers and has about 500,000 stockholders. About 300 major retail stores (including Levitz furniture and Montgomery Ward) use its credit card system, and its NBC television network has about 200 affiliated stations.

The third largest defense contractor in the United States, GE has been involved in the development of most major weapons systems over the past two decades, including the MX missile, the B-1 bomber, the Stealth aircraft, and the "Star Wars" (satellite defense system) program. GE is also a major builder of nuclear weapons. It even received government contracts to estimate Soviet military strength. On GE's board of directors sit General David Jones, retired head of the Joint Chiefs of Staff, and William French Smith, former attorney general of the United States. GE is the nation's second largest plastics manufacturer. Among its holdings are RCA, a cable television network, the Kidder Peabody stockbrokerage firm, and a bank, GE Capital, which has $91 billion in assets (Greider, 1992:335). In part because GE sells many items to the government, it maintains a highly active Washington lobby. General Electric is also among the most lawless American corporations.

Item: Between 1981 and 1983 GE had nets profits of $6.5 billion, but tax legislation brought it a tax rebate of $283 million from the debt-ridden federal

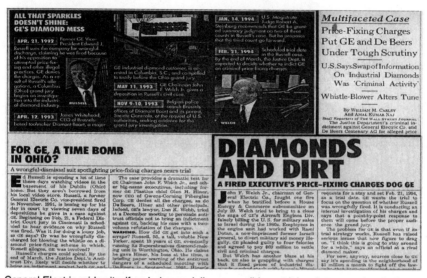

General Electric prides itself on being socially responsible, yet it has been convicted of criminal violations stretching back many years. If General Electric were a person instead of a corporation, it would be considered an habitual criminal.

government. In fact, from 1981 to 1987 GE saved over $1 billion on its taxes but created virtually no new American jobs. It was busy shrinking its American workforce by 50,000 employees, selling off its American subsidiaries, and aggressively buying other firms. In 1986 alone GE spent $11.1 billion to buy 338 companies, while it closed 73 of its own plants and offices (Greider, 1992:341–42). As we shall see, such corporate "restructuring" has contributed mightily to the economic decline of the United States since 1970.

Since the repeal of the law that gave GE all those tax advantages, the company has been carrying a $3.5 billion tax deferment on its books. It does so legally because, as a defense contractor, it doesn't have to pay its taxes until some future date.

In 1988 the government indicted GE on 317 counts of fraud in connection with a $21 million army contract for a logistics computer.

GE has a very long history of corporate crime:

• In 1961 GE was convicted of price-fixing and other charges in connection with the sale of electrical equipment valued at $1.74 billion a year. This was the largest price-fixing case since the Sherman Antitrust Act was passed in 1890.

• In 1981 GE was convicted of paying a $1.25 million bribe to a Puerto Rican official to obtain a contract for an electrical plant. Three GE executives were imprisoned.

• In 1986 GE officials at a machine tool company were charged with paying kickbacks to three former GE purchasing employees to obtain Pentagon subcontracts.

• In 1987 it was revealed that GE supplied thousands of defective airplane engines to military and civilian customers. The defects included cracks in tubing and brackets in the F-404 engine used in the F-18 navy fighter, the T-700 helicopter, and the CT-7 for small commuter planes (Simon & Eitzen, 1993:178–79).

• In 1989 GE's stockbrokerage firm, Kidder Peabody, paid $25.3 million to settle an insider trading complaint to the Securities and Exchange Commission. GE Capital paid a $275,000 civil penalty in 1989 for discriminating against low-income consumers, the largest fine ever levied under the Equal Credit Opportunity Act. GE itself paid a $32 million settlement to women and minorities in an employment discrimination case, and its Canadian subsidiary was convicted (along with Westinghouse and other firms) of conspiring to fix the prices of lightbulbs (Greider, 1992:350).

Item: GE is also a major polluter of the environment. Four of its factories are on the Environmental Protection Agency's list of the most dangerous industrial sources of air pollution. In addition, GE is responsible for contributing to the damage of forty-seven environmental cleanup sites. The company has paid tens of millions of dollars in out-of-court settlements for its dumping of chemicals that can cause cancer and birth defects in humans (Greider, 1992:351–52).

If GE were an individual, it would be considered a habitual criminal under American law. Instead, it tries to undo laws and cultivate a favorable public image by engaging in a host of image-enhancing activities.

Item: GE acts as a social philanthropist by giving away about $19 million a year through its tax-exempt foundations. Most of the money goes to scholarships for poor and minority college students. It also donates money to such charities as the United Way. Even charitable contributions further GE's political and economic aims. Some of GE's tax-exempt contributions go to a variety of lobbying groups:

• Chris Walker's American Council for Capital Formation, an "educational" front group that campaigns against the corporate income tax and for a national sales tax.
• The Institute for International Economics, a think tank that promotes corporate positions on economic policy and trade.
• Americans for Generational Equity, which campaigns for curtailment of the social security program (Greider, 1992: 338).

GE also finds other ways to promote its political views:

• It sponsors *The McLaughlin Group,* a right-wing TV talk show.
• It is a member of the Business Roundtable, which disseminates the views of the largest 500 American corporations.

• It is a member of the Committee on the Present Danger, a group financed by the defense industry, whose propaganda promoted the massive defense spending of the 1980s.

• It tripled its advertising budget to about $30 million a year in the mid-1980s, after the firm came under attack for its production of nuclear weapons and its involvement in various corporate scandals.

GE cultivates the image of a company that cares about its employees and "brings good things to light" by making lightbulbs and jet engines, inventing night baseball games, and helping liberate Hungary from communism. (GE got an exemption from U.S. antitrust laws so it could buy Hungary's state-owned Tungsram Company, Eastern Europe's major maker of lightbulbs.)

Many other corporations and organizations make visible contributions to the Public Broadcasting System and Jerry Lewis's Labor Day telethon, and many of them begin doing so after they have been involved in an embarrassing scandal. Spending on public image advertising by major American firms annually runs about $1 billion (Grieder, 1992:339). Evidence indicates that such public relations efforts do increase the public's trust in companies that are in danger of losing it (Winters, 1988).

Many large corporations also cultivate political goodwill by contributing to the campaigns of members of Congress. In 1988 GE's political action committees gave $595,000 to various congressional campaigns. GE paid an additional $50,000 directly to representatives and senators as speaking fees before the practice was ended (with a huge congressional pay raise) in 1990. Most of these speeches are given to members of the armed services and defense-related committees. The company has about two dozen permanent lobbyists and a large support staff in Washington to oversee its contributions. Indeed, the number of political action committees (PACs) in Washington rose from about 600 in the 1970s to 4585 by 1992, and all but about 365 of them are sponsored by corporations. "Candidates have become so dependent on PAC money that they actually visit PAC offices and all but demand contributions" (*The World Almanac of U.S. Politics,* 1993:19). The beer distributors' PAC is called Six PAC. There are also a Beef PAC and an Ice Cream PAC. These PACs may donate up to $5000 to each congressional candidate in both primary and general election campaigns. During the 1991–92 campaigns all Democratic congressional candidates raised $360 million, while Republican candidates raised $293 million. The Republican National Committee raised an additional $85.4 million while the Democratic National Committee raised $65.7 million. About 80 percent of these funds came from PACs.

General Electric is a symbol of a much more widespread condition that affects the structure of mass society and the contradictions and social harms it causes. General Electric's vast wealth and its influence on government policy suggest that American corporations and political organizations are intertwined in a political economy whose contradictions give rise to social problems. The idea of contradictions remains controversial in some respects (see Box 2-1), but there is solid evidence to support the proposition that the central contradiction of the modern social structure is inequality of wealth and power.

BOX 2-1

THE DEBATE OVER CONTRADICTIONS

Contradictions are inherent conflicts within the social structure that cannot be resolved without modification of the system (Mills, 1962:83; Worsley, 1982:10). The contradictions within a social structure vary over time. As social structures (that is, institutions and societies) change, the nature of contradictions likewise changes, as does the nature of the social problems they create. One economic contradiction can be seen in the idea that the way to make a profit is to hold down labor costs (wages and salaries). The conflict here is that businesses also want people (workers) to consume the goods they produce. Before people can consume, they must have money to spend.

The conflict between labor costs and consumption may generate any number of public problems. When a firm lays off workers to cut costs, it may decrease consumer demand for its products, thus creating the conditions that lead to recession or depression. Unemployment itself is linked to a host of personal troubles and social problems, including increased rates of suicide, mental illness, divorce, crime, and imprisonment. Unemployment may also devastate communities, as when a single-industry town is virtually shut down when a plant closes. Thus institutional contradictions generate public issues, and these public issues directly parallel personal troubles suffered by ordinary people.

Such contradictions may seem obvious, but the very idea of contradictions is troubling to many social scientists (Knapp & Spector, 1991: 319–24). The idea was first brought to sociological analysis by Karl Marx. Marx believed that contradictions were located in the economic substructure of societies in the form of class conflict. Under capitalism, the class of property owners (the bourgeoisie) was in conflict with the class of propertyless factory workers (the proletariat). These two classes form relations of production in which owners pay wages in exchange for the workers' labor (skills and time). The conflict inherent in this relationship is that workers end up exploited: the wages they are paid are disproportionately low in relation to the wealth they create. Marx believed that the labor it takes to create (manufacture) a product accounts for the entire worth of that product beyond the costs of raw materials and tools. Of course, the difference between those costs plus what workers are paid and the price that the products they manufacture sell for is called profit by capitalists. Marxists, however, call it surplus value; profit is merely exploitation.

This situation does not represent a social problem unless it results in demonstrable harm. Marx insisted that real harm was being inflicted on workers. As he and his colleague Friedrich Engels repeatedly demonstrated:

1 Workers were so poorly paid that they were barely able to afford basic necessities and lacked adequate medical care.

2 Workers labored under very dangerous conditions that often resulted in injury or death. Workers were injured by machines and by breathing in toxic chemicals and coal dust. In his *Capital* Marx describes one supervisor's testimony at a hearing to investigate the death of one of her employees. The employee died after working "26½ hours, with 60 other girls, 30 in one room, that afforded only one third of the cubic feet of air required for them" (Marx, 1952:123). The supervisor describes her disappointment that the worker failed to finish the dress she was sewing before she died!

3 Work was not only poorly paid and physically dangerous; it was stressful and boring. Workers had no voice in the quality of the products they produced, their prices, or the work process itself. Laborers were simply required to keep up with the pace of production, or they were fired and replaced by other workers, who were competing for the same jobs. Marx termed these working conditions that psychically and physically harmed workers alienating, and related how they contributed to workers' feelings of isolation, loneliness, powerlessness, and self-estrangement. In short, working conditions under capitalism did not allow workers to exercise their own human nature, to be creative.

Much of what Marx saw as problematic in nineteenth-century capitalism was of concern to Charles Dickens and many other writers. Contradictions exist and cause problems in all social structures, not just economic institutions. Some of Marx's observations about capitalism's structure and contradictions still seem relevant, yet capitalism's structure and its contradictions have changed dramatically since Marx died in 1883. Thus Marx's insights have limited utility today, and they are made more limited still by "vulgar" Marxists, who believe that every aspect of society is economically determined. One problem with such reductionism is that it overlooks other social structures that also generate contradictions, which in turn cause social problems.

THE POLITICAL ECONOMY AND THE POWER ELITE

In 1956 C. Wright Mills warned the America people of a growing centralization and coordination of wealth and power in the United States. He wrote (1956:7–8):

The economy . . . has become dominated by two or three hundred giant corporations, administratively and politically integrated, which together hold the keys to economic decisions. The political [system] has become a centralized, executive establishment which has taken unto itself many powers previously scattered, and now enters into each and every cranny of the social structure. The military . . . has become the largest and most expensive feature of government, and, although well versed in smiling public relations, now has all the grim and clumsy efficiency of a sprawling [bureaucracy]. . . . There is no longer, on the one hand, an economy, and, on the other hand, a political order containing a military establishment unimportant to politics and to money making. There is a political order linked, in a thousand ways, with military institutions and decisions. . . . If there is government intervention in the corporate economy, so there is corporate intervention in the governmental process.

Collectively the people who head these institutions of great power (large corporations, the executive branch of the government, and the military apparatus) form what Mills termed the *power elite.* Six years later, in 1961, President Dwight D. Eisenhower called them the *military-industrial complex.* These two terms are interchangeable.

The Corporate Sector

The corporate component of the power elite's structure is made up of the largest 100 to 200 industrial corporations in the nation and the insurance companies, banks, and other financial entities (such as mutual funds) that own stock in them. The largest 100 firms are usually awarded about 75 percent of the contracts for major weapons systems by the Department of Defense (the Pentagon). Weapons systems account for about 30 percent of the nation's military budget.

The 100 largest industrial corporations dominate the entire corporate sector of the American economy. They control more industrial assets than the next 199,900 corporations combined (about 60 percent of such assets are controlled by the 100 largest firms). The five largest industrial corporations (General Motors, Exxon, Ford Motor Company, IBM, and General Electric) alone control 15 percent of the nation's industrial assets (Dye & Zeigler, 1993:98).

The largest 100 corporations are also multinational: they own factories and contract for labor and raw materials in many nations throughout the world. They also tend to be interlocked. The Clayton Antitrust Act of 1914 forbids any company to own stock in another company in the same industry. Thus General Motors (GM), for example, cannot own stock in Ford. However, if a large bank buys a 5 percent interest in GM and a 5 percent interest in Ford, the bank can sit on both boards of directors. This practice is known as an *interlocking directorate.* This is the story of much corporate ownership.

One study of the 250 largest American corporations found that all but 17 of them have at least one chief executive sitting on the board of another corporation. Over 250 directors of the top 500 American corporations hold seats on the boards of competing firms. Much of this interlocking stems from the fact that the 50 largest banks (which control 66 percent of all banking assets) hold seats on the boards of America's 500 largest firms. As of the late 1970s, one large New York bank, Morgan Guarantee Trust, was the single largest stockholder in 122 of the largest American corporations. The Rockefeller-owned Chase Manhattan Bank is interlocked with the nation's 100 largest corporations. Finally, large banks and financial institutions own blocks of one another's stock. Citibank and Chase Manhattan are the largest owners of Morgan Guarantee Trust (Simon & Eitzen, 1993:16).

What all this means is that the 200 or so largest corporations and some 50 financial institutions control about two-thirds of all business income and half of all bank deposits. These firms are interlocked by directorships controlled by less than one-half of 1 percent of the nation's population (Simon & Eitzen, 1993:16–17). This great concentration of corporate ownership and the immense political influence corporations exercise have enabled corporate America to escape effective regulation by government.

The nation's 500 largest corporations account for 90 percent of all prime-time television advertising. These large firms also hire the nation's largest and most prestigious law firms, many of which employ former members of the president's cabinet. And defense contractors have hired over 4500 high-ranking retired military officers and 350 retired civilian Pentagon employees.

Defense contractors employ almost 16 percent of the civilian workforce, including nearly 20 percent of all U.S. corporate managers and adminstrators (Simon & Eitzen, 1993:167).

The Military Sector

The military component of the complex consists of the major branches of the military services (army, navy, and air force), as well as the nation's intelligence community (the National Security Council, the Central Intelligence Agency, the Defense Intelligence Agency, and the intelligence arms of the various branches of the military). Involved as well are the Veterans Administration and organizations representing the nation's veterans (the Veterans of Foreign Wars, the American Legion). The secrecy of the intelligence apparatus and its web of affiliations with the military services have created something of a "secret government" (Moyers, 1988). Since 1945 the actions of this secret government have had immense consequences for the nation's foreign and defense policies.

The Political Sector

The political sector includes defense contracting lobbies, members of Congress who sit on the appropriations committees of the U.S. Senate and House of Representatives, the Joint Chiefs of Staff, and the civilian administrators (the secretary of defense and the secretaries of the various armed services) who oversee the nation's military establishment. Two-thirds of all the nation's congressional districts either contain or border on military installations or defense plants (Simon & Eitzen, 1993: 172).

The Research and Policy-Formulating Sector

The military-industrial complex also possesses a research and policy-formulating sector. The lion's share of Pentagon-funded research goes to twelve elite universities and to a series of think tanks (private research firms, such as the Rand Corporation and the Stanford Research Institute) that do research, much of it highly classified. Through private foundations the nation's largest corporations have also set up a series of policy-formulating associations that publish journals and issue white (position) papers on various policy questions.

Many Americans wonder if there is still a military-industrial complex in the post–Cold War world. While the Pentagon's budget has been cut somewhat, weapons are still being produced in significant numbers and varieties. Domestic orders for weapons are declining, yet the United States' defense budget is still "larger than most national economies" (Evans, 1993:14). Moreover, 60 percent of all weapons purchased by foreign nations are produced by U.S. corporations.

Many of these sales are paid for by your tax dollars as part of foreign aid. In 1994 Israel alone received $1.8 billion in foreign aid to purchase military aircraft. Thus the export arm of the defense industry is thriving. In short, there is no evidence that the arms complex has disappeared or will do so any time soon. The 1994 defense budget, in 1994 dollars, is $33 billion more than it was in 1975, at the end of the Vietnam War (Evans, 1993:18).

WHO RUNS THE MILITARY-INDUSTRIAL COMPLEX?: THE NATIONAL UPPER CLASS

The power elite is dominated by a group of people that compose a significant segment of America's national upper class. One can spot members of the upper class by a few characteristic indicators:

1 Their names and addresses appear in the *Social Register,* a list of socially influential people published in major U.S. cities. About 138,000 Americans are listed in the various editions of the *Social Register.*

2 They have attended private elite preparatory schools and universities. Among the favored preparatory schools are St. Paul's in New Hampshire, Hotchkiss in Connecticut, Foxcroft in Virginia, and Chapin in New York (Gilbert & Kahl, 1993:211). (The elite universities are listed in Figure 2-1.)

3 They belong to exclusive social clubs and attend upper-class vacation retreats (Bohemian Grove, Knickerbocker Club, Pacific Union).

4 They sit on the boards of directors of the nation's largest corporations (Domhoff, 1967: 87–96).

5 Their annual income is typically in the millions of dollars and their

Great wealth has always existed side by side with grinding, widespread poverty in America. People carrying signs like this one are plainly visible in every major American city. Recent government estimates place the number of homeless in America at around 7 million. No other industrial democracy in the world allows its citizens to go without shelter. (Edwin Remsburg/Gamma Liaison)

wealth typically totals tens of millions of dollars. These 0.5% of Americans possess 25 to 30 percent of all privately held wealth (Domhoff, 1993:174), an increase of 6.7% between 1979 and 1989 (Dowd, 1993:223). The ramifications of this increasing inequality are explored in Chapter 4.

Item: A study of the president's cabinet from 1897 to 1973 found that the percentage of cabinet members coming from big business increased from 60 percent (in William McKinley's administration) to 95.5 percent (in Nixon's administration) (Freitag, 1975).

Item: Another study found that 63 percent of the secretaries of state, 62 percent of the secretaries of defense, and 63 percent of the secretaries of the treasury have been members of the national upper class (Kerbo, 1993:227). Among the members of the power elite we find:

• John Foster Dulles, secretary of state from 1953 to 1960. Before his appointment he was senior partner in a prestigious law firm, Sullivan &

Cromwell, and sat on the boards of numerous corporations: Bank of New York, American Bank Note Company, United Railroad, International Nickel of Canada, American Cotton Oil Company, and European Textile Corporation. Dulles was also a trustee of leading civic organizations: the New York Public Library, the Rockefeller Foundation, and the Carnegie Endowment for International Peace. His brother, Allen, was director of central intelligence (1953–1961) and was a member of the Warren Commission, the panel set up by President Lyndon B. Johnson to investigate the assassination of President Kennedy.

• Alexander Haig, secretary of state in 1981–82, is currently president of United Technologies Corporation, a major defense contractor. Haig is a former four-star general and former supreme commander of NATO forces in Europe; former assistant to President Nixon; former deputy commander of the U.S. Military Academy at West Point; and former deputy secretary of defense. He is the man most responsible for the terms set down in the pardon of President Nixon after the Watergate scandal.

• George Bush's secretary of the treasury, Nicholas Brady, was a former chairman of Dillon Read, a major Wall Street investment firm, and a member of the boards of directors of Purolator, NCR, Georgia International, and Media General.

• Jimmy Carter's secretary of the treasury, Michael Blumenthal, is president of the Bendix Corporation, former vice president of Crown Cork, and trustee of the Council on Foreign Relations.

Bill Clinton promised the American people a cabinet that would "look like America," with women and minorities represented; but he did not promise us a cabinet that would look like America in social class makeup. President Clinton has appointed more millionaires to cabinet posts than Reagan and Bush (Savio, 1993: 24–26). Among them:

• Treasury Secretary Lloyd Bentsen, champion of tax breaks for corporations during his Senate career. Of the $2.5 million in Bentsen's campaign fund for his last Senate bid, 89 percent came from corporate PACs. Bentsen's personal worth exceeds $10 million, and his holdings include a number of businesses in Texas. His deputy secretary, Roger Altman, comes from a Wall Street investment firm, the Blackstone Group, which has been involved in the four largest acquisitions of American firms by Japanese firms, including Sony's takeover of Columbia Pictures and CBS Records.

• Commerce Secretary Ron Brown, former head of the Democratic National Committee. As a partner in an elite law firm, Patton, Boggs, & Blow, Brown has represented many major corporations, including Japan Air Lines and American Express, and his firm represents such clients as Mutual Life Insurance, New York Life, and the former dictator of Haiti, "Baby Doc" Duvalier.

President Bill Clinton promised to appoint cabinet members who resembled America. However, cabinet members such as Treasury Secretary Lloyd Bentson (upper left), Commerce Secretary Ron Brown (upper right), and Secretary of State Warren Christopher (lower left) are all multimillionaires with many ties to the associations that make up the American power elite. Clinton's appointments resemble the 0.0004 percent of the American upper class that occupies key positions in American governmental and corporate life. (Upper left: Cynthia Johnson/Gamma Liaison; upper right: Reuters/Bettmann; lower left: Diana Walker/Gamma Liaison)

• U.S. Trade Representative Mickey Kantor, law partner in Manatt, Phelps, Phillips, & Kantor, which has represented Occidental Petroleum, ARCO, Martin Marietta, and Philip Morris. Kantor represented tobacco-industry groups in their efforts to prevent passage of a smokefree restaurant bill in Beverly Hills, California.

• Secretary of State Warren Christopher, lawyer from O'Melveny & Meyers. He represented Exxon in the lawsuits stemming from its pollution of Prince William Sound, Alaska. He also represented E. F. Hutton when it was revealed that Hutton had regularly taken advantage of the lag between the time checks were written and the time they actually cleared, thus giving themselves millions in interest-free loans. Christopher has also served on the board of Southern California Edison, Lockheed, United Airlines, Banker's Trust (New York), Occidental Petroleum, and Japan's Fuji Bank and Mitsubishi Corporation.

It makes little difference, then, whether the White House is occupied by a Republican or a Democrat. Most of the people who run the government have corporate backgrounds and shares remarkably similar educational and cultural experiences and affiliations.

Numerous additional studies support the finding that the upper class not only is overrepresented in governmental circles but runs corporate America as well.

• 54% of members of boards of directors of the twenty largest American corporations are from the upper class.

• 62% of members of the boards of directors of the nation's fifteen largest banks are from the upper class.

• 44% of members of boards of directors of the nation's fifteen largest insurance companies are from the upper class.

• 53% of members of boards of directors of the nation's fifteen largest transportation companies are from the upper class (Kerbo, 1993:225).

The power elite makes certain its wishes are given every consideration in Washington and in other governmental circles by exerting an influence on the policy-making process (Domhoff, 1974; Kerbo, 1993; Greenberg, 1985; Greider, 1992). The policy-making process is composed of a series of interrelated practices engaged in on an ongoing basis by corporate, political, and military elites. The corporate rich exert their political influence by:

1 Donating substantial sums of money to political candidates.
2 Occasionally running for office.
3 Holding posts in the executive branch of the federal government.
4 Establishing private foundations and elite associations and sponsoring university research. The policy position statements that issue from these activities are readily given to politicians the corporate elites wish to influence.
5 Spending billions of dollars in "institutional" advertising and "charitable" ventures in efforts to create a favorable public image and socialize the public in the ideology of free enterprise.

Major corporations are not the only institutional players in the policy-making process.

1 Twenty-five elite universities and colleges annually garner half of all educational endowment funds, and some 656 corporate elites sit on their boards of trustees. A mere 50 foundations (out of over 1200) control 40 percent of all foundation assets. Foundations account for a large proportion of funds devoted to university and foundation research. Foundation executives usually have experience in either corporate America or the federal government.

2 Elite civic associations (such as the Council on Foreign Relations) bring together national (and sometimes international) elites from the corporate, educational, legal, and governmental worlds. The political scientist Thomas Dye (1990) views these associations as coordinators of national policy. These organizations typically issue white papers on domestic and international policy matters. Membership in them is often a prerequisite for a high-ranking cabinet post. Twenty of the last twenty-one secretaries of state, for example, have been members of the Council on Foreign Relations (Simon & Eitzen, 1993:20–23)

3 The mass media are central to the policy-making process because they set limits on the breadth of ideological views that will enter the policy-making debate in the United States. The media also choose which stories to emphasize and which to ignore. The major media almost completely ignored the savings and loan scandal, for example, until the industry's losses became so overwhelming that Congress had to vote billions of dollars to bail it out. Finally, the media are merely a group of corporations that are owned by other corporations and financial institutions. Controlling shares in the three major television networks are owned by five large New York banks (Citibank, Chase, Morgan Guarantee, Bank of New York, and Banker's Trust). The 500 largest American corporations account for 90 percent of all prime-time television network advertising revenues.

4 Twenty-eight large law firms do much of the legal work for corporations and the upper class. Ninety percent of all the legal work in the United States is done for a mere 10 percent of the population. These law firms are also heavily involved in the lobbying process in Washington, and many of their partners are former members of the president's cabinet, as we have seen.

5 The research institutes known as think tanks typically receive money from corporate and governmental sources. The Rand Corporation and the Stanford Research Institute (owned by Stanford University until 1970) are annually awarded about 5 percent of the Pentagon's research and development budget (Simon & Eitzen, 1993:23). The process by which the power elite makes public policy is described in Figure 2-1.

Numerous studies have confirmed the power of elite networks in America and other modern democracies (Olsen & Marger, 1993:153–249; Greenberg, 1985; Domhoff, 1990). No one has described the current policy-making

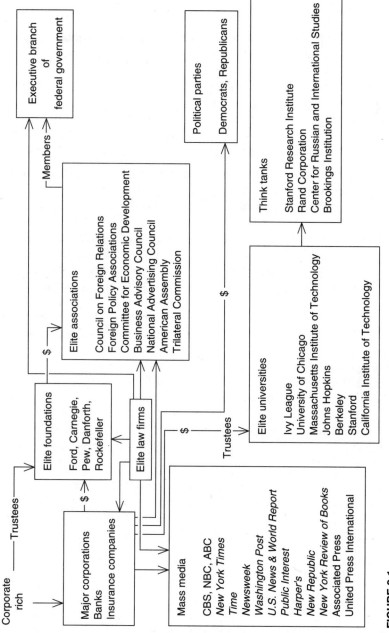

FIGURE 2-1
POLICY MAKING AMONG THE POWER ELITE.
(Adapted from G. William Domhoff, "State and Ruling Class in Corporate America," *The Insurgent Sociologist* 4 (Spring 1974): 9. By permission of G. William Domhoff and *The Insurgent Sociologist.*

process better than the journalist William Greider (1992), who notes a funda-mental contradiction in American political and economic life: the public has great contempt for its politicians and politicians are contemptuous of the pub-lic. The two are locked in a dance of mutual distrust, cynicism, and alienation. Politicians know full well that "the people" are not their constituents. The elites who finance elections are their real constituents. Democracy has be-come a ritual dance in which politicians profess to care about the common people and their needs (jobs, health care, homelessness), but behind the scenes the interests of organized money groups call the tune.

What has emerged in Washington is a shadow government made up of public relations firms, think tanks, and polling organizations, all funded by corporate interests. The results are staggering:

• Fifty-one U.S. senators and 146 members of the House of Representa-tives are either founders or officers of tax-exempt organizations that produce either research statistics or corporate propaganda for lobbying purposes (Greider, 1992:51).

• In 1960 fewer than 400 lobbyists were registered with the U.S. Con-gress. By 1992 40,000 were so registered (Perot, 1993:120). Those 40,000 people represent mostly American and foreign corporations. Much of this growth came in the 1970s and 1980s, when the capitalist class decided it was underrepresented in the nation's capital. Eighty percent of the *Fortune* 500 corporations established "public affairs offices" (lobbies) in Washington.

• In the 1970s new think tanks were established and richly endowed by corporate money. The right-wing Heritage Foundation was started with a $250,000 donation from the Colorado beer tycoon Joseph Coors (Gilbert & Kahl, 1993:224–25). The patrons of the American Enterprise Institute include AT&T ($125,000), Chase Manhattan Bank ($125,000), Exxon ($130,000), General Electric ($65,000), General Motors ($100,000), and Procter & Gam-ble ($165,000). The "institute" quickly became a "primary source of Wash-ington opinion," shaping the policy positions of Washington politicians and the mass media (Greider, 1992:48).

Elite rule has not only made the United States less democratic by convert-ing American democracy into what Greider terms "a busy commerce in deal making" (1992:112); it has also converted much of American society into what C. Wright Mills described as "a network of rackets" (1960:17).

BEYOND THE UNITED STATES: THE NEW WORLD ORDER

The world's societies are interdependent economically, politically, culturally, and environmentally. Consequently, conflict anywhere on the globe affects conditions in other nations. A fundamentalist religious sect in Egypt can now easily bomb the World Trade Center in New York. Starving Somalis can appear on U.S. network news programs and soon spur the mobilization of U.S. troops.

The post–Cold War world system—Bush's "new world order"—began in 1989 with the fall of the Berlin Wall and the disintegration of the communist bloc. The Soviet Union itself fragmented into a fluid alliance of regions that barely hang together as a "commonwealth of independent states." The American news media remain fixated on the old Soviet Union in an effort to convince the American public that the Cold War was worth the sacrifices of Vietnam and $4 trillion in military spending. Thus inordinate attention has been paid to the various crises in the nations of the former USSR since 1989:

- The 1992 military coup that toppled the government of General Secretary Mikhail Gorbechav.
- The 1993 revolt against Russian president Boris Yeltsin that culminated in an assault by Russian troops on the parliament building (the "White House") and purged Yeltsin's critics four months before new elections were to be held.
- The civil wars raging in Georgia, Azerbaijan, and other remnants of the old Soviet empire.

The real power blocs of the new world order, however, gain their strength more from economic prowess than from military might. These blocs are composed of three groups of nations, popularly known as the First, Second, and Third Worlds (Perdue, 1993; Russell, 1992:52).

The First World

The First World includes the advanced capitalist democracies of North American, Western Europe, and Japan. Within the First World are actually three formidable economic alliances in Europe, Asia, and North America.

The European Communities (EC) In 1967 the European Common Market was created by the merger of three organizations: the European Coal and Steel Community, the European Atomic Energy Commission (Euratom), and the European Economic Community. Today the European Communities consist of Belgium, Denmark, France, Germany, Greece, Ireland, Italy, Luxembourg, the Netherlands, Portugal, Spain, and the United Kingdom. The European Act of 1987 committed these nations to form a single European market by the end of 1992, eliminating all barriers to trade and the free movement of people and investment capital. The EC is composed of 340 million potential consumers. The nations that have become independent with the collapse of the Soviet empire (Hungary, Romania, Poland, and so on) have also expressed an interest in joining the EC.

The Asian Pacific Bloc   A second bloc of advanced capitalist powers is found among the rapidly developing nations of the Pacific. Popularly known as "the flying geese," they are Japan, South Korea, Singapore, Thailand, Taiwan, and Malaysia. These nations have achieved huge trade surpluses since 1980. Each year from 1984 to 1993 the United States imported goods worth over $100 billion more than those it exported, and most of these imports came from Japan. The Asian "geese" nations all trade with one another and have developed extensive joint ventures. They are also economically active with the People's Republic of China, the nation with the fastest-growing economy in the world.

The Americas   A free-trade agreement signed by the United States and Canada in 1988 created a potential $6 trillion consumer and manufacturing zone. Mexico joined the North American Free Trade Agreement in 1993. The potential of this alliance rivals that of the EC and the Asian Pacific nations.

The Second World

The Second World of nations consists of the formerly communist nations of Eastern Europe and the old Soviet Union. Russia is now in turmoil. The other Eastern European nations are struggling to make the transition to a market economy with varying degrees of success, but there is every chance that at least some of them will be integrated into the EC in future decades.

The Third World

The Third World is composed of the poorest nations of Asia, Africa, and Latin America. Economically, politically, and culturally the world system is dominated by the First World. While First World nations often come into conflict (witness Japan's "invasion" of the American automobile market), they also cooperate. There is now essentially one international capitalist economy, which is the basis on which all national economies function. Countries in the Second and Third Worlds have progressively lost sovereignty over their own economies. The more powerful the capitalist world system grows, the more that system, rather than any national economy, becomes the focus of economic and class conflicts.

Inequalities of wealth and power within and between the three groups of nations cause numerous social problems. The Third World is desperately poor, and much of it is starving. About 10,000 people die of starvation each day and 1.5 billion people lack medical care. The average per capita income in 1991 ranged from less than $350 a year in Ethiopia and Kenya to under $3000 a year in Mexico, Turkey, and Chile (the U.S. per capita income in 1991 was nearly $22,000) (*The World Almanac and Book of Facts,* 1993:742,

This densely crowded Third World slum in Rio de Janeiro, Brazil, is fairly typical of the living conditions experienced by the hundreds of millions of urban poor in the Third World. Daily life in many nations is a constant struggle for food and survival. An estimated 30 million Third World women have been sold into prostitution in recent decades. (Claudia Andujar Love/Ford Foundation)

752, 778, 811). In most Third World nations, about 3 percent of the population own 60 to 90 percent of all private wealth, and military dictatorships attempt to keep the poor masses from making revolutions that might bring a better life. These dictatorships are kept in power in part with military and other aid from the United States and other advanced capitalist nations. Collectively, Third World nations owe First World governments and banks over $1.3 trillion (Dowd, 1993:391). This debt makes Third World nations vulnerable to First World demands regarding wage levels, trade practices, and a host of other policies. Meanwhile, multinational corporations make substantial returns on investments in Third World nations, but do not reinvest their profits in these poor lands. Instead, profits tend to be paid to stockholders or invested in other overseas ventures in First and Second World nations.

As a result, the Third World is plagued by numerous social problems, many with global consequences: overpopulation, illegal emigration to First World nations, pollution, wars, violations of human rights, famines. Moreover, American elites have at times supported Third World governments that have engaged in serious violations of human rights. Human rights are defined in two treaties of which the United States is a signatory, the United Nations

Declaration of Human Rights of the 1940s and the Helsinki Agreement of 1975. Among these rights are freedom from arrest without probable cause, freedom from kidnapping and torture, and freedom of speech and of the press. Yet the United States has played an important role in supporting regimes that violate human rights, all in the name of anticommunism.

Guatemala   In 1954 the CIA directed a coup that toppled the government of Jacobo Arbenz in Guatemala. After it was learned that Arbenz planned to implement a land-reform program by requiring the United Fruit Company to sell land not under cultivation at the low valuation it had claimed for tax purposes, the Eisenhower administration, recklessly branding Arbenz a communist, replaced him with a U.S. Army–trained officer, Carlos Castillo Armas. Castillo Armas issued a decree giving himself all executive and legislative functions, halted the land-reform program, canceled the registration of more than 500 labor unions, and required all unions to be certified free of communist influence by a government committee. He was assassinated in 1957, but his policies lived on. Between 1963 and 1993 his U.S.-backed successors tortured and killed 150,000 of their own citizens and kidnapped 50,000 more. Guatemala's human rights record was so grotesque that in 1990 the Bush administration was forced to suspend aid under congressional pressure (Johnson et al., 1993: 13; Simon & Eitzen, 1993: 201).

The Bush administration claimed in 1991 that the Guatemalan human rights record was improving, but the evidence contradicted this assertion. Human rights groups documented 730 assassinations and 100 disappearances (an average of three a day) between January and September 1991. A Guatemalan Indian woman, Rigoberta Menchú, was awarded the Nobel Peace Prize in 1992 for her efforts to get the government to stop relocating and killing her people (the government forcibly relocated a million Indians between 1982 and 1991). The Reagan and Bush administrations provided Guatemala with over $77 million in aid during this period.

Chile   In 1973 the CIA supported a coup that ousted the democratically elected government of the Marxist Salvador Allende. Allende was murdered in the overthrow and replaced by a brutal dictator, General Augusto Pinochet. Two years later, one of every 125 Chilean citizens had been arrested and detained for more than a day. People were routinely held for twenty days or more without notification of their families. A wide range of torture methods were reported: rape, shocks applied through electrodes on knees and genitals, sleep deprivation, mock execution, submersion in water, live rats shoved into victims' mouths. Pinochet built himself a 15,000-square-foot house with an infared security system at a cost of between $10 and $13 million, and secured it with a private force of eighty guards. He finally left office in 1989 after losing a plebiscite (Neier & Brown, 1987; Simon & Eitzen, 1993:202–3).

El Salvador Between 1978 and 1993 more than 40,000 people were killed in El Salvador by government-supported right-wing death squads, and 800,000 people (20 percent of the population) became refugees. Between 1979 and 1984 the Reagan administration gave El Salvador six times more aid than it had received in the previous thirty years. In 1980 the government's death squads raped and murdered four American nuns, and Amnesty International declared the death squads' activities a gross abuse of human rights. Over the years such multinational corporations as Chevron, Kimberly-Clark, and Texaco have invested over $100 million in El Salvador (Kwitney, 1984: 10–11; Caldicott, 1984:160). Human rights abuses in El Salvador continue in the 1990s. A United Nations observer mission reported 105 assassinations, 15 kidnappings, and 281 illegal captures by security forces in 1992. In January 1993 the widow and children of a former head of the Salvadoran Human Rights Commission were fired on by government troops. The children had personally witnessed their father's murder by the government in 1987 (Johnson et al., 1993: 54–55).

Foreign Aid The U.S. government still supplies some of the world's most oppressive regimes with foreign aid and weapons. Much of this aid is obtained with the help of highly paid Washington lobbyists.

• In 1991 Guatemala received $91 million in American aid, even though arms sales to that nation had been ordered suspended because of human rights abuses. The Guatemalan government paid $680,000 to public relations firms (one of which was Commerce Secretary Brown's law firm).
• Turkey receives about $800 million annually in U.S. aid. It spends $3.8 million on lobbying efforts in Washington. Political killings in Turkey increased 600 percent between 1991 and 1992, many of them committed by government security forces (Gozan, 1993:6–7).

U.S. support for regimes that violate human rights is an indication of a much more fundamental problem both inside and outside the United States.

BUREAUCRACY AND THE HIGHER IMMORALITY

The power elite have become the most dominant force in American life and in that of other advanced capitalist nations. As we have seen, their influence holds Third World nations in a tight grip. These institutions are shapers of social character. Their ethical and moral priorities have become the central values of American culture. Indeed, a central contradiction among the power elite is that they frequently violate the very laws they are sworn to uphold. This set of deviant practices has been termed the *higher immorality* (Mills, 1956:343–61; Simon & Eitzen, 1993:49–90). These violations take place in part because of the way corporate, political, and military intelligence institutions are structured: they are bureaucracies. Bureaucratic organizations are structured in ways that regularize crime and deviance.

Forms of the Higher Immorality

First, bureaucratic organizations are goal-oriented. They exist to make money or to expand their power. This means that bureaucracies are amoral entities: they recognize no moral constraints, only goals, and there is often nothing moral about their goals. From time to time most organizations want to achieve goals they cannot pursue within the limits imposed by existing rules, laws, or ethical codes. When this happens, organizations secretly engage in illegal or unethical behaviors. Power in bureaucracies is concentrated at the top. The people who head the organizations are shielded from their workers and from the public by layers of secretaries, public relations departments, and lawyers. It is this hierarchical structure that makes secrecy a central characteristic of bureaucratic life. This combination of goal orientation and secrecy makes scandal a frequent occurrence.

Item: In the 1970s Ford hurriedly rushed its Pinto automobile into production. This car contained an unprotected gas tank that would explode if the car were hit from the rear at speeds as low as 5 miles per hour. Ford executives wrote a secret memo (subsequently leaked to the press) comparing the estimated amount of money the company would have pay out in wrongful death claims with the estimated amount it would have to pay to fix the gas tanks in all the vehicles. The memo clearly demonstrated that it would be more profitable to let people die or be seriously injured than to insert an $11 rubber bladder inside the gas tank. The result: Ford let the unsafe Pinto roll off the assembly line and hundreds of people were either killed or maimed.

Item: After the Nicaraguan Contras mined the harbor in Managua in 1982, the U.S. Congress voted to cut off all military aid to them. The Reagan administration, determined to continue sending aid to the Contras, set up a secret operation that sold arms to Iran and funneled part of the profits to the Contras. As a result of the Iran-Contra scandal, several members of the Reagan administration resigned from office or were sent to prison.

These are not the only instances of the higher immorality. Socially patterned deviant and criminal acts among the power elite take many forms.

Violations of Antitrust, Advertising, and Pollution Laws Corporate crime in the form of violation of antitrust, advertising, and pollution laws costs American consumers an estimated $200 billion a year, forty times more than estimated losses from street crime (Donahue, 1992:16). Studies reveal that only about 2 percent of corporate crime cases result in imprisonment. Moreover, a study conducted in the 1970s (Clinard, 1979) revealed that:

- 60 percent of the 582 largest American corporations committed at least one crime in a twenty-four-month period (a rate confirmed by subsequent studies).
- Nearly half of the crimes were committed in just three industries: autos, petroleum, and drugs. These industries comprise some of the largest and most politically active firms in the nation.
- Of those firms charged with at least one crime, the average number of crimes charged was 4.2—a rate approaching habitual criminality.

Amitai Etzioni (1990:33) found that between 1975 and 1984, 62 percent of the *Fortune* 500 companies were involved in one or more incidents of corrupt behavior (bribery, price-fixing, tax fraud, or violations of environmental regulations). A study of the twenty-five largest *Fortune* 500 corporations found that all were either found guilty of criminal behavior or fined for civil violations between 1977 and 1990 (Donahue, 1992:17–18).

Corruption, Violations of Civil Liberties, and Unethical Campaign Practices The Watergate scandal of 1972–74 is the classic example of political corruption. Watergate was actually an endless series of miniscandals:

- Burglars, bankrolled by the Committee to Reelect the President, broke into the headquarters of the Democratic National Committee in the Watergate complex in Washington, D.C., and planted eavesdropping devices for reasons still unknown. The burglars, all former CIA agents, some associated with the 1961 Bay of Pigs fiasco, were promised executive clemency and hush money by the White House.
- Another burglary was committed at the office of Daniel Ellsberg's psychiatrist. Ellsberg, who had leaked the Pentagon Papers to the *New York Times,* was standing trial at the time. While the trial was in progress, the judge in the case was approached with an offer of the directorship of the FBI. The judge declared a mistrial.
- President Nixon had placed microphones in his own office and in the offices of his top aides to record every conversation.
- Nixon's vice president, Spiro Agnew, confessed to accepting kickbacks on government contracts from Maryland contractors and resigned from office as part of a plea bargain.
- A White House secret intelligence unit, called "the plumbers" because they were intended to stop leaks to the press, engaged in a host of dirty tricks aimed at discrediting potential Democratic presidential candidates. They wrote and distributed letters that allegedly came from Senator Edmund Muskie's campaign charging that Senator Henry Jackson was a homosexual. They hired prostitutes and planted them at campaign rallies to embarrass opposition candidates.
- Nixon's administration generated an "enemy list" of its critics inside and

outside government and illegally misused the Internal Revenue Service by requesting tax audits of those critics. The FBI and CIA were manipulated into cutting short the investigation into Watergate, and the head of the FBI even destroyed vital evidence in the case by burning files along with Christmas wrappings.

• Nixon lied repeatedly to Congress concerning both his involvement in the case and his possession of evidence that would reveal his involvement. Nixon offered his two top aides, John Erlichman and H. R. Halderman, money in exchange for their silence. He had his personal attorney solicit illegal campaign contributions in exchange for promises of ambassadorships. Money from these contributions was illegally laundered to conceal the donors' identities.

• Attorney General John Mitchell helped plan the bugging of the Democratic National Committee. Mitchell and numerous other Nixon administration officials were convicted of perjury and other crimes and sent to prison.

Unfair Compensation, Tax Advantages, and Subsidies American corporate executives make 300 times more on average than do their employees, and some of the special benefits they receive have caused major scandals. This is especially the case with regard to the $500 billion savings and loan scandal of the 1980s.

Several S&Ls paid their executives fabulous sums while they were losing considerable amounts of money. During the period when the Lincoln S&L was losing $300 million, its owner, Charles Keating, paid himself and his staff (which included several members of his family) some $4 million in salaries.

Under the charter of the Resolution Trust Corporation, formed by Congress to bail out ailing S&Ls, all S&L assets are guaranteed profitable for ten years by direct federal subsidy. Among the big winners:

• Arizona businessman James Fall received $1.5 billion in government subsidies to buy fifteen failed S&Ls while putting up only $1,000 of his own money.
• Trammel Crow, a Texas billionaire, and his partners invested $128 million in 1989 and received $3.2 billion in thrift assets and $1.49 billion in federal aid. Crow donated $128,000 to the 1988 Bush campaign.
• Robert Bass invested $550 million in American Savings and Loan and in return received ownership of a $30 billion S&L along with $2.5 billion in cash for a profit of $31.95 billion. Bass promptly created a separate S&L branch for the institution's bad loans and used $1.5 billion in S&L deposits to finance corporate mergers (*San Diego Times Union,* September 1, 1991, p. A-2).

The Creation of Phony Crises and the Manipulation of Public Opinion   The power elite are adept at creating "crises" and manipulating public opinion for financial and political advantage.

- In the 1970s, American oil companies used the excuse of an embargo by the Organization of Petroleum Exporting Countries (OPEC) to quadruple the price of gasoline, even though there was no evidence of a shortage of gasoline in the United States.
- After a televised speech on Vietnam, President Nixon claimed his views were shared by an overwhelming majority of Americans and substantiated his claim by holding up some of the 10,000 telegrams he said he had received in support. Actually, Nixon had his staff send the messages.
- In the late 1980s President Bush portrayed Iraq's Saddam Hussein as an evil dictator who was creating a huge military machine that threatened the peace of the Middle East and the world. In truth, the United States had been selling weapons to Iraq for years, in violation of its own laws. Just before Hussein marched into Kuwait, the U.S. ambassador to Iraq told Hussein that the United States would not object if he invaded Kuwait.

The Hiring of Prostitutes to Close Business and Political Deals   Corporations and politicians are highly appreciative of the efforts of prostitutes to make their clients happy. Karen Wilkening of San Diego, the notorious Roledex madam, supplied Don Dixon, head of Vernon S&L, with prostitutes for the S&L's "staff meetings" in San Diego County. The S&L paid the bill. In April 1991 Dixon was sentenced to three consecutive five-year prison terms. He was also fined $611,000 for using. depositors' money to hire Ms. Wilkening's call girls and to build the house where he and his staff partied with them (Simon & Eitzen, 1993: chap. 2).

Cooperation with Elements of Organized Crime   The crime syndicates are often happy to cooperate with corporations and governments. It has frequently been claimed that the CIA laundered drug money through Mafia-linked S&Ls in order to buy arms for the Contras. Much of the information regarding CIA/Mafia activity in the S&L crisis was uncorked by the *Houston Post* reporter Pete Brewton. Brewton almost singlehandedly discovered that the failure of at least twenty-two S&Ls was linked to a small group of operatives, men such as Herman Bebe, a former casino owner with ties to the New Orleans crime boss Vincent Marcello, and Mario Renda, a financier with ties to Bebe.

Bebe had ties to Neil Bush, son of the president and board member of Silverado Savings of Denver. Silverado lent money to Bebe and to Howard Corson, Houston developer and CIA operative. Some of the funds lent to Corson may have been used to pay for the CIA's covert operations in Nicaragua.

Renda and the CIA were involved in the 1984 failure of the Indian Springs State Bank of Kansas City, Kansas. Indian Springs hired Anthony Russo, attorney for the Civella Mafia family of Kansas City. Russo was also a consultant to Global International Airways, whose owner, Farhad Azima, was loaned $600,000 by Indian Springs, in violation of a $349,000 borrower limit. Global flew missions under contract to the CIA. Indian Springs also lent $400,000 to Morris Shenker, owner of the Dunes casino in Las Vegas, former attorney to murdered Teamster president Jimmy Hoffa, and associate of the Civella family. At the time loans were being made to the Civellas, the family was under indictment for skimming $280,000 from Las Vegas's Tropicana casino.

Renda also brokered deposits to S&Ls that agreed to lend them to phony companies. In return, Renda and his business associates, men with ties to New York's Lucchese family, received "finders' fees" of from 2 to 6 percent of the loans. Most of the borrowers with Mafia ties defaulted on the loans, hastening the demise of the S&Ls.

In one trial involving a former Mafia stockbroker, it was revealed that the broker's partner was a CIA pilot. The pilot confessed that the CIA had laundered drug money through unsuspecting S&Ls, and obtained S&L loans just before it sent money to the Contras in violation of the Boland Amendment (Simon & Eitzen, 1993: chap. 2).

The Higher Immorality as a Master Trend

In their efforts to amass profits from military and nonmilitary spending and to secure access to overseas markets, the corporate elite have created a permanent war economy that is always either fighting or preparing to engage in armed conflict. This structure is not a conspiracy. It evolved from the nation's triumph in World War II and has grown ever since. These elites have increasingly centralized wealth and power. Less than one ten-thousandths of 1 percent of the nation's population now controls corporate America and the executive branch of the federal government (Dye, 1990:30ff.).

The elites have become so powerful that they now undemocratically make the big decisions regarding war and peace, inflation and unemployment. By employing what Mills termed "enveloping techniques of political domination" (1959:13)—ideological persuasion, propaganda, advertising, and a host of media distractions—they keep the masses of people from resisting either the maldistribution of resources or their undemocratic government. When these noncoercive forms of social control fail, a host of control institutions (jails, prisons, mental hospitals) await those who threaten the status quo. If repressive institutions are unable to handle disruption of the system, armed force by the police (or the military if necessary) remains a last resort (Hellinger & Judd, 1991).

Inside these huge corporate, political, and military organizations people without much power are easily manipulated and mobilized to realize the goals of the organization. Workers in large organizations tend to feel powerless. One of the first lessons corporate and governmental bureaucracies teach workers is that they are replaceable (Coleman, 1992).

I experienced powerlessness most dramatically during a tour of duty in the U.S. Air Force. Upon reaching my first post, I was shown to my office. On the desk was the base phone book. The names in it were not of people but of positions within the various squadrons: squadron commander, administrative officer, first sergeant, and so on. According to the phone book, people did not exist, only positions and offices. The feeling of powerlessness engendered by the very structure of bureaucracy also represents a social problem that manifests itself in various forms of work alienation and mental illness.

No bureaucracy openly admits that it treats people with indifference and even cruelty. All bureaucracies constantly issue official pronouncements about morale, compassion, concern, and so on. As we shall see, these public relations efforts are a part of the mystification that characterizes mass societies.

THE SYMBIOTIC NATURE OF SOCIAL PROBLEMS

The inequalities of wealth and power, and the higher immorality to which they give rise, cause many types of social problems. The macro social problems caused by corporations and centralized government and the micro social problems of the powerless are symbiotic; that is, they are interdependent. The powerless—the poor and the working classes, nonwhite minorities, women, gays, the elderly, and children of the lower classes—suffer the most from the inequalities inherent in our social system. The powerless and the powerful are interdependent in several senses.

Physical Harm

The power elite can directly inflict harm on the powerless.

- The war that began secretly with the CIA's training of the South Vietnamese police resulted in the deaths of over 158,000 American men and women and cost nearly $160 billion to fight. Many people who served in Vietnam thought the war was immoral and did not want to serve but were forced to do so (Thio, 1988:96). Money needed to alleviate poverty went instead to conduct the war.
- More than 40,000 Vietnamese civilians were murdered in the CIA-sponsored Phoenix program, most of them without trial.
- More than 5 million acres of South Vietnam were sprayed with defoliat-

ing chemicals. Agent Orange caused high incidences of cancer, birth defects, and other diseases in American service personnel. The government withheld information on the dangers of Agent Orange until 1993 (Simon & Eitzen, 1993:6–7).

Physical harm caused by the power elite is not confined to military activities. The National Commission on Product Safety estimates that dangerous products injure 20 million Americans each year in home accidents, resulting in 110,000 permanent disabilities and 30,000 deaths. One dangerous drug alone, Eli Lilly's Darvon, has been associated with 11,000 deaths and 79,000 emergency room visits (Simon & Eitzen, 1993:126).

Approximately 100,000 American workers die each year from diseases attributable to exposure to dangerous chemicals at work. An additional 3.3 million workers suffer work-related injuries that require medical treatment, and almost 400,000 workers suffer occupational diseases.

The American food supply contains more than 1500 chemical additives, only a few of which have been tested for their carcinogenic properties. One slice of white bread can contain up to 93 chemicals. Unfortunately, it takes twenty to thirty years to learn which additives can cause cancer and what level of ingestion is safe.

The largest industry in America is the food industry, in which 50 of 20,000 firms make 60 percent of all the profits. Much of the industry consists of fast-food restaurants, which currently serve about 50 percent of restaurant meals in the United States. Much fast food contains high levels of saturated fat, sodium, and sugar. These substances are associated with the most common causes of death in America: heart disease, cancer, and high blood pressure. After Americans became enamored of fast food in the 1950s, consumption of saturated fats in the United States went from 45.1 pounds per person per year in 1960 to 60.7 pounds in 1989.

Another serious form of physical harm is industrial pollution. This nation, with a mere 5 percent of the world's population, is responsible for 50 percent of the world's industrial pollutants. The results are increasingly serious.

In 1993 the Environmental Protection Agency (EPA) and the Harvard School of Public Health estimated that particle pollution from factories causes 50,000 to 60,000 deaths each year. Most vulnerable are children with respiratory diseases, asthmatics of all ages, and elderly people with such ailments as bronchitis. It is the poor and the working class that tend to live close to chemical factories, and they suffer the highest rates of pollution-caused cancer. Indoor pollution from cigarette smoke and radon gas causes 5000 or more cases of cancer annually (Hilts, 1993:A-1).

In response to a congressional inquiry in 1990, the EPA identified 149 industrial plants in thirty-three states where the surrounding air was known to be "quite dangerous" (Greider, 1992:124). At one facility in Port Neches, Texas, the lifetime risk of contracting cancer was one in ten. A risk of one in a million is unacceptable by EPA standards. Yet at forty-five other plants the risk of contracting cancer was one in less than 100, and at all the others the risk was greater than one in 10,000.

Financial Harm

Some harms caused by the power elite are less physical but no less far-reaching.

Item: Price-fixing, a criminal act in which two or more firms conspire to rig prices, costs American consumers about $60 billion a year.

Item: Price gouging is especially common in the prescription drug industry. For example, 100 tablets of Abbot's brand of the antibiotic erythromycin wholesales for $15.50, but the generic tablets wholesale for $6.20 per 100 (Simon & Eitzen, 1993:100–102).

Item: Fraud, the crime of inducing people to part with valuables or money by lies, deception, and misrepresentation, is the most common nonviolent crime in the United States. It costs American consumers tens of billions of dollars every year. Repair fraud alone costs consumers approximately $20 billion a year (Simon & Eitzen, 1993:99).

Perhaps the largest fraud in American history is the savings and loan scandal. Investigators estimate that 60 percent of the $500 billion to $1 trillion lost in the scandal is due to fraud. Since late 1990 the FBI has been investigating some 7000 of these cases, 100 of which were selected for priority prosecution. The scandal could cost each American taxpaying family about $5,000 (Simon & Eitzen, 1993:53).

Moral Harm

Wrongdoing by the powerful may serve as a model of behavior for the powerless. Scandal in high places provides a rationalization for powerless people that neutralizes any guilt that may arise from the victimization of other people. This moral harm causes citizens at all levels of society to become distrustful of their political and corporate leaders. They don't care about me, they think, so why should I care about them? This attitude makes it more likely that people will cheat on their taxes, especially if they believe the government wastes their money or spends it only to benefit the wealthy and powerful. People who work for corporations are more likely to steal from them if they do not trust them. Moreover, the homicide rate increased during the Vietnam War, and it generally increases after an execution has been publicized (Thio, 1988:96).

Immorality and Inequality

Many aspects of the higher immorality, especially subsidies, tax breaks for the wealthy, and excessive corporate salaries, have only worsened inequality in the United States, and a great degree of inequality makes many micro social problems into macro problems. During the 1980s, the poorest 40 percent of Americans saw a decline of $256 billion in their wealth. The wealth of African Americans declined from 24 to 19 percent of the wealth held by white Americans (Gozan, 1993:8). From 1973 to 1993, the number of young people living in poverty increased by 51 percent. Between 1983 and 1993, crime among youth increased 50 percent (Males, 1993:18).

Great inequalities of wealth and income also worsen social problems of relative deprivation. That is, people who are not so destitute that they are forced to steal for food or rent may steal to obtain consumer goods they cannot afford. In the 1980s gold jewelry, $100 sneakers, and Mercedes cars were conspicuous parts of the "lifestyle" of the rich and famous. Such items are status symbols, and in a culture that has made a fetish of materialism, one proclaims one's status by conspicuously parading one's possessions. Thus the more ostentatious the powerful, the more their showy ways will be copied by the less powerful. This is one of the leading contradictions of inequality in America: the more the powerful stress the American dream of material success, the more crime the powerless commit. Thus by displays of wealth and material goods, especially through advertising and movies, the powerful can intensify the social problems suffered and inflicted by the powerless.

The behavior of the powerful not only influences that of the powerless but also is influenced by it. The social problems caused by the powerless also influence the social problems caused by the powerful.

First, the problems of the powerless "help to deflect, weaken, or nullify the social control over the powerful, thus freeing the powerful to engage in their own deviant pursuits" (Thio, 1988:97). Street crime is defined as "the crime problem." The vast majority of the resources of the criminal justice system are devoted to apprehending, prosecuting, and incarcerating street criminals. The powerful believe their own ideology, which holds that the "real" criminals are muggers, rapists, and burglars, not corporate executives who fix prices or politicians who lie to the public. Thus the powerful judge the acts of the powerless as morally wrong and rationalize their own wrongdoing.

When the powerful are caught, their punishment pales in comparison to that of the powerless. Between 1987 and 1992, for example, 75 percent of the cases of criminal fraud referred by federal regulators to the Justice Department in connection with the savings and loan scandal were dropped. In those cases that were prosecuted, the average prison sentence was 2.4 years. The average prison sentence for bank robbery in the United States is 7.8 years (Pizzo & Muolo, 1993:56). The powerful thus have little incentive not to do wrong. The chance of getting away with it is good. If they are apprehended, the punishment is often a fine or a brief stint in a federal minimum-security facility with golf course and tennis courts.

Finally, most victims of street crimes are residents of poor areas. This risk is part of what sociologists term their "life chances"—their opportunities for the good things in life. Acts of victimization reflect the culture and social institutions in which they occur. The likely victims are not merely people who happen to be in the wrong place at the wrong time. They are, tragically, members of victimization-prone groups whose life chances are adversely affected by their social statuses—their class, race, and gender, in these cases. Indeed, people at the bottom of the class structure in the United States (and nearly everywhere else) are "more frequently the victims (and perpetrators) of violent crime, less likely to be in good health, and more likely to feel lonely. Those at the top [of the class structure] are healthier, safer, and more likely to send their children to college" (Gilbert & Kahl, 1993:2).

Indeed, people at the bottom of the class system even have a greater risk of being victims of so-called "natural disasters that presumably threaten all alike." In 1912 the ocean liner *Titanic* sank on its first crossing of the Atlantic. Among the ship's female passengers (who were expected to be given priority in the few lifeboats available) only 3 percent of first-class passengers drowned, in comparison with 16 percent of the second-class and 45 percent of the third-class passengers. Sadly, these differential rates of victimization were no accident. The third-class passengers were ordered to stay belowdecks, some at gunpoint, and were kept away from the lifeboats (Lord, 1955:8).

All of the life-enhancing opportunities within a society may be viewed as lifeboats. When opportunities to enter society's lifeboats are perceived as unequal and in fact are unequal, social problems occur. Victimization by elites, street criminals, and organized crime syndicates reinforces inequality by keeping the poor poor (or making them poorer), thus diminishing their life chances.

THE SOCIOLOGICAL IMAGINATION AS A PARADIGM

Our lack of sociological understanding has created an age of confusion, characterized by forms of alienation that blind the public to solutions to social problems. This deficiency of knowledge also keeps individuals from realizing that the sources of many of their troubles, including feelings of inferiority and insecurity, are sociological rather than personal.

In this chapter we have explored the aspects of postmodern mass society that cause social problems and mystify their causes and solutions. Social problems are caused by conflicts over the distribution of wealth, political power, and the power to determine the nature of culture. Postmodern life is structured by impersonal institutions:

1 A world system composed of capitalist economies and competing nation-states.

2 Mass societies in which wealth is concentrated in the hands of elites and power is exercised through bureaucratic organizations.

3 Impersonal local communities in which people feel no sense of belonging, of values, or of order.

The centralization of wealth and power in the hands of a fortunate few who own much of corporate America and have inordinate influence over government policy has given rise to a host of social problems. The most important of these problems is a set of institutionalized deviant and criminal practices that can be called the "higher immorality." The people most adversely affected by these acts tend to be the poorest members of their societies.

In a variety of ways the social problems created by the powerful and those caused by the powerless are interdependent and mutually reinforcing. The powerful can sometimes order or manipulate the powerless into victimization. The powerful's definition of morality tends to create an ethic that emphasizes the wrongdoing of the powerless and lessens the social control over acts of powerful individuals and organizations. The wrongdoing of the powerful creates a role model for the powerless whereby powerless people become cynical about elite behavior and desirous of the materialism of elite lifestyles. Crime and other deviant acts by the powerless become easy to rationalize. The wrongdoing of the powerful increases inequality by victimizing the powerless. Many deviant acts of the powerless also victimize other powerless people.

REFERENCES

Caldicott, Hellen. 1984. *Missile Envy.* New York: Morrow.

Clinard, Marshall. 1979. *Illegal Corporate Behavior.* Washington, D.C.: U.S. Department of Justice.

Coleman, James S. 1992. "The Asymmetric Society." In *Corporate and Governmental Deviance,* 4th ed., eds. M. David Ermann and Richard J. Lundman, pp. 95–106. New York: Oxford University Press.

Domhoff, G. William. 1967. *Who Rules America?* Englewood Cliffs, N.J. Prentice-Hall.

———. 1974. *The Bohemian Grove and Other Retreats.* New York: Harper & Row.

———. 1990. *The Power Elite and the State.* New York: Aldine-DeGruyter.

Donahue, J. 1992. "The Missing Rapsheet: Government Records of Corporate Abuses." *Multinational Monitor,* December, pp. 16–19.

Dowd, Douglas. 1993. *Capitalist Development since 1776.* Armonk, N.Y.: M. E. Sharpe.

Dye, Thomas. 1990. *Who's Running America?: The Bush Years.* Englewood Cliffs, N.J.: Prentice-Hall.

———— and Harmon Zeigler. 1993. *The Irony of Democracy: An Uncommon Introduction to American Government.* 8th ed. Pacific Grove, Calif.: Brooks/Cole.

Etzioni, A. 1990. "Is Corporate Crime Worth the Time." *Business and Society Review,* 36 (Winter): 33–36.

Evans, D. 1993. "We Arm the World." *In These Times,* November 15–18, pp. 14–18.

Freitag, Peter. 1975. "The Cabinet and Big Business." *Social Problems* 23: 137–52.

Gilbert, Dennis, and Joseph Kahl. 1993. *The American Class Structure: A New Synthesis.* 4th ed. Belmont, Calif.: Wadsworth.

Gozan, Julie. 1992. "Wealth for the Few." *Multinational Monitor,* December, p. 6.

————. 1993. "The Tortures Lobby." *Multinational Monitor,* April, pp. 6–8.

Greenberg, Edward S. 1985. *Capitalism and the American Political Ideal.* New York: M. E. Sharpe.

Greider, William. 1992. *Who Will Tell the People? The Betrayal of American Democracy.* New York: Simon & Schuster.

Hellinger, Daniel, and Dennis Judd. 1991. *The Democratic Facade.* Belmont, Calif.: Wadsworth.

Hilts, Peter. 1993. "50,000 Deaths a Year Blamed on Soot in Air," *San Francisco Chronical,* July 19, pp. A1, A15.

Johnson, Bruce, et al. 1993. "What Ever Happened to Central America?," *Propaganda Review,* 10 (Summer): 10–13, 53–55.

Kerbo, Harold. 1993. "Upper Class Power." In *Power in Modern Societies,* eds. Marvin E. Olsen and Martin N. Marger, pp. 223–37. Boulder, Colo.: Westview Press.

Knapp, Peter, and Alan Spector. 1991. *Crisis and Change: Basic Questions of Marxist Sociology.* Chicago: Nelson Hall.

Kwitney, Jonnathan. 1984. *Endless Enemies.* New York: Cogdon/Weed.

Lord, Walter. 1955. *A Night to Remember.* New York: Henry Holt.

Males, Mike. 1993. "Infantile Arguments." *In These Times,* August 9, pp. 18–20.

Mills, C. Wright. 1956. *The Power Elite.* New York: Oxford University Press.

————. 1959. *The Sociological Imagination.* New York: Oxford University Press.

————. 1962. *The Marxists.* New York: Dell.

Moyers, Bill. 1988. *The Secret Government.* Berkeley: Seven Locks.

Neier, A., and C. Brown. 1987. "Pinochet's Way." *New York Review of Books,* June, 25, pp. 17–20.

Olsen, Marvin E., and Martin E. Marger. Eds. 1993. *Power in Modern Societies.* Boulder, Colo.: Westview.

Perdue, William D. 1993. *Systemic Crisis: Problems in Society, Politics, and World Order.* New York: Harcourt Brace.

Perot, Ross. 1993. *Not for Sale at Any Price: How We Can Save America for Our Children.* New York: Hyperion.

Pizzo, Steve, and Paul Muolo. 1993. "Take the Money and Run." *New York Times Magazine,* May 10, pp. 56–61.

Russell, James W. 1992. *Introduction to Macrosociology.* Englewood Cliffs, N.J.: Prentice-Hall.

Savio, N. 1993. "The Business of Government: Clinton's Corporate Cabinet," *Multi-national Monitor,* January, pp. 24–26.

Simon, David R. 1992. "Watergate and the Nixon Presidency." In *Watergate and Afterward: The Legacy of Richard M. Nixon,* eds. Leon Friedman and William Levantrosser, pp. 5–22.

————, and D. Stanley Eitzen. 1993. *Elite Deviance.* 4th ed. Needham Heights, Mass.: Allyn & Bacon.

Thio, Alex. 1988. *Deviant Behavior.* 3rd ed. New York: Harper & Row.

Winters, Lewis. 1988. "Does It Pay to Advertise to Hostile Audiences with Corporate Advertising." *Journal of Advertising Research,* June, pp. 1–15.

The World Almanac and Book of Facts. 1993. New York: Pharos Books.

The World Almanac of U.S. Politics: 1993–1995 Edition. 1993. Mahwah, N.J.: Funk and Wagnalls.

Worsley, Peter. 1982. *Marx and Marxism.* London: Tavistock.

EXERCISE 2-1. THE HIGHER IMMORALITY

Look up the categories having to do with corporate crime in the latest complete *New York Times Index* or the *Wall Street Journal Index.* These categories include:

1 Antitrust violations.
2 Pollution law violations.
3 False advertising.
4 Fraud.
5 Sexual harassment.

Do you notice any patterns in respect to which industries have the most violations? Many violations take place in the petroleum, automobile, and drug industries. Do these firms serve as models of corporate behavior for others? Were any specific corporations involved in more than one violation?

EXERCISE 2-2. EXAMINING CONTRADICTIONS: A TERM PROJECT

America's value system is loaded with contradictions. Polls indicate that a majority of Americans:

• Favor a woman's right to an abortion, but do not want women actually to have abortions.
• Think democracy is the greatest political system in the world, but do not trust the politicians who run that system.
• Believe free-enterprise capitalism is the best economic system, but distrust the large multinational corporations that dominate that system.
• Frown on criminal activity, but admire characters such as J. R. Ewing of TV's *Dallas,* who can get away with breaking the rules.

There are numerous other contradictions in the values Americans espouse. Write a paper that examines Americans' contradictory beliefs concerning any of our major institutions:

The economy
The polity
The mass media

The criminal justice system
The military
The family
The educational system
Religion

SUGGESTED READINGS

Dowd, Douglas. 1993. *Capitalist Development since 1776.* Armonk, N.Y.: M. E. Sharpe. An excellent and well-written historical analysis of the American political economy by a passionate radical historian.

Greider, William. 1992. *Who Will Tell the People?: The Betrayal of American Democracy.* New York: Simon & Schuster. The most readable and sensible analysis of the crisis of confidence in the American political system.

Messner, Steve F., and Richard Rosenfeld. 1994. *Crime and the American Dream.* Belmont, Calif.: Wadsworth. A significant work that successfully links the values of the American dream to deviant behavior.

3

ALIENATION AND THE ANTISOCIAL SOCIAL CHARACTER

ALIENATING CONDITIONS AND SELF-ALIENATION

Lying and deception are among the most fascinating and least appreciated of social problems. A recent survey indicates that 91 percent of Americans tell lies regularly, and two-thirds of Americans see nothing "wrong in telling a lie" (Patterson & Kim, 1991:45, 49). Most important to the sociological imagination paradigm, lying is *"an integral part of American culture, a trait of the American [social] character"* (Patterson & Kim, 1991:7).

Lying and deception are social problems because they result in a wide variety of physical, financial, and moral harms. The variety of deceptions practiced on an unsuspecting public is staggering.

• As many as 500,000 Americans may possess fraudulent credentials and diplomas, among them 10,000 questionable medical degrees. As many as one in three employed Americans were hired with credentials that been altered in some way.

• In an FBI undercover investigation called Dipscam (for Diploma Scam), one agent was able to obtain seventeen advanced degrees by mail for little or no work. The late Florida congressman Claude Pepper, cooperating with the investigation, obtained a Ph.D. from Union University of Los Angeles by paying $1780 and mailing in four book reviews.

• A college professor, Paul A. Crafton, acquired thirty-four aliases, seventy credit cards (including four American Express gold cards), and five driver's licenses while teaching at three colleges under different names.

• In 1975 the Equity Life Insurance Company defrauded its investors of between $2 and $3 billion by inventing thousands of nonexistent insurance policies, thereby inflating the company's assets.

• In 1981 Robert Cranberg was reported missing from a fishing boat. His wife filed claims for insurance totaling $6 million. Cranberg had jumped overboard, swum ashore, and flown to England. He was finally indicted for fraud.

Ever since actor Tony Curtis played Waldo Demara in *The Great Impostor* (1960), the role has become a model for would-be impostors. Demara, on whose career the film was based, successfully passed himself off as a monk, teacher, assistant warden of a Texas prison, and Royal Canadian Navy physician and surgeon. (Yes, he performed surgery on sailors.) Since the movie was released, one woman, Dorothy Woods, who lived in an eighteen-room mansion and owned a Rolls-Royce, successfully bilked the government out of $377,500 in welfare, medical payments, and food stamps. Ms. Woods filed for welfare payments under twelve names (none of them hers), claiming a total of forty-nine children. A San Francisco man posed as a game warden for three months, issuing citations and confiscating fish. When he was caught, he told police that he had always wanted to be a game warden and thought he

Tony Curtis played Waldo Demara in the movie *The Great Impostor.* Demara passed himself off as a member of a number of skilled professions, including surgical medicine. Available evidence suggests that fraudulent identities in the United States are disturbingly common, and fraud is the most common nonviolent crime in the nation. (UPI/Bettmann)

would see what it was like. The owner of a Miami novelty shop, pretending to be a flight attendant, obtained $40,000 worth of trips on Pan Am planes (Marx, 1988: 1–2).

Indeed, "deception regarding [individual] identity and biography . . . [is a] common, but little commented upon feature of American life" (Marx, 1988:1). Many people now believe that "if honesty counts for something, it counts for very little" (Ehrhart, 1993). Lying and deception are common practices in American culture. They are so common among the American power elite that they have become institutionalized.

The English language, as these dominant institutions use it, has been thoroughly perverted. George Orwell coined the term "doublespeak" in *1984,* his novel about a future totalitarian state. Doublespeak is language that is incongruous because its elements conflict. Rutgers University English professor William Lutz (1989) has identified five kinds of doublespeak.

A *euphemism* is "an inoffensive or positive word or phrase used to avoid a harsh, unpleasant, or distasteful reality" (Lutz, 1989: 2). Corporate and government organizations use euphemisms to deceive, mislead, or otherwise alter the public's perception of reality.

• In 1984 the U.S. State Department decided to be careful about using the word "killing" in reporting about nations that violated human rights. The People's Republic of China, say, engaged in "killing"; nations that were supported by U.S. military aid engaged in "unlawful or arbitrary deprivation of life" (Lutz, 1989:3).

• Euphemisms pour out of the Pentagon. The killing of civilians is "pacification." Assassination is "termination with extreme prejudice."

• Euphemisms are a lingua franca in advertising. For example, "boxes of pudding announce four generous portions but neglect to mention that this applies only to people no larger than hamsters" (Ehrhart, 1993).

Jargon is specialized language associated with a trade or profession. When it is used to communicate with other members of the same profession, jargon can be a useful shorthand. Often it is used to deceive people who are negatively affected by what organizations do. Nowadays employees are often termed "associates," and when they are fired ("laid off"), "their former employers call it downsizing (or restructuring) and speak boldly of the company's bright future while voting themselves bonuses" (Ehrhart, 1993).

Several years ago the public was outraged by reports that the Defense Department paid $400 each for ordinary hammers that could be bought in any hardware store for a few dollars (Simon & Eitzen, 1993: 170). In an attempt to deceive the public into picturing a complex machine, the Pentagon called them "multidirectional impact devices" (Nader, 1985).

During the Gulf War of 1991 the Pentagon used the term "smart bombs" to describe what were really (92 percent of the time) the same kind of ordnance that was used against Germany in 1944, thus deceiving the public into believing that a new weapon had been developed.

Gobbledygook (bureaucratese) consists of words and sentences designed to overwhelm audiences or to impress them with the speaker's apparent competence and expertise. Former vice president Dan Quayle, explaining the need for the Star Wars weapons system, noted, "Why wouldn't an enhanced deterrent, a more stable peace, a better prospect to denying the ones who enter the conflict in the first place to have a reduction of offensive systems and an introduction to defensive capability?" (Lutz, 1989:5). Bureaucratese is commonly mixed with euphemisms and jargon of all kinds.

Puffery—inflated language, usually in the form of unprovable superlatives and overgeneralizations—is used endlessly in advertising and sales. We encounter puffery every day:

"Every kid in America loves Jell-O brand gelatin."
"Pepsi, the only cola with 'Uh-Huh.' "
"Ford gives you better ideas."
"Coke is it!" (Simon & Eitzen, 1993:111)

Automobile dealers are fond of claiming to be "number 1" in their area, but they seldom define what they mean by "number 1."

Weasel words are words that appear to be making a claim but in reality make no claim at all. They get their name from the fact that a weasel makes a small hole in an egg and sucks out the contents, and then replaces the egg in the nest. The egg still looks whole but it has no substance.

The most commonly used of such words is "helps," as in "Helps relieve your symptoms!" Note that "helps" does not mean cures, stops, or ends. The claim fails to specify how much the product "helps." Another such word is "virtually." A dishwasher detergent can be advertised as leaving dishes "virtually spotless" and still leave plenty of spots. The advertiser escapes responsibility for the spots because "virtually" means "almost," not "100 percent." "New and improved," "acts fast," "works like magic"—all are familiar weasel words. In most cases, such claims are so unspecific as to be meaningless (Lutz, 1989:85–94).

These instances of individual and organizational deception, interesting as they are in their own right, are merely symptomatic of a much more serious condition. Doublespeak is a dangerous weapon of social control, manipulation, and exploitation (Lutz, 1989:xiii). In *1984* Orwell describes an official state language called Newspeak. Newspeak is designed to limit criticism of the government and its activities by getting people to believe things that are inherently contradictory.

Nuclear war is winnable.
We had to destroy the village in order to save it.

Peace through war.
Capital punishment enhances life.

Newspeak results in a type of illogic that has been called *doublethink.* Doublethink is the ability to hold two contradictory ideas in mind at the same time and believe that both are true. The only way one can persist in believing that both things are true is never to put them side by side, so that the contradiction is never revealed. Newspeak, with its capacity to produce doublethink, is a formidable device at the service of the institutions that shape our social character.

C. Wright Mills (1951:viii) believed that one of the great tasks of modern social science was to describe the effects of economic and political institutions (social structures) on people's inner feelings, values, goals, and behaviors. Indeed, the sociological imagination involves the ability to shift from one perspective to another, "from the political to the psychological . . . the capacity to range from the most impersonal and remote . . . to the most intimate features of the human self" (Mills, 1959:7). Moreover, Mills believed that "it may well be that the most radical discovery [of] psychology and social science is the discovery of how so many intimate features of the person are socially patterned and even implanted" (Mills, 1959:161). In other words, many of the personality traits that most people consider to be individual characteristics are actually widely shared products of mass socialization by the communications media and other bureaucratic institutions that dominate postmodern life.

There is a link between societal institutions and micro social problems, between the alienating conditions of the social structure and the feelings of alienation experienced by individuals. Such connections are often described as the macro-micro link, implying a relationship between the most intimate of feelings and the most important structural features of modern life. It is crucial to understand that dominant societal institutions mold social character, but they do not mold it by themselves. Often their influence is indirect. To be sure, child-rearing practices within the family are the principal influences in the shaping of personality traits (Wilkinson, 1992:12). However, the character formation within families and in the schools, religious institutions, and such community organizations as the Boy Scouts, Girl Scouts, and Little League reinforces traits required by economic and political institutions. Finally, in a nation as diverse as the United States, character traits vary widely among social classes, racial and ethnic groups, and geographic regions. Thus, it is not easy to speak of a "national character," a set of traits that applies equally to all Americans. It is reasonable, however, to describe traits for which there is solid empirical evidence.

The issue is not which institutions have the most influence but what kinds of human nature the society as a whole is producing and what sorts of social problems the members of that society experience. One central theme in the writing on American character since the 1940s is the lonely individual who wants to be liked and who packages and sells him- or herself on the job market. In postmodern society, many social critics claim, people suppress their real needs in reaction to social pressures to conform and to achieve (Fromm, 1955; Riesman, 1950; Lasch, 1978, 1984; Wilkinson, 1992:12).

If members of American society are encouraged to develop phony personality traits, such as an inclination to lie, then a condition of alienation may be said to exist. As we shall see, alienation is directly related to a host of social problems—suicide, drug abuse, delinquency, sexual deviance, mental illness. To be sure, alienation is not the only cause of these maladies, any more than any human behavior is caused by a single variable. To think in such terms is to engage in simplistic thinking. Nevertheless, the more alienated people are, the more likely they are to suffer from social problems. If alienation is socially patterned in various groups, it is probably caused by the social structure. The question then becomes: What is there about the social structure that produces feelings of alienation in these people?

There are good reasons to believe that all of us have *basic human needs* (Breed, 1971:203–4; Fromm, 1955:37–39, 61–64; Mecca, Smelser, & Vasconcellos, 1989). Evidence suggests that people in every type of social structure need at least three things:

1 *Love*—physical affection and emotional bonding with other people.

2 *Self-esteem*—recognition of achievement, approval, encouragement, and affirmation that results in a positive concept of oneself and one's abilities. The result is a sense of "power, confidence, agency" that is positive as measured against some standard that may be either absolute or relative (Smelser, 1989:10).

3 *Identity*—context or wholeness, an organizing principle that defines who one is and where and how one fits among the social roles that make up one's environment. An identity provides one with the ability to organize one's perceptions, emotions, and beliefs into a coherent picture of oneself and one's place in the world.

When these three emotional needs are satisfied, one feels secure in a life that has meaning and direction. These needs require frequent gratification, the more frequent the better. Each person is unique in both interests and personality, so the means to satisfy the basic needs vary from person to person. The more freedom of choice the social structure allows among social roles, the lower the alienation in that society (Breed, 1971:204). *Alienation results when the basic human needs—love, self-esteem, and identity—go unmet.*

If societies do not allow their members to meet these needs, resentment and confusion result. Confusion and resentment are subjective reactions to an objective condition that exposes people to forces beyond their control and understanding. Resentment and confusion are frequently accompanied by a variety of other negative feelings of self-alienation.

Thus the negative feelings of the alienated individual are rooted in a societal (institutional) base. "The roots of alienation do not reside in either intrapsychic [individual "personality"] processes or in interpersonal relationships, but in societal structures" (Breed, 1971:197–98).

Alienation is characterized by feelings of estrangement (separation) either from society or from oneself, often from both. Specific feelings are associated with alienation (Seeman, 1961; Israel, 1971:208–15):

1 *Powerlessness* is the "expectation or belief that [one's] behavior will not determine or affect [one's] future" (Rogers & Mays, 1987:167). People who have such feelings see no reason to pursue any goals, since they see their future as shaped by forces beyond their control and themselves as cogs in a wheel (Bernard et al., 1971). People who feel powerless do not feel in charge of their own lives and destiny.

2 *Meaninglessness* is a feeling of "confusion or vagueness about what one ought to believe or about the criteria for making important decisions" (Rogers & Mays, 1987:168). To experience meaninglessness is to lack an understanding of the environment of which one is a part (Israel, 1971:210). To experience life as meaningless is to live in the present and to lack optimism about one's future.

3 *Normlessness (anomie)* is a social situation in which rules (social norms) no longer influence one's behavior. When the culturally acceptable means (such as diligent effort) to achieve the culturally prescribed goals (money and status, for example) appear to be useless, many people turn to deviant or criminal behavior in pursuit of those goals (Merton, 1938/1994).

4 *Cultural estrangement (value isolation)* is rejection of values widely shared in the society. The culturally estranged abandon the goals the culture prescribes; they turn their backs on the pursuit of riches. American history is filled with social movements and subcultures that were formed out of such feelings. The beatniks of the 1950s and the flower children of the 1960s are only two in a long line of such subcultures.

5 *Loneliness and social isolation* result from a lack of acceptance by people within one's environment. People who feel rejected are lonely even in a crowd (Riesman, 1950). Loneliness is common in mass societies, especially in those that stress individualism. It is often a contributing cause of depression and suicide.

6 *Self-estrangement* is the experiencing of oneself as alien, with resultant feelings of resentment and confusion. Self-estrangement often opens people to the possibility of self-deception (Schmidt, 1983: 65). Self-estranged people often feel fragmented, not whole. They tend to hide these feelings behind a mask of self-confidence (they "construct an image" to "sell themselves"). Being strangers to themselves, they lack a stable identity and often feel like frauds. Not trusting themselves, self-estranged people tend to be distrustful of other people and of their society as well.

MEDIA OWNERSHIP AND ALIENATION

Perhaps the best way to view alienating conditions within the American social structure is to study the mass media. The mass media are everywhere in postmodern society. The very structure of the mass media is alienating because the average person is so far removed from their ownership and control. The dominant media institutions—television networks, major newspapers, recording companies, book and magazine publishers, film production companies—are huge multinational corporations. They either own or are owned by other corporations, banks, and insurance companies. In 1936 and for several decades thereafter, most movie studios were owned by New York investment banks controlled by such superrich families as the Rockefellers and the Morgans (Parenti, 1991:181).

Since the mid-1980s, forty-four corporations have controlled "half or more of all media output" in the United States (Berger, 1991:388). This figure is down from fifty companies in 1982, so concentration of media ownership is increasing. The three major television networks combined own more than 1000 local stations, as well as considerable portions of the cable television industry. NBC, for example, owns the CNBC network.

One company, Time-Warner, has over $15 billion in assets and owns major magazines *(Time, Sports Illustrated, Fortune, Mad, Money, People, and Life),* a film studio (Warner Brothers), a recording company (Warner Records), a book publisher (Warner Books), and two cable television companies (HBO and Showtime).

Fewer than one hundred corporate executives now control the major portion of each medium. Twenty corporations control 52 percent of all newspaper circulation. Twenty firms control 50 percent of all periodical sales. Twenty publishing houses control 52 percent of book sales, and another twenty control 76 percent of all compact disk and cassette tape sales. "If one counts the three [television] networks and the ten corporations whose sponsorship dominates prime time, thirteen corporations control two-thirds of the audience in television and radio" (Bagdikian, 1991:389). A mere seven companies control 75 percent of all movie distribution.

Thus media ownership and control are approaching monopolistic proportions. Competition among newspapers, for example, is nearly dead. Ninety-seven percent of all chain-owned newspapers have no competition from another newspaper. Moreover, by the year 2000 a mere ten multinational firms will control most of the world's mass media (Hewitt, 1991:396). The concern of most observers is that increased concentration of ownership restricts the content of news and political opinion disseminated by the media. Observers are also concerned about the content of TV programming, movies, and advertising, and the effects of that content on audiences.

Recent polls reveal a deeply felt alienation from the media. Two-thirds of the people polled in 1993 said that the news media look out for the interests of powerful people rather than for the interests of ordinary people. Many people in the news media are now viewed as celebrities in their own right, and we see them attending presidential inaugurations, gracing the covers of national magazines, guesting on talk shows. Thus nearly two-thirds of the public believe that newscasters have little in common with ordinary people and see no reason to trust them (Shaw, 1993:A-18–19). Unfortunately, no questions were asked concerning nonnews programming, its violence, gratuitous sexual imagery, and manipulative advertising. The effects of these aspects of the media on social character are profound.

THE MEDIA AND SOCIAL CHARACTER

C. Wright Mills once observed that no one knows all the functions served by the mass media, and the media's effects on people's values and behavior are hotly debated. Today the mass media not only keep us informed of what's going on in the world but dramatically shape our perceptions of that world. Indeed, Professor Arthur Asa Berger (1991:328) believes that America has evolved into a "teleculture": television "has become the most powerful socializing . . . force in society." Its influence has replaced traditional sources of socialization and ethics: parents, priests, teachers, and peers. To be sure, the way in which the media influence people is often subtle and indirect, and people's perceptions of media messages are filtered through a variety of lenses— social class, age, gender, race and ethnicity, and earlier socialization experiences with the media. Nevertheless, there is enough evidence to indicate that Berger's idea of the media as the dominant socializing force in the United States is realistic.

The numbers regarding the ubiquity of television are staggering:

• 98 percent of American households own at least one television set, and 30 percent of households have two or more sets (Parenti, 1991:10). Even homes that lack hot water or an indoor toilet have television.

• Since the mid-1980s Americans have been spending 52 hours a week in front of the TV. Households of three or more people have the TV on 61 hours a week.

• The average American is exposed to 100 television commercials, 60 radio commercials, 30 print ads, and countless signs and billboards each day—90,000 ads a year of various types. Moreover, ads are becoming increasingly numerous and diverse in form. (In Chapter 4 we'll explore advertising as a master trend.) The ads equate happiness with material things, display women as sex objects, and contribute to dependency, anxiety, and low self-esteem (Berger, 1991:330).

There is little dispute about the links between certain media themes and various character traits. Violence, for instance, is seemingly everywhere in the American media and in American life, and not by coincidence. Virtually thousands of studies have demonstrated that media violence can motivate people who are predisposed to commit violence to do so. After *The Deer Hunter* opened in movie theaters in 1979, twenty-five Americans committed suicide by Russian roulette. The number of suicides increases significantly after the suicide of a famous person, such as Marilyn Monroe, is reported. Homicide rates also increase immediately after heavyweight boxing matches (Parenti, 1991:7). This is the tip of a very ugly iceberg.

The United States is the most violent industrial democracy in the world, with a homicide rate ten times higher than that of the entire continent of Europe. Half of the American public reports having violent urges, and one-fourth of the population has acted on those impulses (Patterson & Kim, 1991:120). One-third of the entire American adult population now owns at least one gun, and, most frighteningly, 26 million Americans now carry guns with them when they leave home (including nearly 3 percent of ninth- to twelfth-graders). Forty percent of students in grades 6 through 12 say they know someone who has been injured or killed by a gun (Chira, 1993).

Media violence outpaces even the real violence in society. Movie and television role models are much more violent now than they were in the 1950s. Heroes used to need a reason to commit violent acts, but no longer. The heroes of most "action" films are lone wolves, perhaps with a single sidekick. They are cynical macho types who have no respect for society's institutions.

Children's television is the most violent of all, averaging twenty-five violent acts per hour. Ninety-five percent of children's programs feature violent acts (Patterson & Kim, 1991:123). Moreover, studies reveal that children often believe that anything they see on television is real.

The more time people spend watching television, the more likely they are to overestimate the actual amount of violent crime in American life and the number of police.

The mass media also shape some key sexual traits, including the linkage of sex and violence. Recent studies of media advertising and sexual portrayals reveal some disturbing findings:

• Sexual symbols pervade postmodern culture. They are now attached to virtually every product and service that is the subject of media advertising. Sex has become a commodity in itself and is associated with youth, power, and success. Even the children portrayed in ads have become sexual beings, "thrusting their pelvises in suggestive ways to sell jeans, kiddy cosmetics," and even women's underwear (Davis & Stasz, 1990:251).

• Studies of movies and television, men's magazines, and pornography all indicate "increased depictions of violence against women" (Malamuth, 1984; Davis & Stasz, 1990:251). The main effect of such presentations is a public desensitization to the link between sex and violence. Such images reinforce the myth that women want to be raped.

• Movies, magazines, and television shows frequently separate sex from

Violent action movies and television shows are among the most common of entertainment genres. *Terminator 2* is one of the top money-making films in recent years. The film was made with an anti-violence message but contained many violent acts. There is considerable evidence that violent media presentations can and do provoke violence in those so predisposed. (Globe Photos)

emotions and relationships. They depict sex as unrelated to personal responsibility for consequences, to affection, intimacy, or commitment. Many movie heroes seduce multiple partners without ever becoming emotionally attached to any woman.

Much of the content of the media's sexual presentations is mirrored in the sex-crime statistics. Twenty times more rapes are reported in the United States than in Japan, Spain, and England combined. Moreover, 20 percent of American women report being victims of date rape (Patterson & Kim, 1991:120, 129).

INAUTHENTICITY: AN ALIENATING CONDITION

Aside from portraying violence and sex, the media try to tell us what we should look like (we should be young and beautiful). They also attempt to tell us what goals in life to strive for (especially money, power, popularity, sexiness, and prestige) and how to achieve them (Mills, 1956:314). In doing these things, they distract us from, and thereby mystify, the causes of social problems even as they perpetuate those problems.

Much advertising and political propaganda appeals to the need to belong to a human collectivity in which our needs for love, recognition, and identity are met. The promises held out to us are far from authentic. A hallmark of inauthenticity, as we have seen, is the presence of *positive overt appearances* coupled with *negative underlying realities* (Simon & Eitzen, 1993:340ff).

Instances of inauthenticity are seen in the advertisements for cigarettes and liquor, with their implied promises of romance, success, and popularity. What are the consequences of regular smoking and drinking? Smoking kills about 400,000 Americans each year and costs society over $50 billion a year in missed workdays, medical costs, and other expenses—more than all profits and tax receipts from tobacco items. Smoking is associated with heart disease, lung cancer, bronchitis, and emphysema; birth defects in the babies of mothers who smoke; and osteoporosis, a disease involving the reabsorption of calcium from the bones, kills 25,000 women each year (Simon & Eitzen, 1993:134,290). Alcohol figures in 100,000 deaths annually, and about $120 billion in medical bills, lost worktime, and related costs. It is a factor in about half of all homicides, and it is nearly always the first drug to which abusers of illegal drugs became addicted (Inciardi, 1986:123; Simon & Eitzen, 1993:290). These are the negative underlying realities of the consumption of alcohol and tobacco, two products that have killed more people in American history than all illegal drugs combined.

No one is arguing that all people who abuse alcohol and other drugs learned to do so from advertising. What is relevant here is that evidence indicates that the more heavily alcohol is advertised in a society, the more alcohol per capita is consumed. And no rational person would argue that even moderate cigarette smoking is harmless.

There are several important issues here:

1 Advertising is not just a set of messages for products. It is a medium that socializes people to be consumers. Much of the time it does so by deceit.[1]

2 Most advertising plays on the fear of not being loved or on low self-esteem. The ads' appeals testify to the recognition that these basic human needs are widely unmet in American culture. Drugs of all types are very heavily advertised on television (about once every eleven minutes) and in magazines. These ads attempt to increase feelings of insecurity and low self-esteem in

---

[1]Those warning labels on cigarette packages were placed there only after a protracted struggle. The tobacco companies finally agreed to the labels in exchange for relief from legal responsibility for the harm done by tobacco. The tobacco industry kept evidence of the harms of smoking secret for thirty years, and has been successfully sued by people who suffered the ill effects of tobacco before the warning labels were placed on the packages.

consumers, and obviously the people who feel most insecure are most vulnerable to such appeals. The overall message is: if you want to be confident, loved, and successful, to know who you are, where you are going in life, and how to get there, you need us. In short, one trait the media attempts to instill in consumers is dependency.

3 When the themes of lifestyle ads are pointed out to them, many people respond by saying something like "Well, those may be the themes, but I don't take such appeals seriously, and neither does anyone else I know." Jeffrey Schrank has pointed out that 90 percent of America's television viewers consider themselves "personally immune" to commercial appeals, yet these viewers account for 90 percent of all sales of advertised products (Schrank, 1977:84). Moreover, evidence suggests that advertisers' claims are believed much more often than most of us would like to think.

• Research indicates that people perceive more contents in ads than the ads contain. When sweaters were pictured with belts and described with a Scottish flavor, for example, consumers were twice as likely to perceive the sweaters as imported (Rotfeld & Preston, 1981).

• Research also supports the idea that implied deceptions (puffery claims) are believed more than outright lies. In one study of seventeen puff claims, 70 percent of respondents believed the claims were either wholly or partially true (Rotfeld & Preston, 1981:9).

• Evidence also indicates that puffery claims are often indistinguishable from factual claims. When researchers presented 100 people with both puff claims (for example, St. Joseph's aspirin for children is the best children's aspirin) and factual claims (for example, St. Joseph's aspirin for children lowers children's fevers), "many of the puff claims were believed by a large proportion of the respondents," and "the subjects could not tell that these puffs might not be literally true" (Rotfeld & Rotzall, 1984:19–20). This finding is only one of many indications that postmodern culture so confuses people's perceptions that they cannot distinguish fantasy from reality.

• A review of puffery research finds that puffery "has the potential to deceive consumers." Researchers find that a large proportion of their respondents interpret a puff claim as suggesting the superiority of the product being advertised (Wyckham, 1987:55).

Consumers fed a constant diet of puffery ads may confuse fact and puffery claims. They may distrust advertising but be unconsciously manipulated by it (Hemmelstein, 1984:68,271; Rotfeld & Preston, 1981:10).

Advertisers spend over $130 billion a year to get their deceptive messages across. Would you spend this gigantic amount of money on something that did not work? Indeed, the most problematic and profound aspect of all media activities may be their constant mixing of fantasy and reality. There is evidence that mixing fantasy and reality causes confusion in vulnerable groups, especially in teenagers (Calabrese, 1987:935). Inauthenticity is more than an appeal to unmet emotional needs; it is also a cause of confusion because it is based on the logic of doublespeak: it requires us to believe in two contradictory things at once.

INTERPERSONAL INAUTHENTICITY: IMPRESSION MANAGEMENT

Over forty years ago C. Wright Mills (1951) described the inauthenticity of the "cheerful robots," white-collar employees. At work they must smile and be personable, courteous, and helpful. White-collar employees sell not only their energy and time to their organization but their personalities as well. They hide their resentment at the need to interact with people they do not like behind a carefully cultivated good humor.

Sociologists who study the sociology of emotions have found some interesting evidence in support of Mills's claims. Arlie Hochschild (1983:234–41) estimates that one-third of American jobs now involve "emotional labor"—inauthentic behavior, or acting. Hochschild differentiates between superficial acting and deep acting. Superficial acting entails putting on a pleasant expression and repeating the same pat phrases over and over. George Ritzer (1993:134–35) has noticed much superficial acting at fast-food restaurants:

> Rule Number 17 for the Burger King workers is "Smile at all times." The Roy Rogers employees who used to say "Happy Trails" to me when I paid for my food really had no interest in what happened to me in the future, on the trail. (In fact, . . . they were really saying, in a polite way, "get lost!") This phenomenon has been generalized to many workers who say "have a nice day" as one is departing . . . they have no real interest in, or concern for, how the rest of one's day goes. Again, in . . . a ritualized way they are really telling us to "get lost," to move on so someone else can be served.

These are Mills's cheerful robots to the life. They have learned the clichés expected of them; they have not learned to care.

Deep acting (expressions of feelings) is required in jobs that place people in more prolonged contact with the public. Flight attendants, for example, are supposed to project a friendly image no matter what a passenger may do. Hochschild (1983:55) quotes a flight attendant who describes the deep acting she does to keep from expressing feelings of anger:

> If I pretend I'm feeling really up, I actually get into it. The passenger responds to me as though I were friendly. . . . Sometimes I purposely take some deep breaths. I try to relax my neck muscles.
> I try to remember that if he's drinking too much, he's probably scared of flying. I think to myself, "he's like a little child." . . . And when I see him that way, I don't get mad that he's yelling at me. He's like a child yelling at me then.

Approximately half of the positions that require this sort of impression management, or creation of a pseudo-identity, are service-sector jobs occupied by women (flight attendants, clerks, nurses, social and recreational workers, radio and television announcers, teachers).

Most important, Hochschild reports that both men and women who must engage in selling their emotions as commodities experience feelings of powerlessness (an important form of alienation) in reaction to the constant pressure to perform. The language, clothes, and looks appropriate to these roles are modeled in the media. The look for women is described in a *Good Housekeeping* story on Mary Tyler Moore's various "faces." Her "business face" relies on "golden, toasty" colors that are flattering even in harsh fluorescent lighting. Ms. Moore's "evening face" highlights her "flawless skin," smoldering dark eyes, and glistening, molded mouth, all worthy of a "round of applause" (Papson, 1985:225–26).

Such impression management often becomes an important part of private life. "What began as the public and commercial relations of business have become deeply personal: there is a public relations aspect to private relations of all sorts, including even relations with oneself" (Mills, 1951:187). Young professionals often spend a good part of their time in singles bars and other "meat markets" projecting false images, false personalities and statuses. They manipulate one another for monetary or sexual purposes, and some use cocaine in an effort to be accepted by others or to escape feelings of alienation. Their relationships, whether sexual or friendly, tend to be shallow because they keep so many of their true feelings hidden from others and, most sadly, from themselves as well (Bellah et al., 1986).

ALIENATION AS DEHUMANIZATION

Because of the impersonality of bureaucratic structures, the high valuation of material goods and status, and the decline of community, mass societies encourage another form of alienation, dehumanization. As we saw earlier, dehumanization takes two interrelated forms, object-directed and self-directed.

Dehumanization is object-directed when people are regarded as less than human for purposes of profit, exploitation, and manipulation. This type of dehumanization is rampant in the mass media, both in programming and in advertising. Numerous studies have documented the stereotyped portrayals of women and minorities in television and movies.

A content analysis of gender presentations in ads that appeared in the *New York Times Magazine* (Synnott, 1991) revealed that youth and beauty were essential for female models, but not for men. Men were often given names in ads, whereas women were never named, implying they were not real. Women were so severely dehumanized that many ads showed only parts of the female anatomy (hands, breasts, buttocks, feet, faces). Far more women than men were depicted in a state of semi-undress, in panties, bras, and swimsuits. The emphasis on the female body affirms that the body plays a greater role in social life for women than for men (Synnott, 1991:340). Women are thus stereotyped as brainless sex objects and erotic body parts.

Women were featured with strange expressions on their faces, implying that they were crazy. No man was ever pictured in an awkward or strange pose. Men were portrayed as working and physically active; women were almost never working. Women were pictured in positions that made them subservient to men. Typically they looked up at men, implying an inequality of power between the sexes. Finally, ageism and racism were implied themes in the ads. Virtually no African Americans or elderly people were shown.

Michael Parenti (1991) notes that television and films have constructed an unreal world in which minorities and women are continually stereotyped:

• Italian-Americans are shown as either members of the Mafia or dumb gluttons incapable of speaking correct English. Italian women are portrayed as shrieking hysterics.

• Working-class people are pictured as stupid and slovenly in speech and appearance, and the work that they do is almost never shown. Labor unions are depicted as corrupt. Individual heroism is nearly always preferable to collective action (teamwork).

• Native Americans are presented as savages, barbarians, and "devils." These people aren't defending their homeland against invaders and colonizers; they simply have such a lust for killing that they have no regard for human life, not even their own.

• For years the movies portrayed women as either seductive temptresses who endangered the lone, self-reliant hero or passive accessories who kept the hero company.

Thus the media do much more than entertain us. They propagate "images and ideologies that are supportive of imperialism, . . . capitalism, racism, sexism, militarism, . . . violence, vigilantism, and anti-working-class attitudes" (Parenti, 1991:2). Moreover, they do these things in ways that dehumanize us all.

Unfortunately, life in mass organizations is increasingly concerned with impression management and the emotional labor of acting (Lasch, 1984; Hochschild, 1983). Some students of bureaucracy (Kanungo, 1982:157) have noted that certain types of cynical and successful people at the top of organizational hierarchies exude charisma in the form of a superficial warmth and charm, yet make decisions on the basis of an object-directed dehumanization that converts people into categories. Such leaders have few problems in making decisions because of their ability to think in nonhuman black-and-white terms regarding plant closings, layoffs, manipulative advertising campaigns, and organizational deviance. Thus inauthenticity and dehumanization are causes of social problems because these behaviors are so often handsomely rewarded.

Self-directed dehumanization is a symptom of self-alienation. People who turn themselves into cogs in a wheel dehumanize themselves. The results are symptoms of high stress (Harris, 1987) and burnout on the job. It is thought that people who dehumanize themselves in this way tend to stereotype other people negatively as well (Bernard et al., 1971). Thus self-directed and object-directed dehumanization are interrelated on the individual level. Moreover, both dehumanization and inauthenticity are integral parts of the social character of postmodern mass society (Montagu & Matson, 1985; Shrader, 1992).

CHARACTER STRUCTURE IN THE POSTMODERN EPOCH

The historical epoch in which we live is characterized by a "postmodern culture" in which reason and freedom have become increasingly weakened; it is a time of indifference, uneasiness, and cynicism. The American social character is dominated by Mills's cheerful-robot mentality. After an eight-hour workday, most people turn to escapist entertainment on television and alienated consumption during their "leisure time." The cheerful robot is a product of mass urban life, with its emphasis on status seeking, consumption, competition, and dependence on bureaucratic organizations for employment, goods, and services.

All of this requires a certain amount of dehumanization of the self and of others. Self-directed dehumanization and personal inauthenticity are also symptoms of a lack of self-esteem, which is often associated with drug abuse, mental illness, alcoholism, and a host of other social problems. Americans today feel so insecure about their personal identity and status that they are overly sensitive to the opinions of others. This sensitivity to the judgments and values of other people has been termed other-directedness (Riesman, 1950). All of these themes contradict the American myth of rugged individualism (see Box 3-1).

INDIVIDUALISM AND SOCIAL CHARACTER

Americans' idea of the individualized self is so extreme as to be unrealistic. It is a notion loaded with myths and contradictions, and a major cause of many micro social problems. The United States has long been proclaimed the land of individual rights, individual cases, individual personalities, individual egos. As we have seen, all these notions are constantly reinforced by the mass media, especially by its focus on celebrities and hero figures.

Americans are probably the only people on earth who believe in what they call "rugged individualism." This belief holds that people have nearly unlim-

BOX 3-1

RUGGED INDIVIDUALISM OR PSEUDO-INDIVIDUALISM: THE MAKING OF A
SOCIAL PROBLEM

Much of what people think of as rugged individualism is really pseudo-individualism (Adorno, 1974), a mass-produced notion of the self that is sold through the media to make people feel cared about as individuals in a society controlled by impersonal institutions. You can find examples of false individualism for yourself any day of the week. Simply buy a newspaper and turn to the astrology column. Under your sign is some advice that is directed at you. My horoscope for yesterday said that I was to receive a long-distance communication revealing a project that was under way. This project could mean an opportunity for travel overseas. The column also advised me to focus on my ability to rise above obstacles (Omar, 1993). The astrologist implies that he knows what is going on in my life. The references are, of course, so general that they can be made to fit a great many people's situations (Adorno, 1974:29). The idea that this column was written just for me is irrational. Indeed, scientific tests of astrology's validity have revealed no evidence to support the astrologists' claims. Two researchers tested the claim that the planet Mars influenced military careers, and found that being born under the sign of Mars (or any other sign) bore no relation to a career in the armed services (Jerome, 1975:15).

Does this lack of scientific validity stop people from believing in astrology? Not at all. The popularity of astrology and other forms of the occult (Dianetics, Eckankar, and so on) is part of a process of mass socialization and social character formation (Roberts, 1978:276–77).

Thus astrology columns are nearly always about individual success and luck. Never is the collective good of society or the cause of a social problem addressed. Thus astrology is part of a socialization process that reinforces a particular concept of the self: that we are all rugged individualists who paddle our own canoes. Each individual is responsible for his or her own success or failure. The great contradiction here, of course, is that astrology represents a gigantic collective exercise in mass conformity, not individualism. Individualism, as a belief system, may be unrelated to individual taste and style. As a widespread character trait, however, belief in individualism has enormous ramifications for the actual causes of social problems and what people *perceive* the causes of social problems to be. Individualism is a key element of the American social character, and it is widely perceived as a positive value. Taken to an extreme, it becomes selfishness, greed, and narcissism.

American society is dominated by massive institutions in which resources and power are heavily centralized. The decision-making process in bureaucratic organizations is well insulated from the influence of the average person. Being removed from key economic and political decisions tends to obscure the nature of reality, and makes a significant number of people feel alone and insignificant. The horoscope fills a number of needs for insecure, alienated, and lonely people. It is a pseudo-solution for the social insecurity that permeates mass society. The horoscope creates the illusion that someone out there cares about us. It also provides advice about personal decisions, something sorely lacking in a rapidly changing society with few stable values and even fewer moral principles that may serve as guides for the decisions of daily life. As one self-help best-seller puts it, we must constantly make decisions for which we have no guidelines:

> Demands are made for decisions from the moment we awake until our final weary retreat under the covers. Shall we drink coffee or decaffeinated? (But decaffeinated *is* coffee, says the kindly TV doctor who is not a doctor.) Shall we drink it black or with cream? Or with nondairy creamer? Artificial sweetener or sugar? Shall we have eggs or Egg Beaters? Is bacon carcinogenic or is that just another laboratory rat exaggeration?
>
> Having struggled through these decisions, we unfold the morning paper. Does the murderer have "diminished capacity" or is he responsible? . . . Shall we sell the silverware or hide it? Shall we enroll in Weight Watchers or Slim Gym? Shall we put the kids in private school or impeach the school board? Shall we move . . . or buy better locks? . . .
>
> The kids sit at the breakfast table, listless. In response to a parental inquiry about their well-being this fine morning we are told they don't feel like talking. Shall we admonish them or give them a pep talk? Shall we keep quiet or sit on our feelings? Do repressed feelings cause cancer? Doesn't everything? (Harris & Harris, 1985:92–93)

As a belief system, individualism is an illusion, and a dangerous one at that. Human beings are among the most social creatures on the face of the earth. No other species live with their parents for eighteen or more years. Moreover, human social organization guarantees that people will be dependent on and interdependent with other people for the basic material necessities of life—food, clothing, and shelter—as well as for their basic social-psychological needs.

ited freedom to choose the direction their lives will take, and that the exercise of this freedom requires individuals to become self-sufficient and psychologically secure so that they may compete against other individuals in seeking life's material rewards. This ideology is not only mythical, it is downright dangerous.

Americans' extreme view of individualism causes us great problems when we try to establish intimate relations with others. Karen Horney, an early writer on this subject, noted that one of the great problems Americans face is deciding whom they can trust.

> [American] culture is economically based on the principle of competition . . . the psychic result of this situation is a diffuse hostile tension between individuals . . . competitiveness and the potential hostility that accompanies it, pervades all human relationships . . . between men and men, between women and women, and between women and men, and whether the point of competition be popularity, competence, attractiveness, or any other social value, it greatly impairs the possibilities of reliable friendship. (Horney, 1938:284)

One result of the potential hostility between individuals is fear—fear of other people's anger, fear of failure—and lowered self-esteem. Together, competitiveness, the hostility it engenders, fear, and lowered self-esteem result in feelings of loneliness; we feel psychologically isolated. One reaction to loneliness is an intensified need for love and affection. Because romantic love meets such vital needs, it is overvalued in American culture; it is seen as a cure for all ills. Because we have come to expect more of it than it can possibly deliver, romantic love has become an illusion, an illusion that serves to cover up the destructive factors (such as extreme individualism and competition) that created the exaggerated need for it in the first place.

The result is genuine contradiction. Americans' individualized selves need a great deal of affection, but our extreme individualism and competition have made love difficult to achieve. In our excessive need for attention, approval, and affection we fall prey to low self-esteem, destructiveness, and anxiety.

A second contradiction of the American self lies in the tension between the freedom we allegedly enjoy and all the real limitations placed on that freedom. Our myth teaches us that anyone can grow up to be president of the United States, or become a millionaire. Yet in reality the United States has had only white male Christian presidents. Only a tiny percentage of the population acquires millionaire status. The result is that Americans feel constantly pulled between a sense of great power to determine their own destiny and a sense of powerlessness to accomplish much of anything by themselves. A culture that promises boundless opportunities for happiness and success but fails to provide the vast majority with the means to achieve them will inevitably have many social problems, including crime (at all social class levels), alcoholism, and drug addiction. The choice of such deviant activities has been described as an adaptation to the reality of living in a society that prescribes the goal of material success but fails to provide the means to achieve it. This structural anomie is now playing an important role in shaping both social character and social problems.[2]

THE AMERICAN DREAM, SOCIAL CHARACTER, AND SOCIAL PROBLEMS

Steven Messner and Richard Rosenfeld argue that one cause of social problems lies in the same values and behaviors that are usually viewed as part of the American version of success. They define the American dream as a "broad cultural ethos that entails a commitment to the goal of material success, to be pursued by everyone in society, under conditions of open individual competition" (1994:6). The power of the American dream comes from the widely shared values that make it up:

1 *An achievement orientation:* pressure to "make something" of oneself, to set goals and achieve them. Material success is one way personal worth is measured in America (Horney, 1938). This is a shaky basis for self-esteem,

---

[2]This is precisely the argument made by Robert Merton (1938/1994).

yet Americans persist in estimating their personal worth much as they do the value of a stock: it rises and falls in accordance with the money they make.

2 *Individualism:* the notion that Americans have not only autonomy but basic individual rights. Americans make their individual decisions regarding marriage and careers, religion, political outlook, and scores of other matters. The result is that individualism and the pressure for achievement combine to produce anomie. Other people become competitors for the rewards and status one seeks. Intense personal competition increases the pressure to succeed. Often this means that rules about the means by which success is obtained are disregarded when they threaten to interfere with personal goals. The case of Charles Stuart offers an extreme example of anomie and the American dream.

On October 23, 1989, Charles and Carol Stuart, eight months pregnant, were on their way home from a childbirth class at a Boston hospital. Charles pulled the car over, allegedly to check some problem, pulled out a gun, and shot Carol at point-blank range. Stuart told police his wife had been killed by a black gunman. Two months later he confessed that he had killed her in order to collect hundreds of thousands of dollars in life insurance, with which he could realize his American dream of owning a restaurant (Derber, 1992:8).

3 *Universalism:* the idea that the chance of achieving the American dream is open to everyone—and so is the chance of failure. Fear of failure is intense in America, and it increases pressure to abandon conformity to the rules that govern proper conduct in favor of expediency.

4 *The fetishism of money:* the fact that money has attained an almost sacred quality in American life. It is the way Americans keep score in the game of success, and there are no rules that tell us when enough is enough. The American dream stresses ends to the neglect of means. As Elliott Currie notes, the pursuit of private gain has become the organizing principle for all of social life (1991:255). Charles Derber (1992) has argued that during the Reagan-Bush era, increasing inequality and the idea that "greed is good" combined to give the American character an element of narcissism. Narcissism is a personality disorder, a mental illness, characterized by distorted self-love and, most important, selfishness coupled with a lack of guilt. The Reagan-Bush ideology of self-reliance stimulated large numbers of upper-world crooks to engage in a quest for power and status in a money culture. (We shall explore their unrestrained quest for personal gain in Chapter 4.)

Between 1971 and 1991, the top 1 percent of Americans experienced an 85 percent increase in their pretax incomes and a 23 percent decline in their tax payments. The bottom 20 percent of the population, in contrast, endured a decline of 12 percent in their real incomes and a 3 percent increase in their tax burdens. Real incomes of families headed by single parents under 25 years of age dropped by over 23 percent during this period.

As a result of these increasing inequalities, there are 10 million more people living in poverty in the 1990s than there were in the 1980s, and the poor are much poorer. They are also increasingly desperate, so desperate that no one in the United States seems to feel safe from criminal victimization. A 1993 poll by the Harvard School of Public Health reported that 94 percent of Americans fear being victims of crime (*New York Times,* October 24, 1993, p. D-1).

The sociologist Robert Merton pointed out over a half century ago that the great contradiction of American culture lay in its stress on success coupled with a lack of opportunity to achieve it. A portion of this contradiction is due to what Emile Durkheim (1966) described as anomie, the social situation in which norms are unclear. Success in America has no official limits. The private accumulation of wealth is without "a final stopping point" (Merton, 1938/1994:119). No matter what their income level, Americans want about 50 percent more money (which, of course, increases by 50 percent once it is achieved).

The same ideology is found among organized crime figures. When Peter Lupsha (1981) investigated the life stories of these people, he discovered that none of them embarked on a criminal career because there were no jobs to be had ("blocked opportunities"), as some theorists of organized crime suppose. American gangsters divide the population into two categories, "suckers" and "wiseguys." Suckers are working-class people who toil at legal jobs and struggle to make ends meet. Wiseguys are gangsters who do what they want and have plenty of money to show for it.

It is not just Mafia figures who think this way. Achieving success through force and fraud has always been considered smart, so smart that for seven decades our culture has lionized gangsters. Beginning with Al Capone, we have come to admire Mafia dons who do not hesitate to take shortcuts to success. Thus *People* magazine's 1989 cover story on John Gotti, godfather of the Gambino crime family, pictured the don as so tough that he could punch his way through a cement block. A multimillionaire with plenty of charisma, *People* noted, Gotti is also a loyal family man who has never cheated on his wife. The fact that he personally has murdered a number of rivals is talked of largely as an occupational requirement.

Merton (1938/1994:119) noted that crime "is a very common phenomenon" among all social classes in the United States. A study of 1700 middle-class New Yorkers in 1947 found that 99 percent of them admitted to committing offenses for which they could have been imprisoned for at least a year, and 64 percent of the men and 29 percent of the women reported committing felonies. A 1991 survey showed that a large percentage of Americans are still engaging in criminal behavior (Patterson & Kim, 1991). Yet one of our persistent myths is that American society can be divided into two populations, the law-abiding and the criminals.

Mobster John Gotti, nicknamed "the dapper don" by *Time* magazine because of his expensive suits, became a media celebrity. His picture appeared on the cover of *People,* a status usually reserved for show business and other newsworthy types. America's habit of admiring people who take shortcuts to the American dream probably goes back to the founding of the republic. In this century, Al Capone became the first celebrity gangster, a tradition that continues to this day. (Reuters/Bettmann)

The social critic James Adams, who coined the term "the American dream," once remarked that many people who immigrated to the United States were relatively law-abiding before they arrived here. People "were made lawless by America, rather than America being made lawless by them" (1929:44). Their role models have been American elites. Elite deviance permits nonelites to engage in crime without feeling guilty. Elite deviance also sends the message that it is stupid not to commit a crime if one has the opportunity to do so. Many a drug dealer has remarked that he was just doing what the Rockefellers, Carnegies, and other robber barons did in the nineteenth century—establishing a monopoly.

It is important to understand that character structures vary among racial and ethnic subcultures. The character structure derived from a long history of racial oppression and persecution can add contradictions to those of the dominant culture. Sadly, this has been the experience of African Americans. The social character associated with this particular ethnic group is unlike that of any other American minority, as Box 3-2 makes clear.

There are other contradictions related to individualized selfhood. There is

BOX 3-2

MINORITIES AND SOCIAL CHARACTER: THE CASE OF AFRICAN AMERICANS

African Americans occupy a unique place in American culture. They are the only group of immigrants whose members were systematically kidnapped, brought to these shores against their will, and enslaved. The descendants of those people share this legacy of oppression and domination by the larger white culture. The social scientist Andrew Hacker has described what being black in America is like:

In the eyes of the dominant culture, being black is your identity in an all-pervasive and unique way, no matter your social class, gender, or occupation. If you write a book on Euclidean geometry or the Renaissance, you are described as a "black author" (1992:32).

African Americans are torn between being members of white America and seeking their own identity. Most blacks feel they are different from whites. No other ethnic group refers to its own people as "brothers and sisters, . . . in ways whites never can" (1992:34). When famous blacks change their names, they frequently adopt Muslim names: Cassius Clay to Mohammed Ali, Lew Alcindor to Kareem Abdul-Jabbar, and so on.

The preferences of African Americans are at odds with the realities of American life. Polls indicate that 85 percent of African Americans would prefer to live in racially mixed neighborhoods, yet 85 percent of American neighborhoods are racially segregated. When the population of a neighborhood becomes about 8 percent black, whites begin to move out; they cannot accept even a 12 percent mix, which would reflect the percentage of blacks in America's population (1992:36). Thus African Americans, no matter what their status in life, are widely seen as contaminating the neighborhoods where white Americans live. This reaction to their presence opens wounds and leaves psychological scars that never heal, that constantly remind African Americans how far they remain from full American citizenship.

When black Americans are in the company of whites, they feel constantly on display. Tokenism frequently makes them the only black juror, corporate director, member of the class. The presence of one black person frequently makes white people uncomfortable and blacks know it. If black people must be present, whites prefer that they smile; that way the whites can feel reassured that the blacks are being well treated. So blacks feel they must constantly be upbeat, must never show anger, exasperation, or rage. Most people cannot keep tight control over these powerful feelings, and the news is freighted with outbursts of black celebrities and the collective anger of ghetto dwellers.

Even when African Americans are not with whites, they know they are the frequent subject of their conversations. No other group has been so intensely studied, pitied, deplored, reduced to data, and dehumanized. Yet most of the books, television programs, movies, and music that African Americans create are works they have adapted to the tastes of white audiences. One of our society's great cultural contradictions is that white Americans have long admired and adopted the slang and the music of the people whose culture they belittle. These days television and movies present a greater proportion of black doctors and lawyers than have ever existed in real life, and blacks appear in commercials, as long as they are not "too black" and look pleased to be among whites. Until recently, in most history books, if mentioned at all, blacks appear as passive, faceless victims.

No other group has ever had a word

like "nigger" thrown at them to keep them in line. The word reminds blacks of their history of inferiorization by whites, and blacks' long history of being divided and conquered. Today blacks find themselves in a confusing and contradictory position in America, and their attitudes reflect this no-win situation. A majority of African Americans:

- Believe they are discriminated against, and do not take charges of reverse discrimination seriously.
- Believe blacks have the right to attend mostly white schools, yet, once there, think it fine that blacks associate largely with other blacks.
- Believe it important that all-black colleges be preserved, yet object to the preservation of all-white schools.
- Believe that whites often vote for white candidates for reasons of race, yet do not consider it racist for blacks to vote for black candidates.
- Reject censorship, yet do not want *Huckleberry Finn* to be used in schools because it contains the word "nigger."

African American life, especially working- and lower-class life, is loaded with a variety of social problems, from birth to death. Many black women never marry, and the majority of those who do marry eventually divorce. Black women live five fewer years than white women; black men's lives are seven years shorter than white men's. Indeed, a black man who lives in Harlem is less likely to reach age 65 than a man in Bangladesh, one of the world's poorest nations. When black men are compared with white men, the blacks are found to have:

- Three times the risk of contracting AIDS.
- Seven times the risk of being killed, or having their civil rights violated.
- Twice the risk of being a crime victim and a higher risk of insomnia, obesity, and hypertension.

These odds are not due merely to poverty but to all the rage, distrust, and anxiety that come from being an African American.

a real tension between success and competition, on one side, and humility and love, on the other. Careers often require Americans to become assertive, even ruthless and aggressive in their efforts to reach the top. Yet the Judeo-Christian ethic admonishes us not even to covet anything that is our neighbor's and to turn the other cheek. The culture itself alternates between stress on teamwork and community and emphasis on our individual recognition, gain, and greed.

Mills, of course, would have none of the myth of individualism. He criticized it when it was perhaps at the height of its popularity. His *White Collar,* published in 1951, begins with the premise of profound alienation among white-collar employees. "Whatever their future," Mills wrote, "it will not be of their own making" (1951:ix). At work they were individuals, but not rugged. To Mills they were lost souls within the bureaucracies for which they toiled, living life out in "slow misery . . . yearning for the quick American climb [to success]" (1951:xi).

Far from being individualistic, Americans are a living contradiction. We are constantly propagandized as a mass, most of us engage in the same spectator behavior (especially television, movies, sports, pop music), yet we persist in the belief that we are a nation of nonconformists. As we have seen, it is the nature of our conformity that is the issue.

REFERENCES

Adams, James. 1929. *Our Business Civilization.* New York: Holmes & Meier.
Adorno, Theodor. 1974. "The Stars Down to Earth." *Telos* 19 (Spring): 13–91.
Bagdikian, B. 1991. "Statement of the Federal Trade Commission." In *Media U.S.A.,* ed. Arthur Asa Berger, 2d ed. New York: Longman.
Bellah, Robert, et al. 1986. *Habits of the Heart.* New York: Harper & Row.
Berger, Arthur Asa, ed. 1991. *Media U.S.A.* 2d ed. New York: Longman.
Bernard, Viola P., et al. 1971. "Dehumanization: A Composite Psychological Defense Mechanism in Relation to Modern War. In *The Triple Revolution Emerging: Social Problems in Depth,* eds. Robert Perucci and Marc Pilisuk, pp. 16–30. Boston: Little, Brown.
Breed, Warren. 1971. *The Self-Guiding Society.* New York: Free Press.
Calabrese, Raymond. 1987. "Adolescence: A Growth Period Conducive to Alienation." *Adolescence* 88 (Winter): 929–38.
Chira, S. 1993. "Surprising Survey on Kids and Guns—40% Know a Victim." *San Francisco Chronicle,* July 20, p. A-10.
Currie, Elliott. 1991. "The Market Society." *Dissent* (Spring): pp. 255–58.
Davis, Nanette, and Clarice Stasz. 1990. *Social Control of Deviance: A Critical Perspective.* New York: McGraw-Hill.
Derber, Charles. 1992. *Money, Murder, and the American Dream: Wilding from Wall Street to Main Street.* Boston: Faber & Faber.
Ehrhart, W. D. 1993. "On the Virtues of Dishonesty." *San Francisco Examiner,* March 19, p. A-23.
Fromm, Erich. 1955. *The Sane Society.* New York: Holt, Rinehart & Winston.
Hacker, Andrew. 1992. *Two Nations: Black and White, Separate, Hostile, and Unequal.* New York: Scribner's.
Harris, A, and T. Harris. 1985. *Staying O.K.* New York: HarperCollins.
Harris, Louis. 1987. *Inside America.* New York: Vintage.
Hemmelstein, Hal. 1984. *Understanding Television.* New York: Praeger.
Hewitt, J. 1991. "Building Media Empires." In *Media U.S.A.,* ed. Arthur Asa Berger, 2d ed., pp. 396–403. New York: Longman.
Hochschild, Arlie 1983. *The Managed Heart.* Berkeley: University of California Press.
Horney, Karen. 1938. *The Neurotic Personality of Our Time.* New York: Norton.
Inciardi, James A. 1986. *The War on Drugs.* Palo Alto, Calif.: Mayfield.
Israel, Jochiem. 1971. *Alienation: An Integrated Approach.* Boston: Allyn & Bacon.
Jerome, L. E. 1975. "Astrology: Magic or Science?" *The Humanist* 35 (September): 10–15.
Kanungo, R. N. 1982. *Work Alienation: An Integrated Approach.* New York: Praeger.

Lasch, Christopher. 1978. *The Culture of Narcissism.* New York: Norton.

———. 1984. *The Minimal Self: Psychic Survival in Troubled Times.* New York: Norton.

Lupsha, Peter. 1981. "American Values and Organized Crime: Suckers and Wiseguys." In *The American Self,* ed. B. Girgus, pp. 144–55. Albuquerque: University of New Mexico Press.

Lutz, William. 1989. *Doublespeak.* New York: HarperCollins.

Malamuth, N. M. 1984. "Aggression Against Women: Cultural and Individual Causes." In *Pornography and Sexual Aggression,* ed. Malamuth and E. Donnerstein. New York: Academic Press.

Marx, Gary T. 1988. "Fraudulent Identification and Biography." Paper presented at a seminar of the Department of Sociology, San Diego State University, February.

Mecca, Andrew. Neil Smelser, and Vasconcellos, eds. 1989. *The Social Importance of Self-Esteem.* Berkeley: University of California Press.

Merton, Robert. 1938/1994. "Social Structure and Anomie." *American Sociological Review* 3 (October): 672–82. Reprinted in *Deviance,* ed. H. Pontell. Englewood Cliffs, N.J.: Prentice Hall.

Messner, Steven, and Richard Rosenfeld. 1994. *Crime and the American Dream.* Monterey, Calif.: Wadsworth.

Mills, C. Wright. 1951. *White Collar.* New York: Oxford University Press.

———. 1956. *The Power Elite.* New York: Oxford University Press.

———. 1959. *The Sociological Imagination.* New York: Oxford University Press.

Montagu, Ashley, and Floyd Matson. 1985. *The Dehumanization of Man.* New York: McGraw-Hill.

Nader, Ralph. 1985. Speech at the University of North Florida.

Omar, Sidney. 1993. "Astrological Forecast." *Los Angeles Times,* March 26, p. E-11.

Papson, Steve. 1985. "Bureaucratic Discourse and the Presentation of Self as Spectacle." *Humanity and Society* 9 (August): 223–36.

Parenti, Michael. 1991. *Make-Believe Media.* New York: St. Martin's Press.

Patterson. James, and Peter Kim. 1991. *The Day Americans Told the Truth.* New York: Prentice-Hall.

Riesman, David. 1950. *The Lonely Crowd.* New Haven: Yale University Press.

Ritzer, George. 1993. *The McDonaldization of Society.* Thousand Oaks, Calif.: Pine Forge Press.

Roberts, Ron. 1978. *Social Problems: Human Possibilities.* St. Louis: Mosby.

Rogers, Henry, and John Mays. 1987. *Juvenile Delinquency.* New York: Wiley.

Rotfeld, Henry J., and I. L. Preston. 1981. "The Potential Impact of Research on Advertising Law." *Journal of Advertising Research* 21: 9–16.

Rotfeld, Henry J., and K. B. Rotzall. 1984. "Is Advertising Puffery Believed?" In *Understanding Television,* ed. H. Hemmelstein. New York: Praeger.

Schmidt, Richard. 1983. *Alienation and Class.* Cambridge, Mass.: Schenkman.

Schrank, Jeffrey. 1977. *Snap, Crackle, and Popular Taste.* New York: Dell.

Seeman, Melvin. 1961. "On the Meaning of Alienation." *American Sociological Review* 26:753–58.

Shaw, D. 1993. "Distrustful Public Views Media as Them—Not Us." *Los Angeles Times,* April 1, pp. A-1, 18–19.

Shrader, W. 1992. *Media Blight and the Dehumanizing of America.* New York: Praeger.

Simon, David, and S. Stanley Eitzen. 1993. *Elite Deviance.* 4th ed. Needham Heights, Mass.: Allyn & Bacon.

Smelser, Neil. 1989. "Self-Esteem and Social Problems: An Introduction." In *The Social Importance of Self-Esteem,* ed. A. M. Mecca et al. Berkeley: University of California Press.

Synnott, A. 1991. "The Presentation of Gender in Advertising." In *Media U.S.A.,* ed. Arthur Asa Berger, 2d ed., pp. 338–44. New York: Longman.

Wilkinson, Rupert, ed. 1992. *American Social Character.* New York: HarperCollins.

Wyckham, R. 1987. "Implied Superiority Claims." *Journal of Advertising Research* 27 (February/March): 54–63.

EXERCISE 3-1. THE DEHUMANIZATION OF WOMEN AND CRIME

Two excellent videos concerning the dehumanization of women in ads are *Killing Us Softly* and *Still Killing Us Softly.* They are available in most college video collections and in some public libraries. Each is about 30 minutes long. Watch one of them in class, then discuss your reactions in a brief paper (two to four pages).

You may wish to focus on the following issues:

1 What relationship is suggested between the way women are presented in ads and the victimization of women by rapists and murderers?

2 What messages do advertisements send women regarding their independence, beauty, and ability to love their families?

3 What messages does advertising send to men concerning what women want from them?

4 How are men depicted in ads, and what messages do you think men are given by such images?

EXERCISE 3-2. ALIENATION IN THE MEDIA

One way to study inauthenticity and dehumanization is to analyze the contents of magazine ads. Select a series of full-page ads at random from current issues of three types of magazines:

General-interest magazines: *Time, Newsweek, U.S. News & World Report, Vanity Fair*
Men's magazines: *GQ, M, Playboy, Penthouse, Esquire*
Women's magazines: *Cosmopolitan, Redbook, Vogue, Good Housekeeping*

Select ads from one issue of one magazine in each of the three categories. Select only full-page ads that picture people. Do not select ads that show only products.

1 Determine whether the pictures and the words in each ad imply a promise of sexual fulfillment, monetary success, popularity, love, happiness, or other benefits.

2 Search for two types of verbal dehumanization:

• *Sexual dehumanization:* presentation of women or men as objects of sexual desire, either directly or by implication.
• *Nonsexual dehumanization:* presentation of men or women as less than human (e.g., "resources," machines, weapons, plants).

3 Find evidence of dehumanization in pictures that present people as sex objects, as expressed by (*a*) the degree of undress of the pictured models and (*b*) the degree of physical contact between couples pictured.

CODING SHEET

Use a separate coding sheet for each ad. A coding sheet is a kind of scorecard used to count the number of themes in each advertisement in your sample. Observe and record either the number of dehumanization and inauthenticity themes in each ad or the presence or absence of such themes (depending on the instructions of your professor).

01 Magazine:

02 Issue date:

03 Page number:

04–10 Verbal inauthenticity
    04 Sexual fulfillment _____
    05 Monetary success, power, status _____
    06 Popularity, friendship _____
    07 Love, romance, marriage _____
    08 Happy family life, successful parenting _____
    09 Pleasurable experiences, good feeling _____
    10 Other benefits _____

11–17 Pictured inauthenticity
    11 Sexual fulfillment _____
    12 Monetary success, power, status _____
    13 Popularity, friendship _____
    14 Love, romance, marriage _____
    15 Happy family life, successful parenting _____
    16 Pleasurable experiences, good feeling _____
    17 Other benefits _____

18–19 Verbal dehumanization
    18 Sexual: eroticism; description or mention of full or partial nudity; description or mention of gestures, clothing, actions, or physical contact suggestive of sex; description or mention of women or men as objects of sexual desire _____
    19 Nonsexual: description or mention of men or women as less than human ("resources," machines or parts of machines, weapons, nonhuman species) _____

20–27 Pictured dehumanization: representation of women or men as sex objects
    20 Clothing that reveals contours of sex organs or secondary sex characteristics (breasts, buttocks) _____
    21 Partial nudity _____
    22 Full nudity _____
    23 Hand contact _____
    24 Embrace _____
    25 Kiss _____
    26 Sexual or erotic pose (e.g., simulated intercourse) _____
    27 Other dehumanizing pose _____

You may want to calculate the proportion of your ads that contain such themes and show your findings in a table such as Table 3-1. A comparison of ads from the 1950s and 1960s with those being published today will reveal whether ads are becoming more or less inauthentic and dehumanizing.

TABLE 3-1
PERCENTAGE OF ADS REPRESENTING VERBAL AND PICTURED
INAUTHENTICITY AND DEHUMANIZATION IN THREE MASS-CIRCULATION
MAGAZINES

	Time	*GQ*	*Cosmopolitan*
Verbal inauthenticity	75%	85%	95%
Pictured inauthenticity	60	85	95
Verbal dehumanization	75	85	95
Pictured dehumanization	60	85	95

SUGGESTED READINGS

Berger, Arthur Asa, ed. 1991. *Media U.S.A.* 2d ed. New York: Longman. A wonderful collection of readings dealing with all problematic aspects of the American mass media.

Hacker, Andrew. 1992. *Two Nations: Black and White, Separate, Hostile, and Unequal.* New York: Scribner's. One of the most interesting and important books on American racism in a long time.

Ritzer, George. 1993. *The McDonaldization of Society.* Thousand Oaks, Calif.: Pine Forge Press. A provocative study of inauthentic and dehumanizing trends in the processes of franchising and mass consumption in the postmodern economy. Ritzer's book is a profound analysis of the contradictions of mass consumerism.

Wilkinson, Rupert, ed. 1992. *American Social Character.* New York: HarperCollins. The most important reader on American character in a generation. It contains classic articles and a superb set of bibliographic essays.

4

MASTER TRENDS OF THE POSTMODERN ERA

WILDING FOR FUN AND PROFIT

On Valentine's Day in 1929 four Chicago gangsters dressed as police officers killed seven members of a rival crime family. The incident, known as the St. Valentine's Day Massacre, sparked outrage all over the nation. A better government association was formed in Chicago and federal agents under the direction of Elliot Ness began an investigation that eventually brought down the leader of one Chicago syndicate, Al Capone. The incident also resulted in the eventual repeal of Prohibition, which had become associated not only with illegal alcohol but with gang violence.

In the 1990s there is at least one massacre every weekend in most major American cities, but there is no corresponding outrage. In fact, an astonishing amount of deviance is now tolerated as normal in American life.

• In 1992, after four Los Angeles police officers were acquitted of the use of excessive force in the beating of Rodney King, fifty-one people were killed in three days of rioting (Moynihan, 1993:16–19).

• Each year 5000 people are murdered by members of their own family. Two million children and 1.5 million elderly people are assaulted by family members. A husband beats his wife every thirty seconds, and over 40 percent of those wives are pregnant at the time. About 160,000 children are kidnapped by parents who have lost custody of them. About 60,000 youngsters are expelled from their homes each year and refused entry (Derber, 1992:116).

Much crime outside the American home seems to be committed for the sake of inflicting pain and in complete disregard of the welfare of the victim.

• In 1989, ten teenage girls were arrested in New York City after they had jabbed dozens of women with pins. The girls said they just wanted to see how the women would react.
• In 1993, several homeless people in the San Francisco Bay Area were doused with alcohol or gasoline and set afire. Most of the perpetrators turned out to be young people who claimed to be bored and in search of a good time. Some said they set the people on fire just to see if the victims would wake up.

Such incidents are socially patterned. The problem has many names: "social breakdown" (*Dissent,* 1991); "social disintegration," or the rise of "the morally loose individual," (Nisbet, 1988); instrumental and expressive "wilding" (Derber, 1992). Whatever one chooses to call it, the problem is a tragically measurable aspect of contemporary American life. As Robert Nisbet notes, the morally loose individual has no attachment to a spouse or a family, to a school, a church, or a job, or to moral responsibility. Moral looseness simply involves "playing fast and loose with other individuals in relationships of trust and responsibility" (1988:84).

The evidence of such looseness is seemingly everywhere in American life:

• The inventor of the junk bond, Michael Milken, having swindled billions of dollars in the 1980s, was hired to teach business ethics at UCLA in 1993.
• Ronald Reagan's administration was characterized by more corruption than any other in American history. Over 120 of his appointees resigned from office under a cloud. The Bush administration was basically a continuation of the "grab it while you can" ethic that began during the Reagan years.
• In 1960, one in every forty white babies and one in five black infants were born out of wedlock. In 1993, one of every five whites and two of every three blacks were so born (Moynihan, 1993:17).
• Of 200,000 college freshmen polled in 1987, 76 percent said that it was very important to be financially well off. Twenty years earlier, only 44 percent of freshmen held such a materialistic view. In 1976, 83 percent of respondents felt it important to develop a philosophy of life. In 1987, only 39 percent of students expressed such a wish (Shames, 1989:43). A 1990 report by the Carnegie Foundation for the Advancement of Teaching complained of a breakdown of civility on the nation's college campuses. Especially alarming was an epidemic of cheating, racial attacks, hate crimes, and rapes on campus. A majority of students at the University of Tennessee and Indiana University admitted to submitting papers that had been written by someone else, or of copying large sections of a friend's paper (Derber, 1992:101).
• Such elite universities as Stanford, Harvard, MIT, and Cal Tech have all been embroiled in scandals involving the unlawful expenditure of research

funds. Some of the illegal purchases included country club memberships, yachts, going-away parties for administrators, and flowers.

• American family life is increasingly filled with risk and uncertainty. The divorce rate has stabilized at twice what it was between 1950 and 1964, three times the rate of 1920–30. The U.S. divorce rate is the highest among advanced capitalist nations, four times that of Japan, three times that of England and France, and twice that of Denmark and Sweden. The proportion of American households headed by a single parent is likewise four times the Japanese rate, three times the Swedish rate, and twice the English rate (Derber, 1992:116).

• One-third of all children born in the 1980s live in single-parent households and over 7 million children live with stepparents. There is little question that stepfamilies have special problems. The divorce rate for second marriages is even higher than for first marriages: 60 to 70 percent for second marriages, 50 percent for first marriages. Children usually view their stepparents as "permanent guests," and most stepparents' sense of commitment to marriage is tentative. Having already experienced at least one unsuccessful marriage, they keep their guard up (Derber, 1992:122).

What master trend has brought us to this social instability?

Master trends have nothing to do with predictions of specific events.[1] Our concern is about predicting trends, societal conditions that cause social problems or make existing social problems worse. For example, what will happen to the standard of living in the United States, and how will social problems be affected? History is not merely about the past. It is also about the legacy the past has left us, the direction in which it has pointed us. Such legacies are really matters of perception, and there is no consensus about the postmodern era and the forces that will shape social problems in the future (see Box 4-1).

Ideally, such an analysis should stem from the sociological imagination paradigm. The tendencies discussed here are changes in (1) social structure, (2) our historical period (the postmodern era), and (3) the impact of structural and historical change on social character (Gerth & Mills, 1953:456–80).

Three master trends of our age come to mind:

1 The world is suffering a crisis of uncontrolled population growth, especially in Asia, Africa, and Latin America. The world's population could soar from about 5.5 billion people in 1992 to 10 billion in 2050 (Hertsgaard, 1993:23).

---

[1]Predicting events is a game Americans love to play. In all of the tabloids at supermarket checkout counters psychics let readers know the coming fate of their favorite celebrities. (The psychics are wrong about 80 percent of the time, but few readers bother to check.) The problem is that social scientists have not fared much better than the psychics in their predictions.

BOX 4-1

BEST-SELLING VIEWS OF MASTER TRENDS

Consider the opinions expressed in some recent bestsellers about American society and where it is going.

Francis Fukuyama (1992:3–4), a conservative, has argued that the twentieth century has made pessimists of nearly all of us. Most of us now believe that there is no such thing as

> history—that is, a meaningful order to the broad sweep of human events. Our . . . experience has taught us that the future is more likely than not to contain new and unimagined evils, from fanatical dictatorships and bloody genocides to the banalization of life through modern consumerism, and that unprecedented disasters await us from nuclear winter to global warming.

Our pessimism, Fukuyama contends, is largely a reaction to the exaggerated optimism of the nineteenth century, based on faith in "progress," scientific developments, and liberal democracy. He believes that liberal democracy should spread in the future. He stands nearly alone in his optimism among writers about master trends.

Paul Kennedy (1987, 1993), a liberal, views the American future with deep concern. He notes that history teaches us that economic power and military power are interrelated and tend to rise and fall together. America's problem is that it has poured so much of its treasure into military hardware and made so many alliances and treaties that it has become overextended. As a result, America is in relative economic and military decline. About the best Americans can hope for is to "muddle through" (Kennedy, 1993:357), as England did. The problem is that England lost its empire in the process of muddling through, and the English are more accepting of the class distinctions that become increasingly apparent when the economic pie is shrinking. In short, Kennedy views the United States as suffering from serious economic and political problems, in the face of dominance by multinational corporations and dramatic overpopulation in Third World nations.

Kevin Phillips (1993), taking Kennedy's analysis to its logical conclusion, believes the American middle class is in steep decline. He contends that democracy and the existence of a large middle class go hand in hand. The decline of the middle class has come at a time of overall economic decline, rising taxes, and a redistribution of wealth and income upward (the rich are getting richer, everyone else is being made worse off).

Donald L. Bartlett and James B. Steele (1992), two *Philadelphia Inquirer* reporters, won a Pulitzer Prize for their analysis of what went wrong with America's economy in the 1980s. Like Phillips, they stress the decline of the middle class and the increased concentration of wealth and income in the upper class. Bartlett and Steele also worry about the uncompetitiveness of the manufacturing sector of the American economy, the exporting of jobs to Mexico and other Third World nations, and the rise in taxes and health-care costs for the middle class.

William Greider (1992) has issued a political call to arms. He deals not only with America's economic woes but with our political problems as well. American democracy is at risk, he argues, because new and powerful lobby groups dominate campaign financing, the flow of information to members of Congress, and, to a degree, public opinion polling.

In view of the diversity of opinions, how does one begin to discern the master trends of our era, especially those trends that are likely to cause future crises? Sometimes things that look like trends are merely passing phenomena. In the 1960s and early 1970s Charles Reich (1970) and others believed that the hippie and New Left movements were going to bring a new revolution to America, one that would build community and overcome alienation, war, racism, and sexism. Nearly three decades later, we can see that the 1960s did bring some positive changes to American society (Gitlin, 1988) (such as the Civil Rights and Equal Employment Opportunity acts). The great revolution that would unite us all, however, has not yet happened. Thus it is no small task to differentiate passing events from permanent change.

2 The great structural change in the United States has been the increased coordination of political, economic, and military institutions and their control over modern weapons of mass destruction and over the civilian population.

3 The set of values that has emerged as part of postmodern culture will mark our era and its social problems for decades to come. Postmodern culture emphasizes themes that reinforce a host of alienating tendencies in capitalist societies, especially inauthenticity and commodification.

THE POPULATION CRISIS

The predicted doubling of the world's population in less than sixty years would have immense negative consequences in the form of numerous social problems, including poverty and immigration, crime and pollution, famine and war, the repression of human rights and declining standards of living in First World nations.

Poverty and destitution are already tremendous social problems, especially in the Third World, where:

- The average child does not see a doctor before age 5.
- A billion people (30 percent of the population) are unemployed.
- Between 60 and 90 percent of the wealth in most nations is owned by 3 to 20 percent of the population.
- Massive famines and starvation already kill over 30 million people a year.
- More than 700 million adults are unable to read, and half of all school-age children do not attend school (Simon & Eitzen, 1993:203–4).

One result of this immense suffering is political instability. A war or revolution has occurred in the Third World about once a month since 1945, and there is little sign of peace breaking out any time soon. These wars and revolutions influence First World nations in many ways—international terrorism, massive immigration, drug trafficking, and a host of other ills.

The Third World is also a place where military dictatorships brutally repress human rights while seeking aid from the United States and other democratic nations (Simon & Eitzen, 1993:194–202). The United States has been all too willing to support dictatorships in the name of anticommunism. This strategy has served the needs of U.S.-based multinational corporations for cheap labor, new markets, and access to raw materials. Exploitation by multinationals arouses considerable resentment in the Third World. Given the political economies and international position of Third World nations, massive global social problems like those mentioned above can worsen.

INEQUALITIES OF WEALTH AND RESOURCES

The main drift of the American postmodern era, the one from which virtually all other patterns flow, has been the unprecedented increase of economic and political power in the hands of a small group of elites. The scope and ramifications of the interactions of these groups are of interest. Let us begin by examining the distribution of wealth.

Most Americans do not own an appreciable amount of wealth, so they tend to confuse wealth and income. Though the two are related, they are not the same. Wealth consists of property (land, buildings, stocks, bonds, savings accounts, factories) that generates income. Thus it is perfectly possible not to work at any job and still have a substantial income if one owns enough income-generating property. There are two types of wealth. Corporate wealth consists of the assets (property) owned by a company or business. Personal wealth is property that belongs to families and individuals.

The increased concentration of ownership has important consequences. Table 4-1 reflects these sad realities of American life:

1 Between 1982 and 1992 the proportion of wealth owned by the richest 1 percent of Americans increased from 31 to 37 percent—an all-time high. More important, it is now estimated that the richest 10 percent of Americans own as much wealth as the bottom 90 percent.

2 Income distribution has also become more concentrated since the 1970s. During the twenty years between 1970 and 1990, only the top 20 percent of income earners saw their earnings increase. The other 80 percent of families lost ground, and by 1995 fully 90 percent of income earners will have experienced a decline in income.

3 The heart of a democratic society is its middle class, and the American middle class is shrinking dramatically. Between 1969 and 1990 the proportion of families earning middle-class incomes declined by 15 percent, the largest such drop in American history. The reasons for this decline, especially

TABLE 4-1
INCREASING CONCENTRATION OF WEALTH AND
INCOME, 1950s–1990s

Years	Percentage of wealth held by top 1 percent
1962–82	31%
1982–92	37

Income distribution (billions of dollars)

	Top 4%	Bottom 35%
1959	$ 31	$ 31
1989	452	452

Income distribution by fifths

	1950s	1970s	1990s
Top 20%	43%	45.0%	51.0%
Second 20%	24	22.0	21.0
Third 20%	17	16.0	14.0
Fourth 20%	12	10.8	9.0
Lowest 20%	5	4.7	3.0

Families earning middle-class incomes[a]

Year	Percent
1969	71.2%
1990	63.3

Projected increase in family incomes, 1985–95 (percent)[b]

U.S. families	Gain
Top 1%	50–75%
Top 5%	25
Remaining 95%	0 or decline

[a]$28,000–$200,000.
[b]Adjusted for inflation.
Source: Adapted from Phillips, 1993: 22–31; 278.

the loss of jobs and the rise in taxes (Bartlett & Steele, 1992), are of less concern to us here than its consequences. The United States has thus far managed to escape the class conflicts that have traumatized other nations, but whether it can continue to do so is anyone's guess (Kennedy, 1987).

4 The decline of the middle class spawns additional serious social problems: increased numbers of people lack basic health insurance and suffer long-term unemployment. As we have seen, studies in the 1970s (Brenner, 1973) indicated that for each 1.5 percent increase in unemployment that lasts at least eighteen months, the rates of other major social problems rise significantly. Thus any significant rise in the unemployment rate will result in increased rates of homicide, admissions to state mental hospitals and prisons, and deaths from suicide and abuse of alcohol and drugs. Jails and prisons, already overcrowded in more than thirty states, will become more so. Sustained unemployment also spawns homelessness and increases in government outlays for social programs, which in turn increase government debt and probably taxes. These developments may convince nonelites that government is not functioning in their interest. Increasing numbers of people may stop going to the polls on election day or may vote for extremist candidates, and the Republican and Democratic parties as we know them may disintegrate.

The working and lower classes may also react to the decline of the quality of American life. We could be in for more urban riots, hate crimes, and other outbreaks of mass deviance. The result would be an increasingly fearful society characterized by conflict between the haves and have-nots. Elites often respond to mass disorder by increases in propaganda and manipulation. If these measures fail, ruling classes are not averse to calling in riot police and the National Guard. If all else fails, regular troops may be mobilized. The result may be a new civil war, this one made more painful by guerrilla action.

Indeed, recent incidents have already been identified as guerrilla warfare. Fanatical white supremacists have planned to attack several key African American targets in hopes of starting a race war. Today the distinction between war and terrorism has become blurred. The bombing of New York's World Trade Center and the apparent attempt to assassinate former president Bush in 1993 reflect this tension at the international level. The proliferation of weapons capable of immediate mass destruction has allowed small groups of disenfranchised people to become important political actors in the postmodern world order. The bombing of civilians in large American cities, drug-financed weapons caches, and airplane hijackings are all with us, and likely to increase before they lessen.

The crisis in the political economy will not soon go away. Southern California alone lost 96,000 jobs in the aerospace industry between 1987 and 1993. The end of the Cold War has also reduced military spending, and severe economic dislocations are possible because of the absence of economic conversion plans. Hundreds of thousands of workers will need retraining if the middle class is to stave off further decline. Retraining will cost billions and perhaps increase budget deficits, taxes, or both. To understand the many additional implications of this crisis, we must understand how it came about.

THE MILITARIZED ECONOMY: A COSTLY MASTER TREND

The enrichment of the upper class and the decline of the middle class result from political and economic changes that have taken place since World War II. At the war's end the United States did not dismantle the military establishment that had enabled it to overcome fascism. The National Security Act of 1947 created the National Military Establishment, headed by a secretary of defense of cabinet rank who had direct supervision of the secretaries of the three military services (the act separated the air force from the army), and a host of governmental intelligence organizations. National security became the measure of foreign and defense policy as the Cold War against communism began. Between 1947 and 1992 the United States spent about $4 trillion on defense, and entered into alliances with nations on all continents.

The economic results were devastating. Research and development (R&D) of new military technologies, products, and services became the top priority. As of 1988, over two-thirds of all U.S. funds spent on R&D were spent for military purposes. Less than 1 percent was spent to develop products used in the civilian sector of the economy (Kennedy, 1993). As a result, the U.S. economy became uncompetitive with those of Japan and Western Europe. By 1988, manufacturing had nearly become a lost art in the United States. Fully 68 percent of U.S. jobs and 71 percent of the national income were based on service-sector jobs (Kennedy, 1993). Other economic traumas also haunted the United States:

• In 1980 the country had the world's largest surplus from international trade; by 1990 it had become the world's largest debtor nation in international commerce.

• Between 1980 and 1992 the national debt increased from $1 trillion to over $4 trillion, the largest such increase in the shortest amount of time in world history. Much of this increase is due to the Reagan administration's $2 trillion defense spending and $750 billion in corporate tax relief.

Ever since the end of World War II, the federal government has been an intimate part of the American economic system, performing two contradictory functions. On the one hand, politically influential corporations seek assistance in accumulating capital and profits by pressing demands for tax relief, lucrative government contracts, subsidies, loans, and loan guarantees. The General Accounting Office found that 41 percent of the 2000 largest American corporations (with assets of $250 million or more) paid either no federal income taxes or less than $100,000 in taxes in 1989, when their receipts totaled $544 billion (*San Diego Times-Union,* July 20, 1993, p. A-1). Corporations also receive military protection of their overseas markets and investments. On the other hand, to maintain its legitimacy the state must meet the demands placed on it for public assistance. It must offer social programs designed to aid people suffering from poverty, unemployment, homelessness, mental illness and retardation, drug addiction, and the other social problems that arise in modern capitalist societies (O'Conner, 1973).

So the state is subjected to competing demands for corporate favors and for social programs. As a result, its expenditures consistently exceed its revenues. It can reduce the massive deficit in only three ways:

1 By reducing its support for corporations, especially through defense contracts, subsidies, loans, and tax relief. Corporate influence in the policy-making process makes this course unlikely.

2 By cutting social programs for the unemployed, working poor, elderly, and other deserving groups, thus losing legitimacy in the eyes of ordinary people. A lessening of legitimation could lead to mass refusal to support any future war to preserve corporate holdings, a tax revolt that would increase the national debt, or a new political movement designed to redistribute wealth, income, and political power in a more democratic fashion.

3 By increasing personal income taxes. This course is so unpopular among voters that no candidate for election will propose it.

The situation is made all the worse by the competitive sector of the economy, the 12 million small and medium-sized businesses that suffer the crises of farm foreclosure, bank failures, and bankruptcy. These businesses have suffered from the high interest rates of the 1980s and declining demand for their goods and services in the 1990s.

The economic result of these massive structural changes has been a dramatic decline in middle-class living standards, a dramatic increase in homelessness, and the worsening of numerous social problems.

ELITE POWER, THE HIGHER IMMORALITY, AND CRIMINAL BEHAVIOR

Corporate crime also plays a role in these economic processes. Harold Barnet (1981) has argued that the marketing of unsafe products, the polluting of the environment, and violations of health, safety, and labor laws all help increase corporate profits by transferring various costs to either consumers, workers, or the public in general. Moreover, the appalling lack of enforcement of laws against corporate crimes and the lenient sentences imposed on the few who are convicted serve further to indicate that the state functions largely to encourage the accumulation of capital, not to repress wrongdoing by the elite. Such deviance is part of the higher immorality that C. Wright Mills described in 1956—the institutionalized set of values and practices that encourage the corporate and political elite to commit acts that in fact are criminal.

Since Mills wrote about the higher immorality in 1956, the nation has experienced unprecedented forms of corruption, including increased cooperation with organized criminal syndicates. No longer are national scandals confined to the bribing of politicians by corporate elites in search of favors. Today these practices run the gamut from unprecedented self-enrichment and abuse of political power (as in Watergate) to deception of the public and sexual perversion.

What Mills perceived in the 1950s was the beginning of a "secret government" (Moyers, 1988) consisting of a set of intelligence agencies, foremost among them the Central Intelligence Agency and the National Security Council. From time to time the CIA has hired former military personnel, arms dealers, drug smugglers, terrorists, former Nazis, and Mafia members to carry out its objectives. The result has been unprecedented scandals of the kind the Constitution was designed to avert.

AMERICA THE SCANDALIZED

Between 1860 and 1920 the United States suffered only two major crises involving corruption at the federal level—an average of about one scandal every thirty years. Beginning in 1963 with the investigation into the assassination of President Kennedy, however, the federal government has experienced repeated scandals. The scandals themselves are serious social problems, causing all manner of social harm.

Item: When President Kennedy was assassinated in Dallas, Texas, on November 22, 1963, a cover-up of the investigation into the crime was personally ordered by President Johnson, Assistant Attorney General Nicholas B. Katzenbach, and FBI director J. Edgar Hoover. They allegedly suspected that Communists in either Cuba or the Soviet Union or both might be involved, and feared a war would result. These officials agreed that the public must be convinced that Lee Harvey Oswald acted alone in killing the president (Simon, 1992). This was President Johnson's motive in setting up the Warren Commission in December 1963. The Warren Commission did indeed find that Oswald had acted alone, and that Dallas nightclub owner Jack Ruby had acted alone in killing Oswald (who at the time was surrounded by nearly 200 armed law-enforcement officers) in the Dallas police station.

Subsequent investigations into the crime by the House Special Committee on Assassinations (HSCA) from 1975 to 1978 found numerous inconsistencies in the case. The HSCA found that President Kennedy "was probably assassinated as a result of a conspiracy" (Summers, 1989:14). Probable suspects included members of organized crime (U.S. House of Representatives, Select Committee on Assassinations, 1979:53). The HSCA concluded that Mafia bosses Carlos Marcello of New Orleans and Santos Trafficante of Florida had the "means, motive, and opportunity" to assassinate the president, and that anti-Castro Cubans may have been involved.

The precise nature of the conspiracy and the identities of the conspirators were never determined. Numerous theories have been advanced. Between 1966 and 1993 more than 600 books and 2000 articles were published about the Kennedy assassination. The dominant view is that government agencies killed their own president because he intended to make peace with the Soviet Union and end the Cold War. There is also speculation that Kennedy was going to disengage the United States from its involvement in Vietnam. Kennedy's assassination not only was the first major postwar scandal but marks the beginning of a drastic decline in public confidence in government agencies and politicans.

After Kennedy's death the United States escalated its military activities in Vietnam. As we know, the Vietnam War produced a number of scandalous incidents that divided public opinion and contributed to Americans' distrust of their government. The Watergate scandal caused public trust to decline even further.

After Watergate in 1975, investigations into the postwar activities of the CIA and the FBI revealed that both agencies had systematically violated the civil liberties of thousands of American citizens. Such violations have continued to this day:

• Since 1947 the FBI has committed more than 1500 illegal break-ins of headquarters of American organizations and foreign embassies. During the Reagan administration (1981–88), the FBI spied on the United Auto Workers, the Maryknoll Sisters, the Southern Christian Leadership Conference, and various other groups and citizens opposed to the administration's policy in Central America (Simon & Eitzen, 1993:257).

• After Dr. Martin Luther King's "I have a dream" speech in 1963, the FBI illegally spied on the Reverend Dr. King, bugging his house and hotel rooms. The FBI even tried to induce Dr. King to commit suicide by threatening to reveal evidence that he had carried on adulterous affairs.

The CIA has been involved in a variety of illegal activities both inside and outside the United States. From 1947 to 1975 the CIA:

• Illegally experimented on a variety of American citizens, scientists from the Army Chemical Corps, and some of its own agents (without their knowledge or consent) with knockout drops, incapacitating chemicals, and LSD (a hallucinogenic drug). The CIA even hired San Francisco prostitutes to give their customers drugs.

• Between 1950 and 1974 the CIA was involved in various plots to assassinate foreign heads of state, including Fidel Castro of Cuba, Patrice Lamumba of Zaire, Rafael Trujillo of the Dominican Republic, Ngo Dinh Diem of South Vietnam, and Salvador Allende of Chile. This practice continued into the 1980s. In 1985 Director William Casey secretly arranged for the murder of the Shiite Muslim leader Fadlallah in a deal with Saudi intelligence (Simon & Eitzen, 1993:270–72).

In 1987 news broke concerning what was to be the most damaging scandal of the Reagan administration, the so-called Iran-Contra affair. The root of the scandal involved the sale of weapons to the Iranian government and the diversion of the profits to the Nicaraguan Contras, a counterrevolutionary force virtually created by the CIA (Moyers, 1988). At first the entire episode was blamed on a marine lieutenant colonel, Oliver North; most high-ranking officials of the Reagan administration claimed they had no knowledge of the events. Subsequent investigations and trial testimony, however, pointed to a massive cover-up by White House aides and others.

Item: North's trial in 1989 revealed that in 1984 a meeting of a national security group composed of Vice President Bush, the Joint Chiefs of Staff, several cabinet officers, and President Reagan discussed the feasibility of soliciting foreign governments to aid the Contras, as a means of getting around the Boland Amendment, which prohibited further military aid to the Contras (Draper, 1989).

Item: President Reagan personally solicited the largest contributions for Contra aid from foreign nations, and a number of Latin American governments were asked to cooperate by falsifying documentation of arms sales to hide the fact that the weapons were destined for the Contras. Nations that cooperated were promised increased U.S. aid.

Item: Both illegal arms sales and illegal solicitation of funds were orchestrated by a secret group, dubbed the Enterprise, set up apart from the CIA and other governmental agencies to ensure secrecy. The Enterprise was composed of retired military and intelligence personnel, arms dealers, and drug smugglers.

According to *Webster's International Dictionary,* "scandal" has various meanings. A scandal can be conduct that encourages loss of religious faith or a violation of a religious precept or rule by a religious person. A scandal can also be the spreading of true or false gossip that damages a person's reputation, or conduct that so seriously violates moral standards that it arouses anger, or the use of impertinent remarks or improper tactics in a court of law. While these definitions of scandal are suggestive, they seem to bear little resemblance to the scandals that have plagued American life since 1963.

What do these events tell us about scandal as a modern social problem and about the structure and contradictions of contemporary American government? All of the government scandals we have reviewed have common characteristics.

1 They all involved secret actions by government agencies (especially the FBI, CIA, and the executive office) that were either illegal or unethical, and all caused severe physical, financial, or moral harm to the nation.

2 All were the subjects of official government hearings or investigations. The Watergate and Iran-Contra hearings were nationally televised.

3 The original causes of most of these episodes are still unknown. Thus motives for President Kennedy's assassination, the reasons for the Watergate break-in, and the possible involvement of Vice President Bush, President Reagan, and Director Casey in planning the sale of arms to Iran and diversion of funds to the Contras remain matters of heated debate.

Though these scandalous episodes do not fit the dictionary definitions very well, they do provide valuable insights into the structure of our government and the social problems it generates.

The Constitution grants the power to declare war to Congress. War has not been officially declared since 1941, yet the United States fought dozens of secret wars between 1954 and 1993, many of them without the knowledge of Congress or the American people. Abroad the secret government has continually backed corrupt military dictatorships and death squads. At home the CIA has violated the civil rights of millions of Americans by collecting dossiers, opening mail, and enlisting the FBI in efforts to burglarize the headquarters of organizations that merely oppose the government's policies.

The effects of the secret government have destroyed the trust of the American people in their government and American prestige in many Third World nations. Beginning with the overthrow of the duly elected government of Iran in 1953, the CIA has repeatedly destabilized democracies unfriendly to U.S.-based multinational corporations. American military intervention has gone hand in hand with the militarization of the economy and increasing secrecy in the making of defense and foreign policy.

The secret government has repeatedly withheld evidence of crimes, committed criminal acts, used classified budgets for illicit purposes, and violated the civil liberties of thousands of Americans. It would be naive to expect all this to end now that the Cold War is over. The institutions that did all these things are still intact. Many social critics believe that the scandals that have erupted in the United States since 1963 are interrelated in some interesting and important respects. Several CIA agents thought to be connected to the assassination of President Kennedy, for example, were also involved in the Watergate break-in in 1972.

The secret government is staking out new territory in the new world order. Robert Gates, the current director of central intelligence, has already stated that the CIA needs to ensure corporate security as well as governmental security. The CIA is stressing the need for domestic counterterrorism, involvement in the drug war, and "crisis management" of low-intensity conflicts around the world. The CIA and its sister intelligence agencies are operating with classified budgets of about $35 billion (Baker, 1992:81). Such practices tend to have antidemocratic effects at home as well.

Both the Watergate and Iran-Contra scandals involved mechanisms developed by the CIA abroad. Moreover, there is disturbing evidence that the

FBI's spying on and harassment of activist organizations have dramatically increased in recent years (Berlet, 1992:82–84). None of these developments bode well for America's democratic processes.

Likewise, America is emerging from a period of self-concern, personal survival, and greed. The Reagan and Bush administrations made greed seem moral and corruption an everyday fact of political life. Yet sociologists usually consider deviant behavior to be abnormal, or as characteristic of a minority of people.

Deviance and crime are commonplace among many segments of the nation's economic, political, and military elites. Moreover, their deviance differs markedly from that of other social classes because it involves so much more money, power, and resources than people in other strata have access to.

LINKS BETWEEN VARIOUS TYPES OF CRIME

Corporate crime and political scandal are related not only to each other but to other types of crime and deviance, most obviously to organized crime.

The American drug problem is a classic example. Drugs are smuggled into the United States only with the cooperation of the banks that launder drug money and the political elites who accept payoffs both here and in the countries where the drugs originate. Thus General Manuel Noriega, the leader of Panama, was indicted in 1988 for accepting bribes from the Columbian cocaine cartel. At the same time, he was a long-time employee of the CIA, which for years had known of the general's involvement in the drug trade. Moreover, the CIA has trafficked in drugs for over forty years in Europe, Southeast Asia, and, most recently, Central America (as we saw in Chapter 2).

The drugs are distributed to street gangs and peddlers by organized criminal syndicates, among them the Italian-American Mafia. At its lowest level, the American drug problem is tied to the vast majority of property crimes committed by street criminals, who seek money to support their drug habits. Moreover, hundreds of murders each year are now committed by gangs seeking to control territory in the drug trade. Thus crimes at all levels of American life are now interrelated. Moreover, the high crime rates at all levels of American society have also had a major influence on our popular culture.

POSTMODERN CULTURE AND AMERICA'S MAIN DRIFT

Many people perceive that we live in a dangerous world. Everyday life is loaded with concerns that a generation ago never entered the consciousness of most middle-class people. Among such concerns:

- Is my job safe or will a worsening economy result in layoffs?
- Are my children practicing unsafe sex? Are they using drugs? Are they at risk for AIDS? Will they be victims of gang violence?
- When does discipline turn into abuse?
- Will my marriage last? Should it?

The problems of daily life have helped create a longing for solutions or for escape. Postmodern themes in advertising, movies, television, pop music, and literature represent new forms of social control. The themes of postmodern culture now dominate the mass media and advertising:

- Preoccupation with the self and neglect of the larger social good.
- Blindness to the effects of institutions and historical events on the individual, and a yearning for an ideal past that never existed.
- Preoccupation with sex and the separation of sex and love.
- Increasing reliance on violence to resolve conflicts.
- Commodification of virtually every human impulse, moral principle, and sacred belief into a product that is capable of being advertised.

All of these tendencies stem from the inauthenticity and dehumanization in advertising. The result, as we have seen, is a decline of traditional values.

Item: From 1950 to 1990, worldwide advertising expenditures increased sevenfold, from about $7 to nearly $50 per person. Advertising revenues have grown one-third faster than global economies and three times faster than the world's population (Durning, 1993:12).

Item: The people most heavily exposed to advertising live in the advanced capitalist nations, especially the United States. Advertising expenditures are 50 percent higher per person in the United States ($486) than in the nearest competitor, Japan ($300), and more than twice as high as in Europe ($200) (Durning, 1993:14; Baldwin, 1992:55). Practically no public place is untouched by advertising. Ads now appear in public restrooms, on huge video screens at shopping centers, on hot dogs, even at the bottoms of the holes on golf courses. In 1991 Americans were the targets of a $130-billion barrage of ads that included 3000 television commercials daily, 65 percent of all newspaper space (up from 40 percent fifty years earlier), and 36 billion pieces of junk mail (Baldwin, 1992:54). Research firms have gone so far as to assemble data on the spending behavior of 80 million consumer households from their credit records, a unique invasion of privacy (Smith, 1992:64).

Advertising exacerbates two troubling social problems that are almost certain to reach crisis proportions in the decades ahead. First, consumers in advanced nations consume many more resources than people in nonconsumer societies, thus hastening the depletion of those resources. Consumers in rich nations use up ten times more energy, thirteen times more iron and steel, four-

The polluted air in this large American city (New York) is not associated by most people with the consumption of mass-produced goods. Yet pollution, along with resource depletion, and massive consumer debt are just some of the negative underlying realities stemming from the constant advertising that haunts daily life in First World nations. (Porterfield/Chickering/Photo Research)

teen times more paper, eighteen times more synthetic chemicals, and nineteen times more aluminum than citizens of less developed countries. The technology that produces the advertised products accounts for "the lion's share of resource depletion, environmental pollution and habitat degradation," thus endangering rare species of animals. The goal of the international advertising industry is to create a world of consumer societies. This is an "ecological impossibility" (Durning, 1993:12), and the attempt at worldwide consumerization will almost certainly trigger a variety of environmental problems.

The detrimental effects of advertising are only now beginning to be understood, and it is becoming clear that advertising makes certain social problems worse:

1 Advertising increases envy, anxiety, and insecurity, especially among the poor and racial minorities. The United States in recent years has witnessed numerous murders by minority young people who wanted the victims' $100 sneakers (Baldwin, 1992:54). Thus advertising may increase racial as well as class antagonisms.

2 Advertising qualifies as what C. Wright Mills (1959:13) described as one of the new "enveloping techniques of political domination." The language of advertising contains "images, sloganeering," and other forms of irrational speech (Collins & Jacobson, 1992:56), and these mechanisms offer a dangerous substitute for rational choice, especially among the status-conscious, celebrity-worshiping young.

Because of its irrationality and widespread use in political campaigns, advertising constitutes a genuine threat to democracy. A candidate for office becomes merely another consumer commodity, and this effect is reinforced by the way the media cover elections. A study of the 1972 presidential election found that 73 percent of the news coverage focused not on issues but on who was ahead in the polls (Hellinger & Judd, 1991:65). Similar studies could have been done on virtually any major election since 1960, when presidential candidates first used television. The net result of expensive ads in political campaigns is that important issues are further and further removed from the citizenry's consideration. Public debate, a cardinal principle of democracy, is compromised, and with it citizens' ability to reach informed judgments.

Finally, there is the near-universal presence in postmodern culture of gratuitous violence and empty sexuality (not to mention sexism). Though the evidence that media violence contributes to violent behavior is overwhelming, the amount of violence on television has not decreased since 1978. Indeed, violence occurs in 70 percent of prime-time television programs (Cannon, 1993:10). There is also evidence that the violence that most desensitizes the young and disposes them to react violently is the kind presented as interesting and fun—in short, TV cartoon violence and commercials for R-rated movies (Cannon, 1993:10). In view of the fact that there is now a cable channel devoted exclusively to cartoons and that expenditures for advertising of all types are continuing to increase, increases in television violence and consequently in violent behavior can be expected in coming decades. These trends have had a major influence on the shaping of the contemporary American social character.

SOCIAL CHARACTER IN AN AGE OF CONFUSION

Social character is the great dependent variable, shaped by both the political economy and the dominant culture. The master trend in the American social character is identity confusion and uncertainty about the future of the nation and its values. Since 1945 the literature on social character has come full circle (Wilkinson, 1988, 1992). The social critics of the 1940s and 1950s complained that Americans were too conformist and insecure. They described the American people as "cheerful robots" (Mills, 1951), "other-directed" (Riesman, 1950), and overly receptive to the opinions of other people. In short, the fear of the fifties was that Americans had lost their independence under the pressures of bureaucratic and suburban life.

The 1960s and 1970s saw a cultural revolution that stressed "doing your own thing." A self-help movement that stressed consciousness expansion, sexual freedom, and experimentation sprang up. Many members of the middle classes, influenced by the civil rights, antiwar, and women's movements of those years, eagerly adopted a lifestyle devoted to self-awareness and self-fulfillment. No sooner had these seemingly independent streaks emerged than the literature of the day began to criticize Americans for their narcissism (selfishness and self-concern) and neglect of the common good.

By the time the yuppies emerged in the 1980s, social critics had become alarmed over the new lifestyle enclaves based solely on material gratification, designer drugs, and greed. Robert Bellah and his colleagues (1986) noted with alarm the inability of new members of the upper middle class to form emotional bonds of any kind. Even such conservative social critics as Charles Sykes (1992) complain that Americans have tried to pass themselves off as victims so they can scam their way into lucrative lawsuits.

Thus in the literature, at least, one notes conflicting trends cited from one decade to the next. Perhaps the greatest change during the past forty years has been a virtual end to the affluence the generation of the 1950s took as a birthright. Such critics as Christopher Lasch (1984) noted the rise of a survival mentality among middle-class victims of inflation and unemployment.

Uncertainty and confusion are new to the American character. Many Americans now profess conflicting attitudes toward their most basic institutions or no faith in them at all. They are fearful about the nation's future but haven't a clue as to what will solve its problems. Americans no longer have faith in any political ideology or political figure. Business executives are every bit as distrusted as politicians. The main drift of the American character is toward cynicism and alienation.

Much of this alienation stems from the inauthenticity and dehumanization that are the hallmarks of postmodern culture. Americans live in a world where it is increasingly difficult to separate fiction and fantasy, image and substance, lasting values from fads. The result is an unprecedented confusion about life's most basic questions. Such confusion serves to spread a diffuse anger toward American institutions. Thus Americans will remain hostile to politics and big business for a long time to come. Such hostility is usually met by slick new forms of propaganda and advertising. These efforts serve to raise up candidates who prove to be ineffective as leaders and deeply enmeshed in the higher immorality.

The public reacts by turning away from politics or by responding to any new and probably dangerous candidate who promises simple answers to com-

This gun was found in the book bag of a third grade student in California. An alarming number of grade school and high school students now carry guns to school on a regular basis. The number of shootings and deaths in America's urban schools has risen dramatically in recent years. Moreover, guns are eleven times more likely to kill people than are attacks with knives or blunt instruments. (John O'Hara/The San Francisco Chronicle)

plex structural problems. We live at a dangerous moment. A decline in economic well-being often triggers extremist political movements and the scapegoating of minorities (now gays and Asian immigrants). The result could conceivably be some ugly moments in America's future. We could see civil rights repressed, hate crimes increase, and many people fall victim to demagogic appeals of irresponsible power seekers. Such events will have profound consequences for the social characters of the scapegoated groups and for us all.

Other changes have contributed to our confusion. The family, often touted as the backbone of the nation, has undergone dramatic change in the last forty years. Women no longer stay home and take care of children while men go off to work. Today over 60 percent of married women work outside the home, and unprecedented numbers of unmarried women are working and raising children alone. The divorce rate has doubled since the 1950s, from 25 to 50 percent of first marriages. Conflict over the custody of children is more complicated than ever, and some children are now choosing to divorce their parents. All this means that trust and stability are on the decline among families, as is the self-esteem of children of divorce (Smelser, 1988).

There have also been dramatic changes in American economic life. Physical labor was valued when the U.S. economy was based on manufacturing and agricultural. The changes in technology and the coming of the service economy have seriously decreased the value of manual labor. Today only one-third of the American workforce produces products, and we now have more college students than farmers. Many people who lack the skills that come with higher education are unable to obtain work. High unemployment and attendant social problems result. In the 1960s, an unemployment rate of 3 percent or less was considered normal. In the 1990s, normal unemployment is placed at 7 percent, and this figure may soon rise.

All of these changes have altered the perceptions of both children and adults. Adults remember when the middle class was more prosperous and daily life was not assaulted by the social problems that result in traumas and national crises. Children live in the present, with little sense of the past. Often they must find their way through a confusing thicket of media messages, parental admonitions, and peer pressures. The results have been dramatic increases in the suicide rate, in drug addiction, and in pregnancies (over a million a year) among teenagers. These trends have contributed to Americans' loss of optimism.

Convicted former S and L official Charles Keating has come to symbolize the greed and selfishness of recent American history. Many conservative and liberal social critics have expressed alarm over the dramatic rise in deviant behavior at all levels of the American social structure. Yet Americans do not seem to understand that deviance among the wealthy and powerful may also motivate middle- and lower-class people to engage in deviant acts as well. (John Barr/Gamma Liaison)

THE AMERICAN FUTURE

Predicting future trends is a risky and uncertain business, and neither social critics nor social scientists have proved very adept at it thus far. Because we cannot predict the future, very few texts on social problems have ever discussed future trends. Nevertheless, our society's main drift is an important topic, if only because citizens' perception of their society's future profoundly affects their attitudes and behaviors today.

Having duly noted the limitations of any attempt to predict master trends, one can still point with some confidence to some institutional conditions that will continue to cause numerous social problems. Increasing inequalities of wealth and political power will worsen unemployment, economic conditions, corporate crimes, political corruption, and related woes.

Disturbing trends in postmodern culture and social character have been evolving since the late 1940s:

1 The emergence of postmodern culture with its emphasis on sex, violence, and materialism and its lack of humane values.

2 A decline of the optimism that was once the hallmark of the American character.

3 The institutionalization of the higher immorality among the national power elite.

As a result of these trends, Americans yearn for stable moral values that will serve as a guide to decision making in daily life. The rapid social changes brought by a slowing economy, cultural fads, and breakthroughs in birth-control devices, medicine, and invasive technology make stable values seem a long way off at best. Moreover, there is every reason to believe that the current mass disrespect for political and economic elites will continue, perhaps to culminate in collective social movements that will effect the basic structural reforms necessary to resolve the great social problems of our age. Such solutions and the means to achieve them are the subjects of Chapter 6.

REFERENCES

Baker, R. W. 1992. "CIA Out of Control." *UTNE Reader,* January/February, pp. 81–84.

Baldwin, D. 1992. "The Hard Sell." *UTNE Reader,* January/February, pp. 54–61.

Barnet, Harold. 1981. "Corporate Capitalism, Corporate Crime." *Crime and Delinquency* 27 (January): 4–23.

Bartlett, Donald L., and James B. Steele. 1992. *America: What Went Wrong?* Kansas City: Andrews & McNeel.

Bellah, Robert, et al. 1986. *Habits of the Heart.* New York: Vintage.

Berlet, C. 1992. "Activists Face Increased Harassment." *UTNE Reader,* January/February, pp. 85–88.

Brenner, Harvey. 1973. *Mental Illness and the Economy.* Cambridge, Mass.: Harvard University Press.

Cannon, C. M. 1993. "Hollywood Shoots to Kill." *This World,* July 11, pp. 7–10.

Collins, K. L., and M. F. Jacobson. 1992. "Are We Consumers or Citizens?" *UTNE Reader,* January/February, pp. 56–57.

Derber, Charles. 1992. *Money, Murder, and the American Dream: Wilding from Wall Street to Main Street.* Boston: Faber and Faber.

Dissent. 1991. (Winter).

Draper, Hal. 1989. "Revelations of the North Trial." *New York Review of Books* 27 (August 17): 54–59.

Durning, Alan T. 1993. "Can't Live Without It." *Worldwatch* 6 (May/June): 10–18.

Fukuyama, Francis. 1992. *The End of History and the Last Man.* New York: Avon.

Gerth, Hans, and C. Wright Mills. 1953. *Character and Social Structure.* New York: Harcourt, Brace & World.

Gitlin, Todd. 1988. *The Sixties.* New York: Random House.

Greider, William. 1992. *Who Will Tell the People?* New York: Simon & Schuster.

Hellinger, Daniel, and Dennis Judd. 1991. *The Democratic Facade.* Pacific Grove, Calif.: Brooks/Cole.

Hertsgaard, M. 1993. "Still Ticking. . . ." *Mother Jones,* March/April, pp. 20–23, 68–74.

Kennedy, Paul C. 1987. *The Rise and Fall of the Great Powers.* New York: Random House.

———. 1993. *Preparing for the Twenty-first Century.* New York: Random House.

Lasch, Christopher. 1984. *The Minimal Self.* New York: Norton.

Mills, C. Wright. 1951. *White Collar.* New York: Oxford University Press.

———. 1956. *The Power Elite.* New York: Oxford University Press.

———. 1959. *The Sociological Imagination.* New York: Oxford University Press.

Moyers, B. 1988. *The Secret Government.* Berkeley: Seven Locks.

Moynihan, Daniel Patrick. 1993. "Defining Deviancy Down." *American Scholar* (Winter):17–30.

Nisbet, Robert. 1988. *The Present Age.* New York: HarperCollins.

O'Conner, James. 1973. *The Fiscal Crisis of the State.* New York: St. Martin's Press.

Phillips, Kevin. 1993. *Boiling Point.* New York: Random House.

Reich, Charles. 1970. *The Greening of America.* New York: Random House.

Riesman, David. 1950. *The Lonely Crowd.* New Haven, Conn. : Yale University Press.

Shames, Lawrence. 1989. *The Hunger for More.* New York: Times Books.

Simon, David R. 1977. "The Ideologies of American Social Critics." *Journal of Communication* 26 (Summer): 40–50.

———. 1992. "Ideology and the Kennedy Assassination." *Quarterly Journal of Ideology* 15 (Autumn): 23–35.

Simon, David R., and D. Stanley Eitzen. 1993. *Elite Deviance.* 4th ed. Needham Heights, Mass.: Allyn & Bacon.

Smelser, Neil. 1988. "Self-Esteem and Social Problems: An Introduction." In *The Social Importance of Self-Esteem,* ed. A. M. Mecca, et al. Berkeley: University of California Press.

Smith, R. E. 1992. "Privacy's End." *UTNE Reader,* January/February, pp. 64–68.

Summers, Anthony. 1989. *Conspiracy.* New York: Paragon House.

Sykes, Charles J. 1992. *A Nation of Victims.* New York: St. Martin's Press.

U.S. House of Representatives, Select Committee on Assassinations. 1979. *Investigation of the Assassination of President John F. Kennedy,* vol. 9. Washington, D.C.: U.S. Government Printing Office.

Wilkinson, Rupert. 1988. *In Search of the American Character.* New York: Harper-Collins.

————, ed. 1992. *American Social Character.* New York: HarperCollins.

EXERCISE 4-1. STUDYING MASTER TRENDS IN THE MASS MEDIA

Most major American newspapers contain a section on trends. The *Los Angeles Times,* the *New York Times,* the *Washington Post,* and other major large-city dailies are especially good sources of such material. These sections are rarely called "Trends"; they are more likely to be called "Lifestyles," "Living," "Cues," or "Modern Living." More often than not, these are the sections that contain movie and television listings and advice columns ("Dear Abby," "Ann Landers"). Weekly news magazines also devote some space to various cultural, political, and economic trends.

These newspaper sections may be analyzed individually or in research teams. Research teams might select three major dailies. Study the trends section of each newspaper for one month. Compare and contrast the articles in the various papers with an eye to the following questions:

1 What are the topics of these articles?

2 Which newspapers pay attention to the types of trends that are causing or will cause major social problems?

3 Which newspapers pay attention only to lifestyle trends (fads, popular culture) and ignore social problems?

4 Which newspapers have a mix of articles devoted to both social problems and pop-culture trends?

An alternative sampling method is to compare trend articles in major newspapers with trend articles in weekly news magazines. Since newspapers are published daily and the magazines are weeklies, it is a good idea to choose several months' worth of weeklies to compare with one month's worth of newspaper articles. Look for the major trends described in this chapter:

1 Increasing inequality of wealth and power.

2 Activities of the secret government and threats to democracy.

3 The population crisis and its consequences.

4 Elements of postmodern culture (the increase in advertising, violence and sex in the media).

This exercise should reveal which publications give evidence of a sociological imagination in their approach to the news. I know that many sociologists will expect to find no such evidence in journalism, but C. Wright Mills thought otherwise, and so do I. By the way, I've noticed that many major papers also analyze trends by running a series of articles on major social problems. Such series frequently appear in the paper's first section, often beginning on the front page. These items would make excellent samples as well.

EXERCISE 4-2. STUDYING MAIN DRIFTS IN SOCIAL CRITICISM

If there is a group of people who consistently write about the main drift in modern mass society, it is social critics (Simon, 1977). The world of social critics is fascinating and unique, and its study can yield important information concerning trend-setting policy proposals as well as the views of various ideological groups on the future. (An exercise in Chapter 5, dealing with the ideologies of social critics, includes the study of trends in social problems.) As an introduction to the study of social criticism, I suggest that students be assigned one of the periodicals listed in Exercise 5-2. If students are assigned to work in teams, two or more periodicals may be compared. I suggest that students study all the articles published during the last full year in monthly publications and analyze the first article in each issue of weekly or semiweekly publications over the same period. If monthlies or quarterlies are assigned, more articles should be chosen at random. The number of articles in the sample can be tailored to the needs of each class. I have students select a dozen pieces initially. Use larger samples to examine social criticism in a term paper or an independent study.

This exercise pertains only to master trends, but it may be used in conjunction with Exercise 5-2 and combined with other categories. Studying master trends easily lends itself to the study of predicted consequences (outcomes) of various social problems, and that is the topic of this exercise. The consequences of a given social problem are often predicted to take one of the following forms:

1 *Benign*—no consequence will befall society, and therefore no action need be taken to solve the problem.

2 A *worsening* of the problem—the numbers of people or degree of severity of the problem will increase unless something is done soon.

3 Imminent *catastrophe.* Some catastrophes often cited by American social critics are:

- A race war, urban riots, etc.
- Possible ecological destruction of the earth, either slowly or relatively quickly.
- Economic depression.
- Nuclear war, limited or global.
- A coup d'état in the United States: the establishment of a dictatorship and the end of democracy as we know it.
  - The decline of the United States as a world economic, political, and military power.
  - The shrinking of the middle class.
  - Social and economic chaos caused by uncontrolled illegal immigration.

Each of these themes is a category in this exercise. It is possible for a single article to predict more than one catastrophe. A separate coding sheet, such as the one below, should be used for each article. The results of the analysis should be presented in a table.

CODING SHEET

---

01 Periodical (see list in Exercise 5-2)

02 Article number (assigned by the coder)

03 Topic(s): the social problem or problems dealt with in each article, usually reflected in its title

04–06 Prediction
04 Benign.
05 A worsening of the problem.
06 Imminent catastrophe.

This analysis can yield interesting data on which periodicals are the most optimistic or pessimistic in regard to the possibility of resolving specific social problems.

SUGGESTED READINGS

Any of the works cited in Box 4-1 are excellent sources of information on master trends. Aside from Greider's book (already recommended), these three I think are great:

Bartlett, Donald L. and James B. Steele. 1992. *America: What Went Wrong?* Kansas City: Andrews & McNeel. This award-winning analysis of the ills of the American economy is interesting, passionate, and essential reading for anyone seeking an understanding of America's economic decline.

Kennedy, Paul C. 1987. *The Rise and Fall of the Great Powers.* New York: Random House.

———. 1993. *Preparing for the Twenty-First Century.* New York: Random House. Kennedy, a history professor at Yale University, has written two of the most important works of comparative history concerning global master trends. His work is very rich with facts and is also compassionate and interesting.

5

THE SOCIOLOGICAL IMAGINATION: USES AND DEVELOPMENT

THE CRISES OF OUR AGE

The world has become a mysterious place to many people. Values and relationships we once thought permanent now easily fall by the wayside. The American dream of homeownership and security seems to be fading. A myriad of social problems, from a declining middle class and poverty to crime, racism, sexism, ageism, overpopulation, permanent recession, and creeping inflation now seem insoluble.

At a more personal level, the social character of our age now seems dominated by unique and insidious forms of alienation. Erich and Marie Josephson (1962:10) noted over thirty years ago:

> The alienation of our age is not found merely in statistics on crime, drug abuse, mental illness and suicide, but in untold lives of quiet desperation that mark our age—the multitudes of factory and white-collar workers who find their jobs monotonous and degrading; the voters and nonvoters who feel hopeless or "don't care"; the juveniles who commit senseless acts of violence; the growing army of idle and lonely old people; . . . the stupefied audiences of the mass media.

Indeed, the very nature of modern life is contradictory and schizoid. "Unparalleled economic growth has occurred side by side with the profoundest human misery; and struggles for freedom and enlightenment side by side with continuing social injustice" (Josephson & Josephson, 1962:9).

All these problems and many others have led many people to adopt a

128

stance of cynicism toward other people and the future. The one great difference between America and the nations from which most Americans' ancestors immigrated was America's optimism. For more than three centuries people have come to these shores believing they would find a better life, and that belief has persisted through wars, depressions, mass poverty, and the violent repression of labor unions. For the first time in the nation's history the optimism of young and old, conservative and liberal, whites and nonwhites is waning. The brilliant psychiatrist Kenneth Keniston (1965:1) described the decline in a positive vision of the future three decades ago:

> Our age inspires scant enthusiasm . . . ardor is lacking, instead [people] talk, growing distant from each other, from their social order, from their work and play, and from values and heroes which in perhaps a romanticized past seem to have given meaning and coherence to their lives. . . . Alienation, once seen as imposed on [people] by an unjust economic system, is increasingly chosen . . . as their basic stance toward society . . . there has seldom been so much confusion about what is valid and good . . . more and more people question what their society offers and asks in return: hopeful visions of the future are increasingly rare.

The reaction of most Americans to their troubled world is to ignore trouble and deny it until it comes crashing in on them. A son is drafted into a war, a daughter is raped or becomes pregnant out of wedlock and obtains an abortion, a father is laid off, a mother develops breast cancer, and soon the family learns that each of their private troubles is merely a symptom of a widespread condition. The awareness of the sociological usually stops at this point. The skill that would allow these people to perceive the relationship between their personal biographies, the historical period in which they live, and the contradictions in the social structure responsible for their various crises remains undeveloped. Is it possible for the public to achieve an understanding of how society functions, and of their place in it? Yes, it is.

If the future is to be better than today, the development of a sociological imagination is essential. Only by relating seemingly personal troubles to social issues will we ever resolve social problems. Only with the realization that the social structure does influence one's personality traits and life choices can an opportunity for true freedom emerge. Only by realizing that the social structure and its dominant values are the ultimate source of social problems can we begin to resolve the crises of our age. Resolving the great crises of our age is a central goal of the sociological imagination.

The sociological imagination is about two issues. The first is how to cultivate and use a set of analytical skills in our personal and professional lives, and the second is how to work for constructive social change that will help to resolve the crises of our age. The sociological imagination is based on the idea that personal liberation and societal liberation go hand in hand. A basic

Periodicals like the ones pictured here have uncovered very important censored stories in recent years. No educated person can ignore the subject matter of such periodicals.

aspect of the sociological imagination is its view of the social world as well as the investigation of that world. The paradigm and methodology of the sociological imagination concern the idea of intellectual craft.

INTELLECTUAL CRAFTING

C. Wright Mills (1959:195) argued that social science is a craft grounded in the classic tradition in social theory. The social scientist's work and private life are one. "Scholarship is a choice of how to live as well as a choice of career; whether [one] knows it or not, the intellectual . . . forms [a] self[-concept] as [one] works toward the perfection of one's craft" (1959:196). Cultivating a sociological imagination is a dual exercise in becoming an informed, active citizen-researcher in a democratic society and a mentally healthy individual with a positive sense of self-esteem. Intellectually, this involves taking an active, ongoing interest in the affairs of the day. Trends and themes in politics, economics, mass culture, child rearing, world affairs, and lifestyle changes need watching for their interrelationships. These themes can be filtered through the concepts that compose the sociological imagination. Psychologically, this means overcoming the severe limitations of Americans' extreme view of individualism, with its constant anxiety and guilt about being "good enough" in relationships and careers.

The sociological imagination is a paradigm through which one perceives and seeks to understand the social world and one's place in it, and an approach to doing research. Above all, it is a paradigm for the analysis of social problems (although sociologists have rarely perceived it in this way). As Mills said, the sociological imagination begins with the study of "problematical situations"; that is, social problems (1959:206).

Social problems are conditions involving socially patterned harms that constitute genuine (not contrived) crises for the society. Genuine crises require the making of choices, usually between competing values. Real crises are too threatening to allow things to be left the way they are. The Los Angeles riot after the Rodney King trial in 1992 was certainly a genuine crisis. Local, state, and national elites perceived the fifty deaths and billion dollars in property damage as an immediate threat. Emergency social programs were quickly instituted.

As we have seen, the sociological imagination rests on basic concepts and definitions regarding (1) the structure of society, (2) the main drifts of the historical epoch in which that society is located, and (3) the types of social character being produced. We have seen the evidence for these central themes:

1 The power elite and its higher immorality.
2 The world capitalist system.
3 The mass society and its postmodern cultural influences.
4 The antisocial character, with its inauthenticity and dehumanization.

The elements of the sociological imagination paradigm are summarized in Box 5-1.

You can use the central themes of the sociological imagination as a model for inquiry. From this model researchers can derive testable theories and hypotheses. This is what Mills means when he advises us to "avoid any rigid set of procedures. Above all seek to develop and use the sociological imagination. Avoid the fetishism of method and technique. . . . Let every [researcher] be his [or her] own methodologist; let every researcher be his [or her] own theorist: let theory and method again become part of the practice of craft" (Mills, 1959:224). What matters most is relating social problems to personal troubles.

The sociological imagination involves a specific set of research strategies and tactics. Let's begin at the most fundamental level, the research process itself. Doing research and writing it up are subject to individual preferences. Some people love to read and collect data but hate to write up their findings.

BOX 5-1

ELEMENTS OF THE SOCIOLOGICAL IMAGINATION PARADIGM

The sociological imagination is a paradigm designed for the analysis of social problems. The starting point is the definition of social problems as socially patterned harms that cause either physical, financial, or moral harm. These harms are problems whether or not the media and governmental elites recognize them as such. The remainder of the paradigm consists of the following elements that either cause social problems or are harmful consequences of such problems.

Structure and contradiction: The power elite and massive inequality

The power elite dominates the American social structure. This elite consists of the people in positions of power in large corporations, the executive and legislative branches of the federal government, and those organizations that make up the military-industrial complex and its "secret government."

Contradictions within the social structure are the causes of social problems. The power elite constitutes a structure that has amassed a disproportionate amount of wealth, political power, and power to define cultural values. Such values include the unlimited accumulation of private property, consumerism and materialism, celebrity worship, and a belief in rugged individualism within an organizational society.

The *higher immorality* is an institutionalized set of deviant and criminal practices within corporate and governmental institutions: deception and manipulation of the public, corruption, corporate crime, and occasionally cooperation with organized criminal syndicates. All the practices associated with the higher immorality are themselves major social problems, and they in turn cause further problems.

Historical epoch: The postmodern capitalist world system

The world's economies are divided into three sectors: modern nations (the First World), the semimodern nations of the old Soviet bloc (the Second World), and poor nations struggling to modernize (the Third World). First World multinational firms increasingly use the cheap labor of the Third World nations and extract from them raw materials and profits. The international debts of Third World nations continue to mount. The capitalist world system tends toward instability at numerous flash points, and wars, revolutions, and terrorism are common in the face of massive inequalities among nations.

Mass society and postmodern culture

Below the power elite structure is an evolving mass society composed of unorganized, relatively powerless masses of people, who lack a sense of community in respect to their neighborhoods and their society. The power elite prevents the masses from exercising democratic power. Elements of postmodern culture, especially advertising, make it difficult to separate fantasy and reality.

Social character: The antisocial character

The typical person in mass society dislikes or is indifferent to work, is alienated from the political and societal systems and from him- or herself, and is prone to engage in various degrees and types of "wilding" (deviant acts). The antisocial character tends to escape into mass culture, and interpersonal relationships are characterized by manipulation and self-deception. The inauthentic and dehumanizing elements of postmodern culture reinforce various forms of personal alienation.

Master trends

While it is difficult to predict the future, we can expect trouble down the road.

Massive inequalities of wealth and power within and between nations constitute genuine harms; so do environmental degradation and unrestrained population growth. The spread of postmodern culture throughout the world is contributing to a crisis of democracy as manipulated masses of people react passively to media propaganda by corporate and governmental elites. Democracy itself is at risk.

Others love to seclude themselves with their typewriters or computers and hate to collect data (they usually leave that chore to assistants).

If you have either of these strong preferences, I highly recommend that you select a work team of a size that suits you. There are great advantages (and some potential disadvantages) to working with others. Partnership can take much of the loneliness and alienation out of the process. If you are passionate about your work, you may engage in stimulating interchanges. While these talks may produce some heated moments, they are often the very essence of growth and change, and of friendship.

Whether you work alone or in a group, you must make some key decisions. The first is how to develop ideas for research. Beginning your research is the most difficult aspect of the process for many students. Where do ideas for projects and topics come from?

Again, all of us have our preferences. All research is about a question regarding a relationship between independent (causal) and dependent (affected) variables. Thus ideas for research grow out of questions about causes and effects. Theories are sets of abstract propositions about causes and effects. Researchers can deduce hypotheses (specific testable statements) from these abstract statements. Causal theories can also be derived inductively from data, observations, and descriptions. Whether one reasons deductively from extant theories or inductively from data, the purpose is to understand causal relationships. C. Wright Mills's solution is highly adaptable.

USING THE SOCIOLOGICAL IMAGINATION

Even if one limits the sociological imagination to the study of social problems, there are still numerous ways to approach such research. Ideally, the sociological imagination explores the relationship between macro and micro social problems, or macro causes of seemingly micro social problems. The following list of such topics is hardly exhaustive.

1 Is the violence on the large and small screens related to rates of violent crime?

2 What is the relationship between America's decline as an economic power and changing traits in the American social character? How does one empirically measure a trait such as alienation?

3 What is the current composition of the American corporate elite? Have recent buyouts of American firms by foreign corporations altered the composition of the elite? What effect, if any, will the changing composition of the corporate elite have on the higher immorality?

How do you study these relationships or others that might interest you? Methodology is the study of research techniques and processes. Methodologies, along with the rules of science regarding data gathering, provide the dictates for sociological studies. C. Wright Mills attempted to provide a blueprint for studying society sociologically. Mills's advice is still among the best ever imparted to sociologists.

Mills advocated keeping a journal, a research log, of "thoughts and speculations about various research projects" (Berger, 1991:15). This is not a diary about your experiences and feelings but a log of your thoughts about research. In his *Media Research Techniques* (1991) Arthur Asa Berger offers the following guidelines for keeping your log:

1 Your log should consist of a bound notebook with numbered pages. Do not add pages to your log or tear pages out of it.

2 Keep notes in ink. Don't worry about neatness. Feel free to cross things out. Don't bother copying things written messily for the sake of neatness; it's a waste of time.

3 Record the date each time you write, so that you can view the evolution of your ideas later.

4 Diagrams and charts are wonderful shorthand means to demonstrate relationships between variables. If you have access to a laptop computer, you can use any of several software programs that draw wonderful charts and graphs.

5 Record ideas in modified outlines. Computer programs can also be useful for this purpose. You may want to divide a page into several vertical columns, and "do a great deal of brainstorming up and down the columns. You can also number the ideas you generate. . . . Later you can take some of these ideas and put them in a more logical or useful order" (Berger, 1991:18). You may also wish to keep lists of tasks vital to your research project. You can do the same with ideas for writing up a project.

6 Berger advocates writing headings in your log, in capital letters, when you record ideas for a specific topic, to keep you focused on that topic.

7 Occasionally you may find it helpful to make small drawings of an inch or two, to stimulate your imagination. Use drawings, outlines, and diagrams in any combination. (You'll find a first-rate case study involving these techniques on pp. 18–22 of *Media Research Techniques.*)

Your log can contain a section headed "State of my problems and plans" (Mills, 1959:197). Once you begin to see the world through the eyes of the sociological imagination, you will develop more ideas for studies than you will ever have time to undertake. This is the mark of a good researcher, and you should not feel inadequate for not doing all of them. Doing them well, one at a time if you work alone or a couple at once if you have partners, is the best strategy. The trick is not to feel overwhelmed by the number of your ideas.

Your log may also contain sections on bibliographic items and excerpts from books. As you learn how to search for key ideas, you will find yourself reading only parts of books for their relevant content. Your log will thus become a "growing store of facts and ideas, from the most vague to the most finished" (Mills, 1959:200). As your log expands to contain a full-blown project, you may wish to establish a separate log for each project you undertake. Again, this is a highly individual matter.

I always carry a small spiral notebook with me in case any flashes of inspiration hit me when I am away from my desk. I usually develop these ideas more fully on my computer. If you can afford a personal computer, I highly recommend it. I find it is a wonderful tool for simplifying the research and writing processes. It allows you to move portions of texts around, sharpen spelling and grammar, and outline your ideas in depth.

Mills advocated keeping files as well as a journal. Your files may be cardboard folders or electronic if you have a computer and a scanner. In your subfiles you may want to keep copies of entire articles, book reviews, book excerpts, and other sources that you find yourself citing in a number of your projects. Once you have your log/journal and a number of subfiles established, review these materials regularly. Otherwise, it is very easy to forget what you have in your files and why it is there.

As you begin to research your project and add to your files, you may want to review your files weekly or monthly. If you are having problems progressing with your project, you can try any of the following strategies:

1 Rearrange your files' contents. This will allow you to synthesize things in new and unimagined ways. Recombining information may lead to new syntheses, concepts, theories, and research questions.

2 Develop a playful attitude toward your work, and the phrases and words that describe the issues with which you are dealing. You can look up synonyms for each key word to understand the full range of their connotations. You may wish to break down complex phrases and words into their parts. See if you can stretch or elaborate their meanings.

3 You might try reclassifying your key themes. This often involves the creation of ideal types—typologies—that can be great tools in efforts to understand the changes taking place in society. All that is necessary is that the classification be exhaustive (cover all possibilities), be composed of mutually exclusive categories (e.g., tradition-directed, inner-directed, and other-directed forms of social character). Such types can serve as theoretical models for empirical testing.

4 Try thinking of the opposite of the concept you are studying. Opposite extremes are useful for comparative purposes, and they frequently lend themselves to insights regarding the contradictions that cause social problems. For example, the only two social classes in American society that have a highly developed sense of class are the upper and lower classes. These two groups have many things in common, but for opposite reasons: both have a great deal of leisure time, both pay low taxes, and each tends to view the other with a good deal of contempt. Such comparisons can be useful in efforts to understand key dimensions of social problems, such as class conflict.

5 There is sometimes benefit in inverting your sense of proportion. Something that seems trivial one minute, such as elderly people's eating cat food, can seem monumentally important the next (an indication of poor people's desperation).

6 Mills believed that for simplicity's sake, thinking should begin in yes-or-no terms, for this practice encourages one to think in extreme opposites. One of the most enjoyable and interesting research projects my students do is to watch a very controversial movie, one that perhaps has been the subject of a cover story in a national news weekly, such as *JFK, Thelma and Louise, Mississippi Burning, The Last Temptation of Christ,* or *Catch-22.* After viewing the movie, students read a sample of reviews in magazines and newspapers from around the nation. They classify each review initially as "liked" or "disliked" by the reviewer. Then they analyze reviews for various subcategories, the specific reasons why each reviewer liked or disliked the film. Controversial movies often tell us a great deal regarding the structure and social character of American life, and they often bring into focus some important contradictions. *JFK* is an excellent example, and the screenplay, along with ninety-four intense reviews of the movie, is now available in paperback (Stone & Sklar, 1992).

7 Another important aspect of the sociological imagination is comparative research. Joseph Scimecca (1977:99) argues that "to possess the sociological imagination is to do comparative work." You might compare different social structures (nation-states) and their respective social characters. Such comparisons can be useful ways to develop policies to address many social problems that other modern democracies have resolved, such as universal health care.

Making historical comparisons is an excellent idea. Comparing the ways in which U.S. industrial workers were treated in the late nineteenth century and in the 1990s can be a very useful way to learn about the mechanisms by which people bring about meaningful social change. Getting a grip on the paramount issues of different eras is also useful for analyzing the main drifts of those eras.

8 Finally, there is the matter of how to present one's findings. The arrangement of a presentation always affects its content. Thus topics are also frequently chapters. A subject such as the careers of corporate executives, the increased power of the top military officers, or the declining presence of society matrons are topics that Mills readily converted into book chapters in *The Power Elite* (1956).

Frequently one divides a chapter into themes. A theme is an idea about what is usually a signal trend, or key distinction, such as freedom and reason (rationality). Sort out key themes and state them in a general way, as briefly and clearly as possible. Brief examples that serve to clarify a theme's meaning are very useful and will make the work more enjoyable to read.

Perhaps the most important question regarding the sociological imagination concerns which topics are appropriate for study and research. This is not an easy question to answer. A great number of concepts, theories, themes, and hypotheses are related to the key concepts of the sociological imagination, especially structure, history, biography, and alienation. What follows is merely suggestive, and is based on my conception of the key elements of this paradigm. Other sociologists (Scimecca, 1977; Eldridge, 1983) have taken slightly different approaches, emphasizing comparative sociology rather than an analysis of social problems.

How does one stay informed in such a world as ours? Perhaps the greatest understanding of public issues can come from an appreciation of differing ideological viewpoints. Ideology is something Americans do not like to think about, but it is a crucial aspect of the analysis of social problems.

THE IMPORTANCE OF IDEOLOGY

Values, preferences, and biases play crucial roles in the study of social problems. Social scientists "are influenced in their definition of what a social problem is by their own backgrounds and values" (Roberts, 1978:4).

Ideologies are sets of proposed solutions on matters of public policy "that form a . . . logically interrelated system" (Ladd, 1986:6). An ideology is like a patchwork quilt, each policy position a patch. Like a quilt, an ideology is more than the sum of its patches (Ladd, 1986:7–8).

The patches of the ideological quilt include beliefs about:

1 What constitutes a social problem.
2 Which social problems are "serious" (i.e., crises) and which are less so.
3 The causes of social problems.
4 The solutions of social problems.
5 The consequences to society if various social problems go unresolved (Simon, 1977b, 1981).

Underlying ideological statements are assumptions about the nature of human nature and the relationship between the individual and society. (Whose rights should take precedence when a conflict occurs, the individual's or the society's?) (See Box 1-2.)

Karl Marx was the first to argue that "ideologies are ideas that do not hold up to the rigors of scientific investigation" (Ferrante, 1992:289). They tend to be more like articles of faith—things that one believes without proof (Walker, 1994:3–5)—and may be far removed from the actual workings of societal institutions. Thus most ideological causal theories suffer from some unscientific dimension. Usually such "theories" are scientifically untestable: they lack a measurable independent and dependent variable. Some theories have been disconfirmed by scientific testing, yet belief in them persists. Others are testable but few researchers have bothered to test them (Bernard, 1990).

It is often difficult, perhaps impossible, to separate ideology from science. As the anthropologist Clifford Geertz notes: "Where, if anywhere, ideology leaves off and science begins has been the Sphinx's Riddle of much of modern sociological thought and the ruthless weapon of its enemies" (1964:48). Indeed, "ideology is the permanent hidden agenda" of the study of social problems (Miller, 1974:21).

Marx also noted that dominant ideologies are those that "support the interests of dominant groups." Because they are backed by those in power, they are taken to be accurate accounts and explanations of social events. On closer analysis, however, dominant ideologies are at best half-truths based on "misleading arguments, incomplete analyses, unsupported assertions, and implausible premises that cast a veil over clear thinking" (Ferrante, 1992:289–90) and allow social problems to persist. Thus to some degree, dominant ideologies mystify the causes of social problems, and this is one reason it is important to deconstruct them and reveal their shortcomings and contradictions.

The two dominant ideologies in American social science and politics are conservatism and liberalism. The two approaches have some elements in common:

1 Both accept the basic institutions of capitalism and American democracy.

2 Both have failed to resolve the many social problems that plague the nation, because neither approach is sociological. Advocates of both approaches do not understand the actual workings of most institutions and the problems those institutions generate.

3 Albeit for different reasons, both have lost their positive vision of the future.

One tragedy of American politics is that most of the criticisms conservatives and liberals level at each other are valid.

The Crisis of Conservatism

Conservatism is the oldest approach to social problems. Conservatives:

1 Emphasize anomie, social pathology, and social disorganization as causes of deviance and social problems, and tend to study lower-class deviants as statistical categories rather than as human beings.

2 Distrust the lower classes and believe strongly in the primacy of traditional institutions and established authority over individual freedom.

3 Reject government intervention to improve the welfare of the poor, but approve of subsidies and tax concessions for corporations and the wealthy.

4 Emphasize punishment and other forms of social control to reduce crime and other threats to established institutions of wealth and power (economic and political systems).

5 Fear a breakdown of the moral order.

Conservatives define social problems as violations of values they perceive as absolute. They believe social problems are caused by the failure of deviant individuals to conform to society's rules. Deviants are people who are "out of adjustment" to society because of some biological or psychological defect or faulty socialization (Thio, 1988:13–15). Deviance consists of acts committed by members of the lower orders of society (variously termed the lower classes, the masses, or deviant subcultures). This "dangerous class" exhibits "defective self-control, self-indulgence, limited time horizons [i.e., an inability to delay gratification] and an underdeveloped moral conscience" (Miller, 1973:35). Conservatives regard human nature as "the secular version of original sin" (Etzioni, 1977:1). Put bluntly, conservatives do not trust lower-class people or people whose values conservatives oppose, such as hippies, liberal intellectuals, and Hollywood leftists.

Conservatives call this supposed lack of moral rules among lower-class deviants "anomie" and label such individuals "anomic." To conservatives, most social problems involve acts by lower-class deviants—juvenile delinquency, street crime, prostitution, mental illness, drug addiction, welfare cheating.

Conservatives fear that too much anomic behavior by deviant people will produce "social disorganization—a lack or breakdown in social organization reflected in weakened social control . . . inadequate socialization" (Horton, 1966:598). If extreme, this lack of social control ("law and order") might result in a complete breakdown of social order (variously described as chaos, the breakdown of authority, and the end of civilization as we know it).

Elite deviance, whether demonstrated by corporations, political parties, or individual corporate executives and politicians, is dismissed as overblown by a liberal press (Garment, 1991). Conservatism is thus elitist. It favors the values of people in key positions in government and in the nation's richest corporations.

The problems with the conservative approach are considerable.

1 Conservatives regard as pathological or abnormal what is simply a lifestyle that differs from "the norms of independent middle-class persons verbally living out Protestant ideals in small-town America" (Mills, 1943:87). They accept the structure of society as "at root, just" (Roberts, 1978:4) and consider its institutions moral and unproblematic. Left unconsidered is the idea that the institutions may be so oppressive that they literally drive people crazy.

This ignoring of the consequences of institutional arrangements is perhaps the most contradictory aspect of American conservatism. Conservatives laud the free-enterprise system and the magic of the market, with its law of supply and demand. But what if the free-enterprise system produces X-rated movies, media violence, and addictive drugs, and encourages gambling? Conservatives blame the popularity of these problematic products on permissive liberals or morally deficient (addictive) personalities. The free-enterprise system's role in making such products available for profit is never mentioned. Moreover, it does not occur to conservatives that the entire basis of American capitalism is gambling with invested money in the form of venture capital, stocks, and bonds.

This is what C. Wright Mills meant when he noted that conservatism is an ideology trying to uphold a liberal tradition (1956:335). What is liberal here is the freedom of expression and creativity required to create the very products that conservatives feel are so decadent.

Contradictory beliefs haunt American conservatism. Conservatives want the government to stay out of people's private lives, yet want government to regulate (even ban) abortions. They proclaim the right to life, yet support capital punishment and freely eat meat. They favor the First Amendment, yet believe political protest will lead to anarchy. In short, conservatism is an ideology loaded with contradictions.

2 There is mounting evidence that most conservative proposals will not work. For twelve years conservatives advocated a "get tough" approach to street crime, for example. The number of Americans in prisons more than doubled between 1980 and 1990, and still the crime rate went up (Walker, 1994). The rich got richer but the economy did not prosper. Between 1982 and 1992 America experienced the longest recession since World War II, and millions of middle-class Americans experienced a decline in their living standards (Phillips, 1993). The defense budget quadrupled and tax cuts for the rich were enacted. Instead of the promised balanced budget, we got a quadrupling of the national debt—the largest such increase in the nation's history (Phillips, 1990). In short, conservatism is an ideology in crisis and disrepute largely because it has failed in practice.

3 Conservatism is contradictory in that its positive vision of the future is an idealization of the past. President Reagan won election in 1980 by promising to take America back to the year 1955, when inflation and unemployment were both running at 1 percent and few people worried about drug addiction, racism, child and spouse abuse, or many of the other crises that haunt contemporary American life. Conservatism is a failed ideology of, by, and for the wealthy and powerful.

The Crisis of American Liberalism

Liberals (according to Sargent, 1993:94):

1 Are ambivalent about human nature: people have both good and bad characteristics, and are capable of changing for the better.

2 Believe that social problems are merely social constructions, based on competing definitions of reality, not absolute values.

3 Believe in government intervention and limited reform to ensure the well-being of the nation's citizens.

4 Lack a positive vision of the future and fear that abuse of governmental power may result in a totalitarian state such as the one described by George Orwell in *1984* (Simon, 1977a, 1981): an all-encompassing dictatorship based on spying ("Big Brother is watching you"), illogical propaganda (Newspeak and doublethink), and constant war and preparation for war.

For liberals, social problems are not violations of rules based on absolute definitions of right and wrong but the outcomes of political contests between conflicting definitions of morality (values). Social problems are merely products of collective definitions and actions by special-interest groups that have successfully pressed their demands in the political arena.

Winners in this process have their "values embodied in . . . law. . . . Deviations from these standards [are] labeled as crimes" (Gibbons & Garabedian, 1974:51). Social problems are conditions recognized by either a significant number of people or a number of significant people (Roberts, 1978:5; Manis, 1974; Rose, 1957). This is the height of value relativism.

Indeed, Herbert Blumer (1971) and Malcolm Spector and John Kitsuse (1973) contend that social problems have careers consisting of recognizable stages:

1 A complaining group (Mothers Against Drunk Driving, say) attempts to define some condition as a social problem (the killing and injury caused by drunk drivers). The complaining group may consist of concerned citizens, social workers, or a pubic-interest lobby. They may begin by calling a press conference. If the press ignores them, they may stage protest demonstrations, hunger strikes, and other displays to capture the attention of the media, the public, and policy makers. If they fail to do so, the issue will not become a social problem.

2 An agency of the government recognizes the problem as real. Its reactions may range from acceptance of the group's demands and investigation of the problem to arrest of the complainants.

3 The complainants may lose faith in the slowness of government action and come to regard investigating bodies as defenders of the status quo who are out to whitewash the problem.

4 Complainants refuse to work with official agencies and attempt their own solutions. Thus neighborhood watch groups attempt to reduce local street crimes. Ross Perot began an alternative political organization for voters fed up with the Washington "gridlock." If successful, these efforts may be co-opted by corporate or government elites. Finally, the cause may become part of a larger revolutionary movement.

Unlike conservatives, liberals tend to distrust elites and sympathize with the underdogs. This view of social problems constitutes less a scientific theory than a description that is resistant to scientific testing. No independent variable is suggested to explain what caused the problem initially.

The same can be said for the liberal theory of deviant behavior. When liberals examine lower-class deviants, they attempt to "humanize" them, to let readers know how it feels to be deviant, to see the situation from the deviant's perspective. Liberals also believe in the labeling theory of deviance: "Deviance is not a quality of the act the person commits, but rather the consequence of the application by others of rules and sanctions to an 'offender.' The deviant is one to whom the label has been successfully applied; deviant behavior is behavior that is so labeled" (Becker, 1963:9). Again we have a description of a process of societal reaction to deviance, not an explanation of the causes of deviance.

Persons labeled as criminals are viewed as "drawn from the ranks of those who lack social power, such as blacks, lower-class individuals, transients [rootless people] and youths" (Gibbons & Garabedian, 1974:65). Liberals view some lower-class deviants as underdogs. Underdogs are in danger of being socially controlled by the overdogs in charge of repressive ("total") social institutions, such as prisons, mental asylums, juvenile detention facilities, and facilities for the handicapped.

Liberals believe that institutions in charge of punishing or rehabilitating deviants are "screwed up" (Gibbons & Garabedian, 1974:52), that the elites who run them must lie about what goes on there because the institutions do not function properly (Becker, 1967). Liberals advocate whistle-blowing as a solution to the problems of defective total institutions. Liberalism offers no solutions to the social problems that are its concern.

The liberal position has its strengths and its weaknesses.

1 The liberal view of social problems as social constructions is valuable. It sheds light on the process by which officials recognize and act upon social problems. Yet this view of social problems goes too far in emphasizing the value-relative nature of reality. There are some actions—homicide, incest, theft, torture—of which most cultures have disapproved throughout history.

2 The social-construction approach is not much of a causal theory. It says very little about why groups of people become upset about social conditions initially. There is no concept of socially patterned harm in liberal thought.

3 Liberals tend to favor endless piecemeal reforms. Liberals accept as relatively unproblematic the basic structure of corporate capitalism and a political system that heavily favors the wealthy and powerful. They recognize occasional slight structural defects (such as pockets of poverty), but overall they believe the system provides equal opportunities for most people. In short, liberalism is an ideology in crisis, but the reasons for its woes are not the same as those that afflict conservatism.

Liberalism is in crisis for two interrelated reasons. First, the perceived failure of the Great Society programs of the 1960s made many liberals cynical about the possibility of social experimentation. For a number of years thereafter, liberal sociologists advocated that liberals merely critique the workings of institutions and remain "on the side" (Gusfield, 1984) when it came to advocating institutional reform. This is one reason why President Clinton ran as "the man from Hope" and portrayed himself as a "centrist," not a liberal. Liberalism is an ideology without a firm agenda of solutions aimed at repairing the nation's ills. It is therefore an ideology without direction.

Second, the failure of the reforms of the 1960s together with the Watergate, Iran-Contra, the savings and loan scandals made liberals cynical regarding the future. Liberalism, in short, experienced "the decline of utopia" (Keniston, 1965): it lost faith in the future of America and the world. An ideology without a positive vision of the future is an ideology in decline. George Bush learned this lesson when he failed to master "the vision thing," as he termed it. Not even liberals advocate liberalism anymore.

4 As C. Wright Mills (1963) noted, liberalism was born during the Enlightenment, an eighteenth-century philosophical movement that stressed the belief that human beings are rational and perfectible. The notion that human beings are rational is questionable. Sigmund Freud, Karl Marx, Max Weber, and Karl Mannheim pointed out the influences on human thought processes by the unconscious mind, one's position in the social class system, and large bureaucracies. Many historical events of the twentieth century (the deaths of over 50 million people in wars, Hitler's genocide of Europe's Jews, the atom bomb) have caused liberals to question our rationality, and in the process they have lost hope. Liberals fear the "police-state methods of totalitarianism" (Wise, 1976:412) adopted by even supposedly democratic governments.

CASE STUDY IN IDEOLOGICAL CONTENT ANALYSIS: The Kennedy Assassination

This case study in ideological content analysis is designed to achieve several ends:

1 It introduces you to the world of social critics. Many social critics— Senator Daniel Patrick Moynihan of New York is one—have become influential in the policy-making process.

2 Examining the ideologies of others gives you an opportunity to examine your own ideological beliefs and values. This can be a meaningful experience in self-reflection.

3 Content analysis, the methodology used in this case study, is a research tool useful in the study of any form of communication. The method itself can serve you well in undergraduate or graduate classes. Content analysis has the great advantage of being easy to learn. Moreover, representative, random probability samples of data are only as far away as the local or college library, video store, or television set/VRC. Few other methods offer these advantages for research. See directions below.

INTRODUCTION: A TRAGEDY THAT REMAINS WITH US

The assassination of President Kennedy remains, after more than thirty years, one of the most hotly debated events in modern American history. The killing's profound impact on the minds and hearts of the public has not ceased. Just as polls at the time indicated, the "crime of the century" (Groden & Livingston, 1990) remains a source of profound "grief, loss, sorrow, shame, and anger" (Light, 1988:167). It marked the beginning of an entire generation's political alienation, which continues to this day (Dionne, 1991).

Three decades later these disturbing questions remain: Who murdered the president? Is there a conspiracy to hide the identity of the killers from the American public? The investigation of the Warren Commission has been challenged on several grounds: its "single-bullet theory," its refusal to interview or ignoring of an entire series of witnesses who claim they heard and saw shots from the "grassy knoll," its refusal to investigate carefully the backgrounds of many of the principal suspects. These criticisms have served as the basis for more than 600 books challenging the Warren Commission and a few defending it (Grunwald, 1991). A congressional investigation into the assassination concluded that President Kennedy "was probably assassinated as a result of a conspiracy" (Summers, 1980:14). Probable suspects included members of organized crime (U.S. House of Representatives, Select Committee on Assassinations, 1979:53). Moreover, the public remains skeptical. In 1988 only 13 percent of respondents in a nationwide poll believed the Warren Commission's version of events, and 66 percent believed there was a conspiracy (*Economist,* November 28, 1988, p. 25). In 1993, 90 percent of the American public expressed belief in a conspiracy.

The sample analyzed here consists of the so-called second-generation critics (Moore, 1990), those who have published books and articles on the topic since 1980. As in any content analysis, the issue of categories is crucial. This study uses ideological categories developed in my study of social critics (Simon, 1977a, 1977b, 1981):

- The causes of a social problem, in this case the identity of the person or persons who caused the president's death.
- The solution of the problem in question.
- The consequences (outcomes) to society if the solution prescribed is not implemented.

The twenty-five books and supporting materials used in this analysis fall into distinct ideological categories. Let us review the conservative, liberal, and radical reactions to the assassination of President Kennedy.

THE CONSERVATIVE POSITION: OSWALD ACTED ALONE

Conservatives are critics of the critics of the Warren Commission. They insist that Lee Harvey Oswald was the assassin and that he acted alone. They accept the single-bullet theory—the notion that one bullet inflicted seven wounds on President Kennedy and Governor John Connally of Texas and emerged merely slightly flattened (not fragmented). Further, conservatives are firmly convinced that Oswald shot Officer J. D. Tippit after he shot Kennedy. David Belin (1988:17–21) views the Tippit murder as the "Rosetta Stone" that confirms Oswald's guilt. Both Belin and Jim Moore (1990) insist that Oswald attempted to murder General Edwin Walker, a noted right-wing extremist and alleged CIA contract agent, several months before the assassination.

The Conservative Solution: Social Control of the Critics

Conservatives accuse the Warren Commission's critics of distortions and omissions in regard to eyewitnesses, fingerprints, and ballistic evidence concerning Oswald's involvement in these killings. For the conservatives, the solution to this problem is for the critics of the Warren Commission to stop distorting the record in efforts to enrich themselves.

Outcome of the Conservative Position

The distortions put forward by the Warren Commission's critics are causing the public to lose faith in America's governmental institutions, a step toward anarchy. According to Moore (1990:208, 211), these critics "need to be bashed by somebody who knows what he's talking about. . . . Why should we continue to believe . . . a handful of greedy individuals intent on destroying the credibility of a system many obviously detest?"

For conservatives, the causes of the assassination are no longer a problem. What upsets them is the lies and distortions of critics. They believe there is conclusive evidence that Oswald killed Officer Tippit, and that Jack Ruby killed Oswald to spare Mrs. Kennedy the trauma of having to testify at Oswald's trial. Belin claims that Ruby passed a lie detector test, substantiating this story and his denial of participation in a conspiracy (1988:40–43).

THE LIBERAL POSITION: THE MAFIA DID IT, MAYBE WITH CASTRO'S ENCOURAGEMENT

The House Select Committee on Assassinations (HSCA) concluded that Mafia bosses Carlos Marcello of New Orleans and Santos Trafficante of Florida, perhaps with the aid of anti-Castro Cubans, had the "means, motive, and opportunity" to assassinate the president. These sentiments have been echoed in many books. Their authors claim the Mafia killed the president for multiple reasons:

1 Carlos Marcello was outraged by his illegal deportation to Latin America by Attorney General Robert Kennedy.

2 Jimmy Hoffa, former president of the Teamsters, was outraged by his imprisonment by the Kennedy administration.

3 Sam Giancana was outraged by the Kennedys' war on organized crime (116 Mafia indictments by the Justice Department) (Magnuson, 1988:43) after the Chicago Mafia boss had "delivered" Illinois, especially Chicago's north wards, to Kennedy in the 1960 election.

4 Numerous mafiosi, still smarting from the loss of their lucrative gambling operations in pre-Castro Havana, were incensed by Kennedy's decision not to invade Cuba again after the Bay of Pigs disaster. They believed they could get the casinos back if Cuba were invaded by the United States.

5 Castro, outraged by CIA plots to kill him, jailed Santos Trafficante and then enlisted his aid. Trafficante in turn enlisted Giancana and Marcello, who hated Kennedy for the reasons we have seen (Anderson & Spear, 1988a, 1988b).

Liberals believe that Oswald, though not the lone gunman, did participate in the assassination (Kaiser, 1983).

1 The House committee found that four shots, not three, were fired in Dealey Plaza, including one from the grassy knoll. Moreover, Oswald's wife, Marina, had discovered a picture of General Walker's home among Oswald's personal effects. The committee, like the Warren Commission, believed that Oswald had tried to kill General Walker.

2 Sylvia Odio, a wealthy Cuban refugee, told the FBI in December 1963 that in September 1963 she was visited by three men, two Cubans and a third man introduced as Leon Oswald. These visitors were allegedly raising money for their anti-Castro activities. Oswald was then supposedly on his way from Mexico City to New Orleans, where he would form the Fair Play for Cuba Committee. The Warren Commission did not believe Odio, but later investigations by the 1979 House committee and by the journalists Edward J. Epstein and Anthony Summers support her story. Specifically, the two Cubans, who were trying to get Odio's father out of a Cuban prison, described Oswald as a former marine, an excellent marksman, and a man who would do anything (including killing Castro).

3 The mobster Johnny Roselli told columnist Jack Anderson in the early 1970s that Santos Trafficante hired Oswald to kill the president. Roselli related that another gunman also fired at JFK from the front (Kaiser, 1983:F-3).

The most recent evidence of Mafia involvement in the assassination was aired in a 1988 documentary by the British director Nigel Turner the week of November 22, 1993, on Bill Kurtis's *Investigative Report* series. Two witnesses, the former French drug smugglers Christian David and Michel Nikoli, support investigator Steve Rivele's claims that three members of the Marseilles-Corsican Mafia, Lucien Sarti (known as "Badgeman" because he was disguised as a Dallas police officer behind the picket fence on the grassy knoll), Roger Bocognani, and Sauveur Pironti, killed Kennedy. Marcello, Giancana, and/or Trafficante recruited the trio. John H. Davis (1989:122–26) also cites evidence that Marcello predicted the assassination in some detail, and Dan Moldea (1986:234–35) claims that Marcello later confessed his involvement in the assassination to an associate.

The Liberal Solution: Reopen the Case

The liberals' solution to the mysteries of the Kennedy assassination is in keeping with their emphasis on reform. They have issued numerous calls for further investigations and even trials for the accused Mafia-linked assassins and their employers (Turner, 1993; Marrs, 1989; Scheim, 1988; Davis, 1989; Lifton, 1988:708; Summers, 1980:522–23). Liberals claim that the Mafia may also have murdered Robert Kennedy and Martin Luther King, Jr. (Davis, 1989: 376–82; 383–98). Robert Blakey, former chair of the HSCA, wants to establish a permanent special prosecutor to look into all the assassinations of the 1960s (Turner, 1993).

The Outcome of the Liberal Position

The liberals point out that the Mafia's fortunes increased considerably after the assassination.

1 The government all but abandoned its crackdown on organized crime between 1964 and 1981.

2 President Nixon commuted Jimmy Hoffa's sentence.

3 Mafia influence over the heroin trade and cooperation with Latin American drug lords increased.

4 Organized crime exercised substantial influence in the Nixon administration. Nixon and his friend Bebe Rebozo invested in the Mafia-dominated Keyes Realty Company (of which Watergate burglar Eugene Martinez was vice president). There is speculation that organized crime may have provided the money with which Nixon bought the silence of the Watergate burglars.

It has also been alleged that the Mafia wielded considerable influence in the Reagan White House. Senator Paul Laxalt of Nevada had intervened to get President Nixon to commute Jimmy Hoffa's sentence. In return, the Mafia allegedly funneled casino profits to Nixon's reelection campaign. Hoffa mysteriously disappeared just before he was to testify about the Kennedy assassination. Laxalt was Reagan's campaign manager in 1976, 1980, and 1984.

Jackie Presser, Hoffa's successor as president of the Teamsters, had numerous links to Cleveland's organized crime family, and was appointed by Reagan as a special economic adviser. Senator Laxalt arranged the appointment. Presser was the Mafia's chief contact for draining the Teamsters' Central States Pension Fund (Scheim, 1988:311–12).

Moreover, organized crime was allegedly allowed to select a number of Reagan cabinet and other appointees, including Labor Secretary Ray Donovan, who allegedly paid off mob hit men and gave lucrative construction contracts to the Genovese crime family through Donovan's construction company.

Then there are the alleged Mafia ties of Reagan's CIA director, William Casey. In 1970 Casey was a partner in an agribusiness firm, Multiponics. The firm filed for bankruptcy in 1971. Carl Biehl, one of the owners, was an associate of Mafia boss and suspected JFK assassin Carlos Marcello. Casey had also represented a New Jersey waste-disposal company, SCA, in 1977. SCA, according to New Jersey State Police intelligence, had deeply rooted ties to organized crime. Two close Casey associates, Max Hugel and William Mc-Cann, whom Casey sponsored for Reagan administration appointments, were also closely linked to organized crime (Scheim, 1988:314)

Finally, there is the great Vatican Bank Scandal, in which Michael Leeden, a CIA agent involved in the Iran-Contra scandal, became associated with the Italian Mafia and other members of the Italian "secret government" organization known as P-2 in the 1980s. Through banker Michele Sindona, a member of P-2, the organization assisted the CIA in its attempts to weaken the Italian political left, was responsible for the failure of America's Franklin Bank (for which Sindona received a twenty-five-year prison sentence for fraud), and defrauded the Vatican of well over $250 million. P-2 also probably killed Pope John Paul I when he was about to expose the fraudulent schemes of Sindona and his associates, and P-2 did attempt to assassinate Pope John Paul II in the 1980s. Michael Leeden participated in a cover-up of the crime designed to blame Bulgarian communists. The discovery of P-2 by the Italian press in 1982 toppled the government of Premier Arnaldo Forlani (Scheim, 1988:318–19). In short, the Mafia benefited both financially and politically as a result of Kennedy's death.

Liberals see the outcome of the Kennedy assassination as increased Mafia power and increased corruption within the American government.

THE RADICAL POSITION: A COUP D'ÉTAT BY THE MILITARY-INDUSTRIAL COMPLEX

The radical position begins with the premise that the Mafia may indeed have supplied the killers for the assassination, but that organized crime could not possibly have covered up the evidence, especially the medical evidence. Radicals postulate a JFK assassination alliance growing out of the CIA-Mafia ties established in the early 1960s. The CIA recruited Roselli, Giancana, and Trafficante to assassinate Castro. Anthony Summers (1980) claimed that JFK was a victim of a right-wing conspiracy made up of anti-Castro Cubans and dissident elements within the CIA. The killing was in retaliation for the Bay of Pigs failure and Kennedy's subsequent pledge not to invade Cuba again. Oswald's New Orleans Fair Play for Cuba pamphlets bore the address 544 Camp Street, where former FBI agent Guy Banister had an office. Banister, who had CIA ties, was involved in right-wing causes (Kaiser, 1983:F2–3).

Radicals insist on government involvement in the cover-up of the assassination. They believe that the Mafia does not have enough influence to suppress government-gathered evidence or to solicit the cooperation of government agencies in carrying out the actual assassination. The likely scenario, radicals believe, is either (1) an assassination by dissident CIA elements with Mafia assistance or (2) a Mafia assassination with mere complacency by government agencies and persons who stood to benefit from Kennedy's death. Finally, Mark Lane (1991) believes the CIA alone, using its disaffected anti-Castro Cubans, committed the murder, and worked with the FBI to cover it up.

Most radicals believe that the conspiracy began soon after the assassination with the transfer of all physical evidence, including Kennedy's body, out of Dallas to Washington. President Johnson, Nicholas Katzenbach, and J. Edgar Hoover all agreed that the public must accept Oswald as the lone killer. The conspirators ignored, suppressed, and destroyed vital evidence, including evidence of the government's involvement in the assassination.

Radical critics of the official version of the Kennedy assassination insist that (among other things too numerous to explore here):

1 Roughly 80 percent of the witnesses at Dealey Plaza ran toward the grassy knoll after the shooting, but the FBI and the Warren Commission ignored their testimony. These incidents suggest at least a cover-up by government investigators. A photo taken by Mary Jane Mooreman has been reanalyzed to reveal a second gunman firing a bullet from the grassy knoll one-sixth of a second before the fatal bullet struck Kennedy's head (Turner, 1993; Marrs, 1989:79–82). The presence of a second gunman suggests a conspiracy in the assassination.

2 Possible illegalities were committed by the president's Secret Service guards. They did not make the usual request for military assistance in guarding the president in Dallas. There were numerous open windows along the parade route. The president's limousine slowed to under 44 miles per hour and made illegal turns. Secret Service personnel violated procedures the night before the shooting by drinking late into the night at a Fort Worth nightclub.

3 The autopsy of the president's body was at best incompetent and very possibly part of the cover-up. Upon arrival in Washington, the president's body was transferred to Walter Reed Army Hospital, where the wounds, especially a massive wound to the back of the head, were surgically altered in such a way that it appeared that all shots came from the limousine's rear. The corpse was then transported to Bethesda Naval Hospital, where two unqualified doctors performed an inappropriate and incompetent autopsy, witnessed by numerous FBI, CIA, Secret Service, and military personnel. During the procedure doctors discovered that the president's entire brain was missing (Marrs, 1989:361–86; Groden & Livingston, 1990:447; Lifton, 1988:425–34, 515).

4 Police arrested and then released three "tramps" along the railroad tracks running behind Dealey Plaza shortly after the assassination. Two of the "tramps" resemble E. Howard Hunt and Frank Sturgis, both of them Watergate burglars, CIA agents, and Bay of Pigs veterans. The Hunt look-alike also closely resembles Mafia hit man Charles Harrelson. Harrelson committed five homicides and had numerous links to the Marcello crime family (Turner, 1993; Marrs, 1989:333–36).

5 Both liberal and radical critics of the Warren Commission report point to many ignored and unanswered questions concerning Oswald's killer, Jack Ruby. Reporter Seth Kantor saw Ruby at Parkland Hospital shortly after the assassination. Ruby claimed he had not been there. The Warren Commission chose to believe Ruby rather than Kantor, and critics believe it might have been Ruby who planted on Governor Connally's stretcher the intact bullet that later became the basis for the single-bullet theory. Doctors removed more bullet fragments from Connally's shattered wrist than are missing from that bullet. Ruby had numerous connections to organized crime, the CIA, and the Dallas police. Just before the assassination, Ruby's phone calls to Hoffa, Marcello, and other mafiosi implicated in the killing increased dramatically. Yet the Warren Commission completely ignored Ruby's links to organized crime, relationships that go back to the 1940s (Marrs, 1989:380–434; Turner, 1993; Groden & Livingston, 1990:137–39, 318–19; Scheim, 1988; Summers, 1980:465–80).

6 Dallas FBI agent James Hosty, under orders, destroyed a note he received from Oswald requesting that the FBI stop harassing Marina Oswald (Groden & Livingston, 1990:125). Hosty had been investigating Oswald after Oswald's alleged visit to the Soviet Embassy in Mexico City. Oswald had left the home of Ruth Paine, where he and his wife had been staying, for a place of his own by the time Hosty arrived there. Marina Oswald was still residing with Mrs. Paine. Upon learning of Hosty's visit to the Paine home, Oswald personally delivered a handwritten note to the FBI's Dallas office (Summers, 1980:370). The rationale for the order to destroy the note was that now that Oswald was dead, there would be no trial.

An army intelligence file on Oswald was also unavailable to the Warren Commission, and the army subsequently destroyed it. The file may have contained information on Oswald's emigration to the Soviet Union. Claiming that he was needed at home to care for his ill mother, Oswald had won a hardship discharge from the Marine Corps and promptly defected to the USSR. A few years later he was back again with a Russian bride, the only living relative of a Soviet intelligence officer the CIA was helping defect from the Soviet Union. Why did the CIA not debrief Oswald after his return from the USSR? Oswald had spent his Marine Corps stint at the Air Force's top secret U-2 outpost in Japan and had had access to classified information about the spy plane. Official investigators also ignored Oswald's relationship with Jack Ruby, as well as Oswald's relationship with his uncle Dutz Murret, an employee of the Marcello crime family (Melanson, 1990).

7 In the weeks before the assassination the FBI ignored two reports of planned attempts to assassinate the president. One, tape-recorded by William Somersett, a Miami undercover police informant, described with startling accuracy a plan to kill Kennedy. Somersett gave his recording of Joseph Milteer, a right-wing extremist, to the FBI. Agents questioned Milteer, then released him (Groden & Livingston, 1990:13–14, 474–77; Marrs, 1989:265–67).

8 Radicals point out that between 1963 and 1966, eighteen material witnesses in the case died under mysterious circumstances, a 100 trillion to 1 chance (Marrs, 1989:555; Groden & Livingston, 1990:127–46)—further evidence of a conspiracy. Jimmy Hoffa disappeared just before he was to testify before a congressional committee investigating the assassination.

9 The FBI never firmly identified Oswald's palm print on the rifle that allegedly killed the president until after Oswald was murdered. The director of the funeral home in charge of Oswald's body, Paul Groody, reported a mysterious visit to the funeral home by an FBI team with camera and fingerprinting kit. The team fingerprinted Oswald's corpse. In 1978 FBI agent Richard Harrison told researcher Gary Mack that Harrison had driven another FBI agent to the funeral home with "Oswald's rifle." "For comparison purposes," the agents placed Oswald's palm print on the gun (Marrs, 1989:444; Turner, 1993; Groden & Livingston, 1990:169–70). Moreover, several witnesses, including a police officer and Oswald's supervisor, saw Oswald calmly eating lunch in the Texas School Book Depository's second-floor lunchroom within ninety seconds of the killing, and other witnesses placed him there from 12:15 P.M. to 12:25 P.M. (Stone, 1991:D3). The president's motorcade passed by at 12:30, but it had been announced to pass at 12:25 (Groden & Livingston, 1990:175).

10 As for Dallas police officer J. D. Tippit's murder, two witnesses to the shooting disagree drastically concerning the size, dress, and direction of escape of the killer or killers. Researchers claim that Oswald's police lineup was extremely biased toward the desired outcome. Others in the lineup included only casually dressed teenagers. Witnesses who saw two gunmen kill the president were threatened into silence (Marrs, 1989:342; Groden & Livingston, 1990:176–79). Radicals also deny that the weapon in question was Oswald's (Oswald's revolver was not an automatic weapon, the kind authorities claimed killed Tippit) and that the jacket found near the murder scene was Oswald's (witnesses claimed the jacket Oswald was wearing was not the one identified by the police) (Marrs, 1989:345–46).

11 Then there is Oswald's alleged attempt against General Walker. Someone fired a rifle bullet into Walker's Dallas home about 9:10 P.M. on April 10 or 12, 1963. The FBI evidently obliterated the number of the license plate on the car Oswald allegedly used that night, a 1957 Chevrolet that may have been stolen. The bullet recovered from Walker's home does not match those fired by Oswald's rifle (Marrs, 1989:255–63; Groden & Livingston, 1990:211–12).

Radicals point to numerous other discrepancies between the official version of the evidence and accounts by witnesses. They also claim that physical evidence was altered and that the House committee sequestered some evidence.

The Radical Solution: Restructure America

Radicals believe that nothing less than a restructuring of the nation's institutions is in order (Marrs, 1989:590). "Former Communist Bloc nations are purging themselves of the secret police who violated their human rights during the Cold War. . . . We should purge ourselves of the antidemocratic elements who came to power during the Kennedy and Nixon administrations. . . . Rule by the intelligence community must come to an end" (Weberman & Canfield, 1992:357).

The Outcome of the Radical Position

Aside from the prosperity of organized crime in America from 1963 to 1980, the death of the president profited a host of other interests, both personal and organizational.

1 The CIA, stopped from engaging in covert operations in Cuba and Vietnam under Kennedy, engaged in covert actions once again. Further, Oswald's murder spared the agency possible negative publicity concerning its ties to Oswald both during his Marine Corps days and during his involvement in anti- or pro-Castro activities on the CIA's behalf just before the assassination (Melanson, 1990).

2 The military-industrial complex undertook the war in Vietnam that Kennedy (perhaps) had planned to stop (Lardner, 1991).

3 Lyndon Johnson, whom Kennedy was planning to drop from the 1964 Democratic ticket, became president, a long-cherished goal. Johnson may have had ties to Marcello, and possibly a history of having opponents physically injured or killed (Marrs, 1989:292–95).

4 Richard Nixon, present in Dallas on November 22, 1963, experienced a political revival and went on to become president.

5 FBI Director J. Edgar Hoover lost two of his most hated political enemies, the president and an effective attorney general, and could continue to focus on dissidents and ignore the Mafia, with which he reputedly had close ties (Scheim, 1988; Marrs, 1989). Oswald's murder also spared the FBI possibly embarrassing revelations concerning Oswald's ties with the agency (he is alleged to have been an informant).

6 Congress allowed the oil industry to retain its depletion allowance, a deduction Kennedy wanted reduced.

In short, powerful undemocratic factions took a large step toward establishing a dictatorship in the United States.

IMPLICATIONS: CRIMINOLOGY AND THE JFK ASSASSINATION

Some theorists of the assassination (Freund, 1988) argue that the event amounts to an exercise in the sociology of knowledge. In this view, theories of the assassination are based on reflections on what is happening currently. Thus the Mafia-did-it theory emerged after the nation's concern about illegal drugs and crime became a "crisis." The latest CIA-involvement theories follow on the heels of the Iran-Contra, October Surprise, and Operation Black Eagle conspiracies (Simon & Eitzen, 1993:311–23). In short, whom we blame for President Kennedy's murder depends on whom we hate at the moment (Freund, 1988), or serves as our response to a Rorschach test on what we think of the American political system (Morley, 1991).

The villain-of-the-moment theory is not inconsistent with belief in accumulated evidence. Why can it not be the case that some people are predisposed to investigate the assassination in ways that match the temper of the times? Over the years, however, new witnesses have come forth, new investigations have revealed new evidence, and new admissions that evidence was destroyed or covered up have been made.

Equally important is the idea of structural rather than personal conspiracy in this case. Could the assassination and its cover-up have occurred as they did without CIA-Mafia cooperation? Is the Mafia an independent power in America, capable of a conspiracy that resulted in the death of a president? Or is it, as radicals claim (Pearce, 1976: 140; Simon & Eitzen, 1993:70–79), subservient to the American power elite, useful for providing various financial and political services on occasion? Did not both illicit enterprise and munitions makers benefit by Kennedy's assassination and the war that followed in Vietnam? Mainstream organized crime texts do not take this perspective seriously (Albanese, 1989; Abadinsky, 1990).

The government's inquiries into the killing have been so inept that they have left the door open to all manner of conspiracy theories. Thus political elites have only themselves to blame for the distrust and doubt their inquiry into the crime of the century has brought. This morass may also explain why so few criminologists have ever written about President Kennedy's death. Some Mafia scholars (Smith, 1975; Albanese, 1989) believe that much of what is believed about American organized crime is based on myths. Doubtless there is something to be said for these criticisms, yet there is evidence that the CIA hired Mafia personnel to assassinate Castro before Kennedy's death. There is very reliable evidence that the Kennedy administration had declared war on the Mafia, and that organized crime figures were both frightened and infuriated by the crusade. There is also evidence that Castro did foil plots against him, and that he did arrest Santos Trafficante in Cuba.

In short, it does not defy either theoretical constraints or the mountain of evidence compiled between 1966 and 1991 to suggest that conspirators mur-

TABLE 5-1
IDEOLOGICAL VIEWS OF THE KENNEDY ASSASSINATION

Ideology	Cause	Solution	Outcome
Conservatism	Anomie: Oswald	Social control	Anarchy
Liberalism	Mafia	Reform	Corruption
Radicalism	Military-industrial complex	Restructuring of society	Dictatorship

TABLE 5-2
IDEOLOGICAL STANCES OF 25
WORKS ON KENNEDY
ASSASSINATION (PERCENT)

Ideology	Percent
Conservative	9%
Liberal	20
Radical	71
All ideologies	100%

dered the president and covered up their involvement, and that American mafiosi were key players in the conspiracy. Conservative critics Belin and Moore too easily dismiss the checkered backgrounds of Oswald and Ruby as irrelevant. While the accounts given by some critics contradict each other, the contradictions tend to be too minor to stop social scientists from seriously looking into this case, either on the secondary (content-analysis) level or on the primary (investigative) level. Who would fund a team of criminologists to undertake such an effort?

Was Oswald part of that team? Did the Mafia, alone or in concert with the CIA, hire the assassins? All the questions remain unanswered.

CONFRONTING THE FUTURE

America is a nation confronted by stark choices. Its current path is leading it to continued economic decline, permanent recession, and rising rates of crime, addiction, and mental illness. Its current emphasis on self-enrichment and such postmodern cultural themes as pessimism, violence, and gratuitous sex only intensifies inauthenticity, dehumanization, and pessimism in an already alienated society. This is a time of increasing inequality both in the United States and throughout the world. Inequality has been the basis of war, suffering, and revolution throughout history.

We are more than just citizens of a nation. We are part of a nation that is interdependent, economically, politically, and culturally, with the rest of the world. The choice that confronts us is between a more democratic, economically prosperous, and mentally healthy world and a world filled with strife, suffering, inequality, and anguish. The sociological imagination can be a valuable tool of scientific analysis, self-help, and political activism.

Many members of the current generation of college students are searching for causes, role models, and the help necessary to cope with the stresses of postmodern America. Chapter 6 suggests ways to use the sociological imagination both to help oneself and to achieve constructive social change.

EXERCISE 5-1. STUDYING THE KENNEDY ASSASSINATION

Gerald Posner's recent book on the assassination of President Kennedy, *Case Closed* (1993), has received much attention from the mainstream mass media. Look up reviews of the book in the *Book Review Digest (BRD)* (usually found in a library's reference section). Do a content analysis of the reviews abstracted in the *BRD*. Use the categories listed in Table 5-1. Instructions for coding the reviews are given in Exercise 5-2. Use a separate coding sheet for each review. Present your findings in a table patterned on Table 5-3.

TABLE 5-3
IDEOLOGICAL ANALYSIS OF 20
REVIEWS OF *CASE CLOSED*

Ideological position	Percent
Conservative	60%
Liberal	20
Radical	15
Other	5
All positions	100%

EXERCISE 5-2. THE IDEOLOGIES OF AMERICAN SOCIAL CRITICS

An expanded version of this exercise appeared in *Teaching Political Science* in July 1981. Three of the periodicals listed in Figure 5-1 are new additions: *American Prospect, Foreign Policy,* and *Tikkun.* Instructors, of course, may add others of their own choosing. I allow students to use such periodicals as *Esquire* and *GQ* when their articles are appropriate.

I see no significant changes in the content of either conservatism or liberalism since 1981, with the possible exception of the so-called neoliberalism championed by President Clinton and the Democratic Leadership Council. Frankly, the only difference between this new liberalism and old-style liberalism is that the neoliberals want to cut government spending and reduce the deficit. I know of no ideological group that does not want to reduce the deficit, so this issue does not make for much of a distinction.

While this exercise is rewarding, it does require a fair amount of instruction, and I suggest that you do a pilot study on one or two articles before you attempt to analyze a sample of a dozen or more. Feel free to alter the size of the sample and the number of periodicals to suit your needs. I suggest students and instructors go through the instructions together, slowly, to clear up any uncertainties that may arise.

IDEOLOGY AWARENESS PROJECT: AN EXERCISE IN ITEM UNIT CONTENT ANALYSIS

This is an exercise in the analysis of the ideological content of writings in journals of social criticism. This will be most students' introduction to such periodicals. Thus the exercise not only teaches you to use content analysis as a research method but introduces you to the ideological statements of America's leading social critics.

Undergraduates often complain about the necessity of writing term papers, most of which end up being merely exercises in regurgitation. The ideological content analysis exercise is a response to this group. Familiarity with the various ideological perspectives among American social critics also allows you to analyze virtually any unit of communication that has some ideological content (newspaper editorials and political columns, commentary on television news programs, television interviews with people holding strong political opinions, and so on).

The phases of the project parallel the phases of most research projects. The sampling universe from which articles may be drawn is taken from Charles Kadushin's (1974) list of the top periodicals of social criticism in the United States. The list of periodicals and the initial choices of samples from which you may draw are described in Figure 5-1.

After selecting articles at random from the journals listed or selected, code each article for its ideological content. Enter the relevant codes on a coding sheet modeled on Figure 5-2, using the codes in Figure 5-3. Use the entire article as the unit of analysis. The coding categories used to determine the ideological orientation of each article consist of causal codes (which refer to the cause or causes of a given problem), solution codes (which refer to the policy or policies proposed to resolve a given problem or set of problems), and outcome codes (which refer to the predicted consequences of a given problem or set of problems if the solution or solutions proposed are not put into effect).

Give each article an overall ideological rating (9 on the coding sheet, Fig. 5-2) in accordance with the following rules:

1 Assign the overall ideological rating of the article on the basis of the *causal* and *solution* codes only; outcome codes at times tend to cut across ideological borders. (All causal, solution, and outcome codes are listed in Figure 5-3.)

2 If an article discusses a cause but suggests no solution, determine the ideological rating of the article on the basis of the causal code only. Though it is possible for an article to discuss only solutions or only outcomes, with no reference whatever to a cause, this is almost never the case. Even pieces that are concerned primarily with prediction tend to begin with a causal analysis as a reference point.

3 Should discussions of either causes, solutions, or outcomes fall outside of the categories used here, code them as "Other" (codes 4d, 5d, and 7d, respectively).

4 In any case, when an article both analyzes a cause and proposes a solution, the cause and solution must be of the same ideological type for the entire piece of writing to be classified as conservative, liberal, or socialist. Should the ideological content of a piece of writing be mixed or fall outside

Adapted from *Teaching Political Science* 8, no. 4 (July 1981): 487–92. © 1981. Reprinted with permission of the Hellen Dwight Reed Foundation. Published by Heldret Publications, 1319 18th St., N.W., Washington, D.C. 20036-1802.

1. Select ten articles for analysis. You may divide your sample in any of the following ways:
   (a) Select ten articles from any one periodical published in 1994.
   (b) Select ten articles from any two periodicals published in 1994.
   (c) Select ten articles from a single periodical, five published in 1993 and five in 1994. This option will allow you to gain an understanding of a change in ideological orientation over time.
   (d) Select ten articles written on a *single topic* that have appeared in any of the periodicals listed below since 1980.

2. Select articles at random; that is, all articles (other than book reviews and editorials) should have an equal chance of being selected. The articles may deal with any of the topics covered in this course.

3. Code all articles for cause(s), solution(s), and outcome(s) in accordance with the codes listed in Figure 5-3. Not all articles will contain examples of all categories listed. If a category is not represented, simply write "None" after that category on the coding sheet.

Periodicals and codes*

01 *American Scholar*	11 *Public Interest*
02 *Atlantic Monthly*	12 *Progressive*
03 *Dissent*	13 *Saturday Review*
04 *Harper's*	14 *Social Policy*
05 *Mother Jones*	15 *Society*
06 *Nation*	16 *Village Voice*
07 *New Republic*	17 *Washington Monthly*
08 *New Yorker* (especially "Letter from Washington")	18 *Yale Review*
09 *New York Review of Books*	19 *American Prospect*
10 *Partisan Review*	20 *Foreign Policy*
	21 *Tikkun*

*Instructors may of course use other periodicals of their choosing.

FIGURE 5-1
EXERCISE IN IDEOLOGICAL CONTENT ANALYSIS

the various causes and solutions outlined in Figure 5-3, code the entire piece as 7d ("Mixed"). This tends to happen in about 6 of every 100 cases.

5 No specific list of social problem codes is given here because such a list is virtually endless, and the rules for coding various categories of social problems, crime, and deviance are extremely complicated. (See Simon, 1975, 1977; Funkhouser, 1973.) However, I recommend that instructors keep such codes as simple as possible: assign an article or other piece of writing a social problem/crime/deviance code on the basis of its major theme; don't assign a separate code for every social problem mentioned in it.

After you have coded each article, select examples of causes, solutions, and/or outcomes in the form of either direct quotes from the materials read or summaries of such passages in your own words. Write your examples on the appropriate lines on the coding sheet.

This exercise often provokes students to examine their own ideological beliefs. Students often report that the exercise has made them much more aware of the ideological content of newspaper editorials, television commentaries, and the like. It is here that the lasting value of this exercise may be found.

1. Periodical no. _____ 2. Article no. _____ 3. Year _____ 4. Page no. _____

5. Topic(s) _____

6. Causal code _____ Example* _____

_____

_____

_____

7. Solution code _____ Example* _____

_____

_____

8. Outcome code _____ Example* _____

_____

_____

9. Ideological rating of article _____

_____

_____

*Continue on back if necessary.

FIGURE 5-2
CODING SHEET

1. Periodical no. (01–21) (see list of periodicals in Fig. 5-1).

2. Article no. (01 to 10).

3. Social problem or problems (to be coded by instructor).

4. *Causal codes*
   (a) Conservative: anomie/bureaucracy. As used by contemporary conservatives, "anomie" refers both to the behavior of individuals who, because of biological abnormality, mental or psychological deficiency, or improper socialization, do not conform to societal (accepted; "normal") rules and values, and to collective behavior involving anomic individuals (e.g., riots, lootings, panics) (see Banfield, 1974; Etzkowitz, 1980: xviii–xxi). "Bureaucracy" refers to the growth of the size of government, "overregulation" of business by government, government waste, and the like.
   (b) Liberal: democracy out of control (special interests). Problems are attributed to undemocratic accumulations of power in the hands of special-interest groups, especially large corporations, law enforcement bureaucracies (e.g., the CIA, the Pentagon), organized crime, etc.
   (c) Socialist: capitalism. Problems are attributed to the political economy of American "monopoly" capitalism; the values of capitalist culture (e.g., militarism, materialism, exploitation, domination, alienation); the contradictions of capitalist society (e.g., "the fiscal crisis of the state").
   (d) Other.

5. *Solution codes*
    (a) Conservative.
    i. Streamline/redefine bureaucracy. Make cutbacks in government spending, bureaucrats, programs; reorganize certain social problems so that they appear less serious (e.g., raise the poverty-level income ceiling so that fewer people qualify as poor).
    ii. Extend social control: take measures to ensure conformity of "deviant" individuals to revailing societal norms (e.g., mandatory prison sentences, capital punishment).
    (b) Liberal: legislative reform. Effect modest redistributions of power and resources in order to overcome the effects of poverty, discrimination, and powerlessness among various minorities (the young, nonwhites, women, the poor); enforce government regulation of powerful interests (e.g., corporate polluters, manufacturers of unsafe products); break up monopolistic economic concentrations; "delabel" certain acts now considered criminal (e.g., prostitution, gambling, status offenses).
    (c) Socialist: Socialism. Lessen the amount of property in private hands, either by nationalization of basic industries or by collective ownership and control of the means of production by the workers.
    (d) Other.

6. Outcomes
    (a) Benign/automatic solution (no negative consequences).
    (b) Anarchy.
    (c) Problem will get worse.
    (d) Apocalypse (e.g., nuclear war, famine, ecocide).
    (e) Problems will worsen, causing collapse of capitalist order.
    (f) None mentioned.

7. *Article ideological rating*
    (a) Conservative.
    (b) Liberal.
    (c) Socialist.
    (d) Mixed/other.

FIGURE 5-3
CODES

References for Exercises 5-2

Banfield, Edward C. 1974. *The Unheavenly City Revisited.* Boston: Little, Brown.
Etzkowitz, H., ed. 1980. *Is America Possible?* Mineola, N.Y.: West.
Funkhouser, Ralph. 1973. "The Issues of the Sixties: An Exploratory Study in the Dynamics of Public Opinion." *Public Opinion Quarterly* 37 (Spring): 62–75.
Kadushin, Charles. 1974. *The American Intellectual Elite.* Boston: Little, Brown.
Simon, David R. 1975. "Ideology and Sociology." Ph.D. dissertation, Rutgers University.
————. 1977. *Ideology and Sociology. Perspectives in Contemporary Social Criticism.* Washington, D.C.: University Press of America.

REFERENCES

Abadinsky, Howard. 1990. *Organized Crime.* 3d ed. Chicago: Nelson Hall.
Albanese, Jay. 1989. *Organized Crime in America.* 2d ed. Cincinnati: Anderson.

Anderson, Jack, and J. Spear. 1988a. "Witness Tells of CIA Plot to Kill Castro." *Washington Post,* November 1, p. C-19.

———. 1988b. "Ask: Who Killed JFK?" *Washington Post,* November 17, p. C-13.

Becker, Howard. 1963. *The Outsiders.* New York: Free Press.

———. 1967. "Whose Side Are We On?" *Social Problems* 14 (Winter): 239–47.

Belin, David. 1988. *Final Disclosure.* New York: Scribner's.

Berger, Arthur Asa. 1991. *Media Research Techniques.* Newbury Park, Calif.: Sage.

Bernard, Thomas. 1990. "Twenty Years of Testing Criminological Theory." *Journal of Research in Crime and Deliquency* 15 (Autumn): 1–18.

Blumer, Herbert. 1971. "Social Problems as Collective Behavior." *Social Problems* 18 (Winter): 298–306.

Davis, John H. 1989. *Mafia Kingfish.* New York: Signet.

Dionne, E. J. 1991. *Why Americans Hate Politics.* New York: Simon & Schuster.

Eldridge, Joan. 1983. *C. Wright Mills.* London: Travistock.

Etzioni, Amatai. 1977. "The Neoconservatives." *Partisan Review* 4 (Autumn): 1–15.

Ferrante, John. 1992. *Sociology: A Multicultural Perspective.* Belmont, Calif.: Wadsworth.

Freund, C. P. 1988. "How the Kennedy Killing Drove America Crazy." *Washington Post,* November 13, pp. C-1, 4–5.

Garment, Susanne. 1991. *Scandal.* New York: Anchor.

Geertz, Clifford. 1964. "Ideology as a Culture System." In *Ideology and Discontent,* ed. David Apter. New York: Free Press.

Gibbons, Don C., and Peter Garabedian. 1974. In *Criminology, Crime, and the Criminal,* ed. Charles Reasons, pp. 50–77. Pacific Palisades, Calif.: Goodyear.

Groden, Robert J., and Harrison Edward Livingston. 1990. *High Treason.* New York: Berkley.

Grunwald, L. 1991. "JFK: Why Do We Still Care?" *Life* 14 (December): 35–46.

Gusfield, Joseph. 1984. "On the Side: Practical Action and Social Constructionism in Social Problems Theory." In *Studies in the Sociology of Social Problems,* eds. John Kitsuse and J. W. Schneider, pp. 31–51. New Jersey: Ablex.

Horton, John. 1968. "Order and Conflict Theories of Social Problems." In *Radical Perspectives on Social Problems,* ed. Frank Lidenfield, pp. 590–602. New York: Free Press.

Josephson, Eric, and Marie Josephson (eds.). 1962. *Man Alone: Alienation in Modern Society.* New York: Dell.

Kaiser, D. E. 1983. "Did Oswald Act Alone?" *Washington Post,* November 20, pp. F1–4.

Keniston, Kenneth. 1965. *The Uncommitted.* New York: Dell.

Ladd, Everett C. 1986. *American Ideologies.* Washington, D.C.: University Press of America.

Lane, Mark. 1991. *Plausible Denial.* New York: Thunder's Mouth Press.

Lardner, George. 1991. ". . . Or Just a Sloppy Mess" *Washington Post,* June 2, p. D-2.

Light, Paul C. 1988. The *Babyboomers.* New York: Norton.

Lifton, David. 1988. *Best Evidence.* New York: Carroll & Graf.

Magnuson, E. 1988. "Did the Mob Kill JFK?" *Time,* November 28, pp. 42–44.

Manis, J. 1974. "Assessing the Seriousness of Social Problems." *Social Problems.*

Marrs, Jim. 1989. *Crossfire: The Plot That Killed Kennedy.* New York: Carroll & Graf.

Melanson, Philip. 1990. *Spy Saga.* Boulder, Colo.: Westview.

Miller, Walter. 1974. "Ideology and Criminal Justice Policy: Some Current Issues." In *The Criminologist: Crime and the Criminal,* ed. Charles Reasons, pp. 19–50. Pacific Palisades, Calif.: Goodyear.

Mills, C. Wright. 1943. "The Professional Ideology of Social Pathologists." *American Journal of Sociology* 49 (September): 165–80.

———. 1956. *The Power Elite.* New York: Oxford University Press.

———. 1959. *The Sociological Imagination.* New York: Oxford University Press.

———. 1963. "IBM Plus Humanism = Sociology." In *Power, Politics and People: The Collected Essays of C. Wright Mills,* ed. Irving Louis Horowitz, pp. 568–76. New York: Ballantine.

Moldea, Dan. 1986. *Dark Victory: Ronald Reagan, MCA, and the Mob.* New York: Viking.

Moore, Jim. 1990. *A Conspiracy of One.* Fort Worth: Summit Group.

Morley, J. 1991. "A Political Rorschach Test." *Los Angeles Times,* December 8, pp. M1–2.

Pearce, Frank. 1976. *Crimes of the Powerful.* London: Pluto.

Phillips, Kevin. 1993. *Boiling Point: Democrats, Republicans, and the Decline of Middle Class Prosperity.* New York: Random House.

Posner, Gerald. 1993. *Case Closed: Lee Harvey Oswald and the Assassination of President John. F. Kennedy.* New York: Random House.

Roberts, R. 1978. *Social Problems: Human Possibilities.* St. Louis: Mosby.

Rose, A. 1957. "Theory for the Study of Social Problems." *Social Problems* 4 (January): 190–205.

Sargent, L. T. 1992. *Contemporary Political Ideology.* 9th ed. Belmont, Calif.: Wadsworth.

Scimecca, Joseph. 1977. *The Sociological Theories of C. Wright Mills.* Port Washington, N.Y.: Kennikat Press.

Scheim, David. 1988. *The Mafia Killed President Kennedy.* London: Allen. Published in the United States as *Contract on America.* New York: Kensington.

Simon, David R. 1977a. *Ideology and Sociology: Perspectives on Contemporary Social Criticism.* Washington, D.C.: University Press of America.

———. 1977b. "The Ideologies of American Social Critics." *Journal of Communication* 25 (Summer): 44–55.

———. 1981. "Exercise in Ideological Content Analysis." *Teaching Political Science* 10 (July): 488–92.

Simon, David R., and D. Stanley Eitzen. 1993. *Elite Deviance.* 4th ed. Needham Heights, Mass.: Allyn & Bacon.

Smith, Dwight. 1975. *Mafia Mystique.* New York: Basic Books.

Spector, Malcolm, and John Kitsuse. 1973. "Social Problems: A Reformulation." *Social Problems* 21 (Fall): 145–59.

Stone, Oliver. 1991. "JFK: A Higher Truth." *Washington Post,* June 2, pp. D-1–3.

Stone, Oliver and Zachary Sklar. 1992. *JFK: The Book of the Film.* New York: Applause Press.

Summers, Anthony. 1989. *Conspiracy.* New York: Paragon House.

Thio, Alex. 1988. *Deviant Behavior: An Integrated Approach.* 3d ed. New York: Harper & Row.

Turner, Nigel. 1993. *The Men Who Killed Kennedy.* Video documentary aired September/October on Bill Kurtis's *Investigative Report,* Arts & Entertainment Network.

U.S. House of Representatives, Select Committee on Assassinations. 1979. *Investigation of the Assassination of President John F. Kennedy,* vol. 9. Washington, D.C.: U.S. Government Printing Office.

Walker, Samuel. 1994. *Sense and Nonsense about Crime.* 3d ed. Monterey, Calif.: Brooks/Cole.

Weberman, Alan, and Michael Canfield. 1992. *Coup d'Ètat in America: The CIA and the Assassination of John F. Kennedy.* San Francisco: Quick American Archives

Wise, David. 1976. *The American Police State.* New York: Vintage.

SUGGESTED READINGS

Berger, Arthur Asa. 1991. *Media Research Techniques.* (Newbury Park, Calif.: Sage). This is an extremely readable and useful introduction to researching the media. It is interesting to contrast Berger's suggestions with those given by C. Wright Mills in the Appendix to *The Sociological Imagination.*

Marrs, Jim. 1989. *Crossfire: The Plot That Killed Kennedy.* New York: Carroll & Graf. This is one of the works on which Oliver Stone's 1991 movie, *JFK,* was based. It is an extremely interesting and detailed exposition of the radical view of the assassination of President Kennedy.

6

FREEDOM, REASON, AND THE SOCIOLOGICAL IMAGINATION

A CHANGING SELF AND A CHANGING SOCIETY

In a beautiful wooded area outside Greensboro, North Carolina, female corporate executives meet in a workshop designed to help them overcome roadblocks to advancement. The most serious barrier to promotion is the "glass ceiling," an invisible barrier that women cannot penetrate. On the other side of the ceiling are top-level management posts. The four-day session is filled with role-playing exercises and psychological tests.

Sponsored by the Center for Creative Leadership, the workshop conveys to those present the results of the Center's own study of the promotion of female executives: the women who get promoted have mastered the rules of the corporate game, built up confidence by knowing their own strengths, learned when to rely on others, and achieved the integration of their personal and professional lives.

When the women are asked to draw pictures to show how they fit into their companies, a curious thing happens. Most of them draw similar pictures. A typical drawing shows a baseball diamond (representing the corporation) with players standing around it. All of the players are men. At home plate stands a woman, but instead of holding a baseball bat, she is bouncing a basketball. A bubble coming out of her mouth asks, "What's the game?" (Webb, 1992:57).

Comparing pictures, the women laugh and express feelings of relief. Each of them thought she was the only one who didn't understand the rules of the game, rules male employees seem to grasp instinctively. These executives

164

have discovered an important aspect of the sociological imagination: that what appears to be a personal problem is really an institutional condition affecting women in general. The ability to relate one's personal troubles to public (social) problems is an important skill. Studying sociology can change one's life. It can help one to understand better the forces that constrain and free. This understanding has a liberating potential; by examining these forces one can stand somewhat apart from at least some aspects of society and exert more creative control over one's own life.

As I have argued from the beginning, what often appear to be personal troubles are merely symptoms of more widespread harmful conditions, such as divorce, drug and child abuse, mental illness, unemployment, and crime. One may try to deny the impact of the social environment on our daily lives, or even escape from it for a time, but such efforts will work only until the realities of our age come crashing through such barriers.

The sociological imagination is more than just a valuable scientific paradigm. First, it is a useful guide to solutions to social problems and to ways to implement those solutions. Rarely has there been a greater need for new ideas regarding the solution of social problems. As we noted in Chapter 5, conservatism and liberalism are ideologies in crisis precisely because their solutions have failed. In addition, these dominant ideologies have lost any vision of a positive future, and an ideology without a positive future orientation is an ideology in crisis. Thus the vision inspired by the sociological imagination offers badly needed hope at a time of cynicism and alienation.

Second, Americans confront a host of personal issues. Many Americans are confused about what values to believe in, what it means to be a man or woman in the late twentieth century, and how to cultivate a positive sense of self in a society steeped in dehumanization and inauthenticity. The sociological imagination, as a worldview, offers a promise of therapeutic transformation for those in need of meaningful self-help.

America's view of extreme individualism and intense competition for scarce rewards that the society values (money, recognition, and power) creates a society in which relatively few people achieve great success. Consequently, many people in America feel they have failed, and their self-esteem suffers. Knowledge about America's reward system and the American sense of individualism is a useful form of self-help. Studying the attitudes and experiences of others—their biographies, as Mills would call them—can be a liberating experience in a society that encourages self-blame and stresses appearance over reality, materialism over caring, concern, and emotional intimacy. Studying these dynamics can give you an important lesson in what is really important and lasting in life, and it can help you to develop a sense of self-worth. Self-esteem is a crucial aspect of one's well-being, necessary for the ability to love and be loved in return. Americans' needs for love, recognition, and identity are not being met. These issues are social problems. The sociological imagination is an ideal paradigm for their analysis. We can combine sociological analysis and self-help in what we may call "sociotherapy," combining the sociological and the psychological. Sociotherapy is about the relationship between collective psychic crises and the crises of your own personal life.

Studying the psychological problems typically experienced by members of American culture will teach you a great deal about the problems of your own life. It will also teach you some important truths about the contradictions of American culture and society. This study should allow you to ease guilt and anxiety because you will learn to blame yourself less and focus on the sociological causes of your personal problems. This does not mean that you'll be able to escape personal responsibility for your actions or violate the norms of society at will, but you'll acquire a greater appreciation for the sociological nature of seemingly personal problems.

USING SOCIOTHERAPY: LOVE

The two most important aspects of most people's lives are their intimate relationships and their work. You can use the evidence gathered by social scientists in these areas to improve your own life and the lives of the people you care about. As we know, the difficulty of attaining satisfying relationships and enjoyable careers is both a personal and a social problem in the United States. Certain structural conditions are important to understand in regard to both of these aspects of daily life.

You may be surprised to know that romantic love is a social invention; most non-Western cultures do not believe in it. Most Americans believe that romantic love has always existed and is common to all cultures. Romantic love was invented at the end of the twelfth century by Queen Eleanor of Aquitaine. She created the rules of love in a calculated effort to gain some of her children's inheritance. Eleanor agreed to teach her children the rules of love in exchange for their financial support (Loudin, 1982).

Originally, romantic love was thought to be possible only outside marriage. Lovers were never supposed to consummate their relationship, in part because the woman, at least, was married or betrothed to someone else: she was unattainable. The rules of love also stressed that love was beyond an individual's control. The rules of love and their consequences resemble what today would be called an obsessive-compulsive disorder.

1 The lovers are obsessed by thoughts of each other. The man writes poetry, gives his lady flowers and other gifts, and pledges his eternal loyalty. The lady's part in this duet is simply to be the object of his adulation, the recipient of his poetry and gifts. The lady is always beautiful, so she must concentrate on making herself worthy of his love by adorning herself with fine clothing, jewelry, and sweet fragrances.

2 When love is obsessive, it is never out of one's thoughts. If the relationship ends, one must always be thinking about the lost love or desperately seeking a new one. Thus the emotional high of having a lover is replaced by the emotional low of being alone, singing the lovesick blues. Courtship (the word comes from the fact that originally romantic love could flower only at the monarch's court) is an emotional roller-coaster ride. Lovers are supposed to be either on cloud nine or in the emotional basement. One can never keep one's life on an even keel when one is in love.

3 Obsessive love is a dangerous game, guaranteed to make the lovers feel insecure. The expectation that one person can meet all of the lover's emotional needs makes monogamous love an enormous emotional investment. Thus the loss of one's lover, whatever the reason, is one's worst nightmare come true. This is why Western literature is replete with suicide (*Romeo and Juliet*), homicide (*Othello*), and other desperate acts when a lover dies, betrays, or leaves. Obsessive love generates fear, which in turn arouses hostility to varying degrees.

4 The more difficult it is to have a love relationship, the more the lovers will want it. This is a central theme of Shakespeare's *Romeo and Juliet*. The feuding families who object to their children's relationship succeed only in driving the lovers together.

The romantic love taught by Eleanor became an important element in the social characteristics of Western cultures. The rules of love assigned specific roles to men and women. Men were to be knights on white horses, competing for the favors of women. Men became active heroes, rescuers of women, and later breadwinners. Women were to be the judges of men's deeds, the guardians of morality. They also were to act like damsels in distress, passive and dependent creatures in need of rescue.

The importance of these roles and the other rules of love lies in their legacy. As the sociologist Inge Bell (1991) notes, the myth of romantic love serves important functions. First, love is depicted as the great equalizer, the utopia open to everyone. The idea that anybody, no matter of what race, class, religion, age, or physical condition, can be loved complements the American values of equal opportunity and justice for all. The egalitarian ideal of romantic love diverts attention from the great inequalities of wealth and power in America.

In reality, marital happiness is highly correlated with one's class position. The higher up the social class ladder one sits, the greater the chances for a contented relationship. The myth of romantic love serves as a form of social control. When a love relationship breaks up, people involved do not blame the social structure; they tend to blame each other and especially themselves. Blaming the self is a great way to avoid looking at sociological factors related to love's failures, such as class inequality. In this way, the myth of romantic love functions to legitimize social inequality by diverting attention toward self-blame.

Romantic love is a constant theme of mass culture. Romantic love is one of the main reasons for buying all manner of consumer goods. The more insecure one is about being loved, the more open one will be to the appeals of advertising. The messages of most ads emphasize dependency. "You are not lovable for yourself. You need this product if you want to be loved." The media in general are destructive of self-esteem. One of their primary functions is to let us know that by ourselves we will never be "good enough." Nowhere is our inferiority more strongly communicated than in messages about attracting the opposite sex.

The modern-day myth of romantic love also influences gender roles. Warren Farrell (1986) argues that men and women both suffer from sexism. Men view women as sex objects, as we noted in Chapter 3. Women, on the other hand, are socialized to view men as "success objects," desirable for the status and financial rewards they can bring to a relationship. The consequences of these different types of sexism are examined in Box 6-1, excerpted from Farrell's book.

Inge Bell believes that these roles affect men and women in other important ways. Women are still taught to repress their ambitions and assertiveness. To express these qualities is to risk being labeled pushy, or worse. Men are taught to repress the "feminine" side of their personalities, those involving intimacy, expressing feelings (other than anger), and caring. To express these qualities is to risk being labeled a wimp.

Often these repressed feelings and desires are projected onto the opposite sex. As Bell (1991:154–55) relates:

Girls begin to repress their ambitions, while boys repress their emotionality and sociability. Through such repression we alienate a piece of ourselves: that is, push the unacceptable trait so far out of consciousness that we begin to believe we actually don't have the censored capacity any more. But we also feel maimed because a piece of us is missing. When we find a member of the opposite sex who likes us, we are prone to project onto that person our own alienated capacities. The woman feels that she has found a man who is ambitious, aggressive and bold, someone who will protect and shelter her poor helpless self. The male, on the other hand, feels that he has found a woman who is sociable, affectionate and emotionally responsive—qualities he longs for in himself but cannot enjoy directly as part of his own personality. Add to these projections all of the little fears by which we live. Are we lonely for friends? Here is a person who will meet all our needs for sociability. Do we regard ourselves as physically unattractive? Here is someone who

BOX 6-1

GENDER ROLES AND SOCIAL CHARACTER

The male primary fantasy versus the female primary fantasy

Playboy and *Penthouse* outsell all [other] men's magazines. They represent *men's primary fantasy:* access to as many beautiful women as desired without risk of rejection. Women's primary fantasy is reflected in the two best-selling women's magazines: *Better Homes and Gardens* and *Family Circle.* Security and a family.

Female primary fantasy		Male primary fantasy	
Magazine	Circulation*	Magazine	Circulation*
Better Homes and Gardens	8,041,951	*Playboy*	4,209,324
Family Circle	7,193,079	*Penthouse*	3,500,275

*All circulation figures and comparisons are based on listings in *The World Almanac 1985*, whose source is *FAS-FAX* (Schaumburg, Ill.: Audit Bureau of Circulation, 1964). Based on total paid circulation over a six-month period.

Both sexes ideally would like to "have it all": an intellectually and sexually exciting partner who provides security; a partner who is a "10" but who is not self-centered; a partner who offers unconditional love, yet pushes our boundaries; a fulfilling job, yet time with the family; income and plenty of time to spend it; and so on. What distinguishes the sexes are our different fantasies of the most important thing the other sex can provide to help us get what we feel we're missing (the primary fantasy) and our second greatest desire from the other sex (the secondary fantasy). The primary and secondary fantasies represent compromises both sexes make with our hidden "have it all" fantasy.

Source: Farrell, 1986:18–23. Footnotes are omitted.

If checkbook stubs reflect values, the *traditional* female values are the strongest. Romance novels comprise 40 percent of *all* paperback book sales. Six of the eleven top-selling magazines are traditional women's magazines (*Better Homes and Gardens* outsells *Playboy* and *Penthouse* combined). *None* of the eleven top-selling magazines are men's magazines. And none are the "new woman" or "working woman" variety of magazine. The more a magazine sells to women, the less it focuses on working.

The primary fantasy magazines all require their readers to work—to work at the role they must play in order to entice the other sex to fulfill their fantasy. *Family Circle* gives a woman recipes to make it worthwhile for a man to keep her and her family secure; *Playboy* gives a man recipes about how to be successful at making women more interested in having sex with him.

After working with 106,000 women and men from all walks of life, I have found that any medium read or watched almost exclusively by one sex creates a remarkably accurate springboard to that sex's world view. I could examine any of the media, but magazines provide the easiest vehicle to study, given the limitations of the book format. An overview of the second-rank best-selling magazines for each sex gives us a view of the differences between the way women and men approach the achievement of their primary fantasies—or, put another way, their *primary means* to their primary fantasies.

The [next table] shows that the female primary *means* to her primary fantasy is glamour/beauty *and* men. Over 90 percent of ads in women's magazines focus on glamour, fashion and beauty.

The articles are divided between glamour/beauty and men: how to get men, and what to do with them. Next to nothing on careers.

To men, the second rank of best-sellers illustrates *men's primary means* to their primary fantasy: heroism—or performance. If he wants *part* of his primary fantasy (*one* beautiful woman), he must be at least a successful performer. If he wants his entire primary fantasy (access to many), it helps to be a hero. His magazines are *American Legion* (war hero), *Sports Illustrated* (sports hero), *Forbes* (business hero), and *Boy's Life* (the childhood preparation to perform). In the [third] table we see there is no alternative to heroism for a man to reach his *primary* fantasy—many beautiful women—and no alternative to performing to reach a part of his primary fantasy. At least, that is the male perception, reflected by his purchases.

Female primary means to primary fantasy: beauty and men		Male primary means to primary fantasy: being a hero*	
Magazine	Circulation	Magazine	Circulation
Cosmopolitan	3,038,400	American Legion	2,507,338
Glamour	2,275,743	Sports Illustrated	2,448,486
Seventeen	1,688,954	Boy's Life	1,452,201
Teen	1,022,552	Forbes	719,906

*The four male magazines represent the four major categories of being a hero. Riflery magazines sell very well, but they are a bridge between the categories of sports and war (*American Legion*) and are therefore not listed separately.

In the past two decades, with the increase in divorce, the female primary fantasy often came tumbling down. Without a man guaranteeing security and a better home, a "new woman" needed to emerge to supply some for herself. To supply an *alternative* means to her primary fantasy. So during the late sixties and seventies, a new group of magazines, the "new woman" magazines, emerged.

The male reality versus the female reality

As we can see from the circulation figures, the greater the emphasis on independence, equality, and working, the lower the circulation. In all of these "new woman" magazines, what women buy (reflected in the full-page ads that run repeatedly) is remarkably similar to the offerings in the ads in magazines like *Cosmo, Glamour,* and *Seventeen.* They have almost no overlap with the ads in men's magazines. This is important insofar as it reflects the gap between the female and male realities, and the gap between conscious and unconscious messages.

There are more computers, financial services, and large office systems advertised in one issue of *Esquire* than in issues of all the top selling women's magazines combined—including *Working Woman, New Woman, Sex* and *Ms.* And if we substitute *Forbes* or *Fortune* for *Esquire,* the gap is even wider.

Is this because women read both types of magazines? Only 5 percent of *Forbes* subscribers are women—about 35,000. Over 8 *million* women subscribe to *Better Homes and Gardens.* Thirty-five thousand is less than half of one percent of 8 million.

The gap between male and female realities can be seen by looking at other contrasts. There's *Bride's Magazine;* no *Groom Magazine.* No ad in *Sports Illustrated* touts a wedding as "The Most Important Day of Your Life," as *Bride's*

Female alternative means to primary fantasy: new woman		Male alternative means to primary fantasy: none
Magazine	Circulation	
Self	1,091,112	No
New Woman	1,055,589	alternative
Working Woman	605,902	to
Ms.	479,185	hero/performer

does. In *Fortune,* Max Factor is an investment opportunity. In a woman's magazine it's a different type of investment opportunity. In *Forbes* an article on slimming down is subtitled, "A Nifty Way for a Banker to Get Smaller"; slimming down in *Good Housekeeping* means "How I lost 283 Pounds." Even when men and women appear to talk the same language, we mean different things.

Determining whether someone has changed means delving under the surface. Both sexes have made surface changes. Under the surface, the underlying values are remarkably unchanged. For example, fifteen years ago boys wouldn't be caught dead with dolls. Now many boys have dolls. Yet when we look more closely at their dolls, we see most of them have just expanded the repertoire by which boys can either perform or kill. G.I. Joe's gun and tank help him fight "an international paramilitary terrorist force," according to the promotional literature. The He-Man doll is muscle-bound, and Luke Skywalker and Lord Power differ "ever so slightly" from Strawberry Shortcake, who comes replete not with a tank but a thank-you postcard. Blithely citing the extraordinary rise in doll sales for boys ignores how boys are just playing out their traditional role with one more medium—cowboys and Indians have switched turf to Star Wars.

Is the same true for the "new woman"? Women's *situation* has clearly changed in the last two decades. But has *what women want from men* changed? Or is more expected of men, because women feel they are giving more?

Do these questions imply that I think men are the way they are merely because of what women want? No. But if a woman, his parents, his peers, and his boss reward a man for success in ways they are unaware of, he gets a very clear message. The only group *overtly* telling

men, "Stop—we want you to be different" is women. Most women do want men to be different and honestly want to know if their message to men is more mixed than they realize. They are not as concerned about what a man's parents or peers did—they want to know what *they* can do—and whether they have a role in perpetuating problems about which they are complaining. . . .

I'm an independent person . . . ads don't influence me

Examining the articles and ads in women's magazines, as well as romance novels, rock stars, soaps, movies, and *Dynasty,* can prompt the objection, "But ads and popular culture don't influence me." That misses the point: whether or not a woman is influenced by them is not as important as the fact that they reflect her values; they could not exist without her financially supporting them. *Her financial support is her choice and therefore her message,* just as *Playboy* and *Sports Illustrated,* which reflect male values, could not be best-sellers without men's financially supporting them. Women's choices create women's magazines.

It is a mistake to assume that we are not influenced by ads. When I buy a Coke I don't consciously say to myself, "I'm being influenced by ads." But there's a reason I buy Coke more often than "Brand X." At $16,000 per second for some television ads no advertiser can afford to operate only on the conscious level. No advertiser will have a pimple-faced, fat woman selling perfume (even in a scratch-and-sniff ad). If we say *"I don't pay attention to these commercials,"* we play right into the advertiser's hands—by not admitting we would be less likely to buy perfume from a pimple-faced, flabby woman. In the process, we also miss the most fundamental message being sold in almost every ad with a woman selling a product: the power of the thin, beautiful, made-up, young-appearing female. So let's look at what women's purchases say about what women value—the real signals men are hearing from women.

What is the reward for understanding all this? Once the female primary fantasy is understood, women begin to under-stand how men adapt to it. They then gain something far more valuable to men than beauty is: an understanding of men.

Many women are beautiful. An understanding of men—from a man's perspective—is rare. And men? Most men aren't quite sure what "getting in touch with feelings" means. Sometimes they ask, embarrassed, "What feelings am I not in touch with?"

finds us attractive and suddenly we feel beautiful. Thus is generated that first "rush" we take to be "falling in love."

The very suddenness of this rush should warn us. Even a person we have only known for twenty-four hours can induce this high in us. Some even experience "love at first sight." It is obvious that we are not responding to another human being whom we really know—in fact, any number of people will do interchangeably and with equal suddenness. Two years down the road we may look at our former love and wonder what we ever "saw" in him. What is really happening is something inside ourselves. Temporarily, we have put in abeyance all the self-criticism which usually saddens us. Temporarily, we have granted ourselves the freedom to feel new feelings which we usually deny ourselves. We love ourselves because some member of the opposite sex seems to accept us. The more we have deprived ourselves of self-acceptance, the more helpless we are in the grip of this temporary alleviation, and the more desperately we feel we need this new partner.

Thus lovers are, at first at least, role players. During courtship lovers do not know each other as real people. They act in ways that are inauthentic; they have their best feet forward. Each dehumanizes the other by objectifying the partner as a sex object or a success object. Mythical love is largely an alienating condition. As a result, many people end up being disappointed in their mates when their "real" personalities emerge. Sex during courtship dramatically alters one's perceptions of the lover, further mystifying the lover's real nature.

The ultimate dehumanization comes when a love object turns into a possession. Possessiveness is often confused with love but really signals an effort at control. The person who truly loves recognizes that the lover is a separate person, with unique needs and traits. To love genuinely is to strive to meet someone else's needs, in and out of bed.

There are plenty of other consequences left over from the days of knights and damsels. Despite all the professed changes since women's liberation, plenty of women still feel they need rescuing. The problem with trying to rescue someone is that rescuers frequently become victims. They are easily manipulated and taken advantage of because of their overpowering need for recognition and approval. Thus rescuers often feel insignificant and dissatisfied with their lives. In rescuing other people they are really attempting to rescue themselves. If you are a male who harbors fantasies about rescuing women, you might want to ask yourself why you feel this way.

The female counterpart to the rescuer is the reformer. This is the legacy of women's role as the judges of men's deeds. Women who came of age in the 1920s and 1930s were taught that their husbands were their "project." A project is something that has to be worked on and brought to fruition. Many women fall in love conditionally. They believe that they can change what they dislike or want to improve about their men.

One of the great truths is that people's basic personalities do not change very much. Trying to reform people in any but superficial ways is fruitless and dangerous. We resent efforts to reform us because we know we are being judged and criticized. Criticism is destructive of love, because it invites resentment and anger. Critical people are critical of themselves as well. They are usually very controlling, have low self-esteem, and tend to project their own perceived shortcomings onto other people. These people are difficult to live with and even more difficult to love.

Wanting to rescue or reform someone else is in many ways unfair. One important way people learn and acquire wisdom is by making mistakes and experiencing failure. To rescue or reform others is to deny them the opportunity to fail and learn from failure. Instead of worrying about someone else's problems, it is best to change those things about yourself that trouble you, beginning with your own lack of self-esteem. When you feel good about yourself, you will see your own shortcomings in a much different light. A fault will simply become something that is part of your humanity, not your entire being. Other people's faults will become much less bothersome as well. If you expect perfection in others or in yourself, you will continually experience disappointment in both. If you expect imperfection, think of how great you'll feel when things go smoothly. Exercise 6-1 will teach you how to increase your self-esteem.

The great truth here is that to love someone is to accept that person for what he or she is, warts and all. The real question is: Can you stand the other person's shortcomings? If you cannot, then you have no business being involved with that person. All of this underscores the importance of getting to know your prospective mate as well as you can.

So how can you really get to know the people you date? How can you increase your chances of having a satisfying relationship? Self-help experts have recommended several strategies:

1 Wait awhile before you engage in sexual intercourse. Stanton Peele and Archie Brodsky (1978) recommend a two-month period of getting to know each other. If you do not want to wait that long, try to wait at least a few weeks before any sexual contact. Anyone who refuses to wait may be signaling a lack of concern about the partner.

2 There is much evidence that a courtship of at least two years dramatically increases one's chances of happiness in marriage.

3 The chances for a satisfying relationship increase when the partners are sociologically similar (are of the same social class, race and ethnicity, religion, and political ideology) and psychologically opposite (extroverted vs. introverted). It also helps to become friends first, and to have interests and activities in common. It is extremely important that two people learn to have fun together.

Another important variable in relationships is power. Power in a relationship is the ability to make decisions about the relationship, including:

• Where you will live.
• Finances.
• Which doctors, dentists, attorneys, tax preparers, and other professionals you will consult.
• In what social activities you will engage together. (Blood & Wolfe, 1968:56)

Interpersonal power is complex. If one partner insists that the other make certain decisions, for example, which one has the power? (It's probably the one who does the insisting.) There is evidence of sociological patterns of power in relationships. A couple's decisions tend to be made either primarily by the man, primarily by the woman, or jointly.

Blood and Wolfe (1968) and Centers and colleagues (1971) reveal that these patterns are associated to some extent with ethnicity. Oriental-American couples are among the most male-dominated, and African American couples are among the most wife-dominated (Centers et al., 1971). Most other ethnic groups tend toward either male domination or the democratic model.

Most crucial, power in a relationship is related to satisfaction within the relationship. Respondents in the study by Richard Centers and his colleagues indicate that a democratic or male-dominated power structure is the most satisfying, and a female-dominated relationship is the least contented.

People learn about power in relationships largely from their parents and other family members. If you did not like the way your parents relate to each other or to you, it will take some deliberate effort on your part to change such patterns within yourself. Therapy with a qualified social worker or psychologist may be useful in such an undertaking.

Abigail Trafford (1984) argues that relationships end when one of the partners wants to change the distribution of power. Power relationships are usually not discussed; they are part of what Trafford terms a "subterranean" (hidden) contract concerning which partner is to be dominant. Now you can see how important it is to discuss issues of decision making early in a relationship. As you have probably concluded, relationships are complicated matters, and need to be approached with patience and commitment.

Many excellent works are available about how to meet people and establish a satisfying relationship; some of them are listed at the end of this chapter.

SEX, LOVE, AND SOCIAL CHARACTER

One of the most alienating aspects of American culture is the values attached to sex and sexual behavior. Americans are the unfortunate heirs of the Puritan and Victorian belief that sex is not to be enjoyed, that it is sinful unless its purpose is reproduction. It is certainly not to be discussed in public, and often it is not discussed in private either. The upshot is one of America's great cultural contradictions.

Because sexuality was repressed for so long in America, really until the 1960s, sex has taken on exaggerated importance. Sex is also steeped in myth. As Vern and Bonnie Bullough (1977) report:

• Graham crackers were invented to keep little boys from masturbating. It was thought that a cracker with less sugar than cookies would keep boys from becoming sexually excited.

• During much of the nineteenth century, it was possible to order antimasturbation devices through the mail. One device was a circular arrangement of sharp metal prongs attached to a belt. The belt was tied around the waist and the device slipped over the penis. This torture, it was thought, would discourage boys from having erections. No doubt it did.

• Menstruation was considered to be something of a temporary mental illness. It was thought that women should not be allowed to attend college because they were incapable of learning during their menses. It was also argued that women should not be allowed to hold public office because their decision-making processes were totally irrational when they were menstruating. This "raging hormone" theory overlooked the fact that men's hormone levels also vary over the course of a month.

These and many other myths have caused serious social problems. Venereal diseases cause suffering and deaths that could be prevented but for religious conservatives' view that sexually transmitted diseases are punishment for sin, not public health issues. AIDS was initially described as God's punishment of homosexuals. When heterosexuals began to contract it, such criticisms faded. Parents' refusal to discuss sex with their children has also contributed to the climbing rate of pregnancy among unmarried teens.

America is a nation of voyeurs. Americans love to watch sexual stimuli.

They are constantly titillated by seductive ads and sexual portrayals in movies and on television. The repression of sex and sexuality has produced an obsessive curiosity about sex, yet sexual behavior is often embarrassingly inept. Over half of the couples in America report that their relationship is marred by a sexual dysfunction, principally premature ejaculation in men and the inability to achieve orgasm in women.

You can learn some important lessons from this sordid history of sexual repression. One of the most destructive myths is that a large sex organ is required for sexual success and satisfaction. In fact, the size of the penis is totally unrelated to orgasm in women. In any case, most penises are about the same size once they are erect.

The most important sex organ you have is your brain. Your attitude toward sex and your sensuality has more to do with sexual satisfaction than any physical attribute. Sex is most satisfying when it is an expression of intimacy between two people who care about pleasing each other as well as themselves. To be truly enjoyable, sexual intercourse must be devoid of the inauthenticity and dehumanization so common in American life.

The mass media use sex as a means to an end, and manipulative people use it the same way in private life. Consider for a moment the sexual slang terms you know. To be "screwed" or "fucked" doesn't just mean to have sex. These words also mean to be taken advantage of, exploited, victimized. Often they mean to have your money or property stolen. These meanings speak volumes concerning America's distrust of sex and its consequences.

You can observe these alienating aspects of sex any day of the week. Simply go to a bar with a reputation as a "meat market" (another dehumanizing term). Sex that begins with a pickup in a bar is usually short-lived (a "one-night stand") and usually very alienating. This is not the stuff of which stable relationships are made. And in the age of AIDS, impersonal sex can kill you.

Sexual alienation almost always involves dehumanization. Many men wish only to "score," and actively keep tabs on how many women they have seduced. Such men usually refer to women in nonhuman terms ("broad," "chick," "pussy," and other terms with which you are no doubt familiar). They use these dehumanizing terms because they are insecure around women, and labeling them as less than human makes them seem less threatening. Women seem threatening because men, as initiators of sexual contact, always risk and fear being rejected. This dehumanization is also a major cause of the widespread sexual harassment of women in American society. It is no accident that among the occupations with the highest rates of harassment of women are those that are traditionally male-dominated, especially medicine, law, and law enforcement (Richman et al., 1993). Men resent intrusion by the people they fear into their previously private enclaves, and harassment becomes a form of retaliation. The truth is that everyone rejects and everyone is rejected somewhere along the relationship trail. Rejection is part of life, and it can lead to real growth and maturity if it is properly perceived.

Sex, then, is no mere physical act. It is the most intimate of experiences, one that can dramatically affect your self-esteem. It is therefore an excellent idea to approach sex with the following points in mind:

1 Be honest about how you feel about sex. Do not let anyone talk you into bed with promises or compliments. If you do not trust what is going on, listen to your feelings. They are the best guide to decision making. The great problem with intuition is not that women seem to have more of it than men but that more people do not listen to it.

2 Love is not about words or sex. It's about action designed to meet one's own needs and the needs of another person. It is important to know your preferences in regard to arousal and the sex act itself. Know what you like and what you do not want.

3 The great contradiction of sexual relations is that women are supposed to express their feelings everywhere except in bed, and men are supposed to be stoic everywhere except in bed (Rubin, 1976). This often makes sexual communication difficult, especially for women. This is why trust is such an important ingredient of intimacy.

4 Sex and relationships in general need to be fun to be satisfying. Sex as fun resembles a dance. It's most enjoyable when feelings of freedom, experimentation, and anticipation are involved. If sex is not fun, it is often perceived as work, as an obligation, or as part of some kind of deal. This makes sex an alienating and emotionally empty experience.

Ironically, almost everything I have just said about sex is true of work as well.

USING SOCIOTHERAPY: WORK

Work alienation is extremely widespread in America. As we saw in Chapter 1, only about 10 percent of the workforce say they really enjoy their jobs. Some reasons for this situation are sociological. Work in America is alienating in part because most people lack the freedom to make decisions about their work. Assembly-line jobs are notoriously monotonous and dull—not only in a Ford plant but in McDonald's as well. There is much evidence indicating that the more control one has over one's work, the more satisfying work is.

Go into any bookstore and you will find a hundred self-help books on relationships for every book about a satisfying career. Most of the books on work are about how to find employment or advance up the career ladder, not about enjoying work. Many people assume that work is simply a means to an end.

They will put up with all sorts of poor conditions if the pay and benefits (extrinsic rewards) are good. The idea that work needs to be intrinsically satisfying is foreign to a great many people.

There is evidence that unsatisfying work can make people mentally ill. Douglas La Bier (1986), a psychiatrist in Washington, D.C., found that many of his clients had exhibited no neurotic symptoms until they had gone to work in the oppressive Washington bureaucracy. La Bier studied people in various government departments and found that the vast majority were successful at their jobs but that the emotional price of their success was often very high. "I find that adaptation to the values, behavior, and mentality best suited for successful career development has a hidden down side that takes the form of a range of conflicts . . . [including] anxiety, rebelliousness, chronic indecisiveness, diminished productiveness, dissatisfaction, . . . guilt, and various unexplained physical symptoms" (70–71). The long hours and devotion to career produced a feeling of inner emptiness, a spiritual vacuum, one of the most prominent symptoms of dehumanization. One has only to look at the number of disgruntled postal employees who have shot up post offices around the nation in the last few years to appreciate the stress that unhealthful working conditions can cause.

So how do you find work that is intrinsically pleasing? Satisfying work begins with knowing what you enjoy. That is one reason why, if you are not sure what career you would like to pursue, a liberal arts education is an excellent idea. It gives you a chance to shop around and find out what interests you.

It also helps to get experience in real work settings. Many college majors allow or require internships or research projects at work sites. These are excellent opportunities to learn about actual working routines and conditions.

Inge Bell (1991) has written an excellent discussion for college students concerning the promise and pitfalls of work in America. Many college students view an education as a ticket to the middle class. Bell makes an interesting distinction between career and work based on the idea of craft.

A *career* is an all-consuming way of life based on a key value associated with the American dream; namely, competitive ambition. People whose lives are dominated by their careers usually have little free time for family life and related activities. The emotional ties they form at work override those of family and personal life. Careerists are often incapable of enjoying the company of other people unless the conversation centers on office gossip. Many people's obsession with their careers is a sad search for approval that grows out of feelings of inferiority and being unloved. Unfortunately, obsession with a career contributes to many divorces.

Careerism is also a cause of another major social problem: white-collar and corporate crime. Michael McCoby (1970) found that the higher executives rise, the more their careers dominate their lives. Their lofty positions made these men incapable of ordinary morality or a loving family life. They will do anything to get ahead and stay ahead. When career executives retire and no longer receive the attention of underlings and co-workers, the experience is traumatic. Retirement becomes a time of loneliness and decay.

What of the rewards brought by a successful career? Bell (1991:135–56) points out that much of the American dream is about status; money and possessions are merely the ways we keep score.

> Americans often accuse themselves of being too materialistic and it is certainly true that we spend enormous amounts of energy acquiring material possessions. But, in reality, most of these possessions are coveted, not for the physical gratification they give, but for the prestige they impart. An expensive house, a Mercedes-Benz, a fur coat are primarily symbols of success. Traditionally, it has been the male's success which has been symbolized, while the female is used as a sort of Christmas tree on which the male can hang the various baubles which signify his rank.
>
> Far from enjoying these goods directly, we are a culture which really despises the sensual pleasures which material goods offer. We are heirs to the Victorian Puritans. The executive who has a business meeting in an expensive restaurant is too busy making a deal to really taste the food. If his position merits an expensive call girl at the end of the day, he is probably too tired to make more than motions in her direction. It is success that we love, not good sex or beautiful objects or a wonderful scene of nature or a delicious meal. We aren't materialists at all. There is something otherworldly in our disregard of the concrete reality around us. A minister who serves the executives of the automobile industry in Detroit says, "These men are monks—monks who've traded in their prayerbooks for a production line." We are so lost in symbolism that, in the words of Alan Watts, "We eat the menu and miss the meal." Businessmen, alas, seldom dance by the light of the moon.

The disease of careerism begins in college. It is part of the great American roller-coaster ride, a series of upward and downward movements that are repeated endlessly. Thus you enter college, as you did high school, as a freshman and work your way up to senior status. If you go on to graduate school, you again begin at the bottom and work your way to the top. After graduate training, you begin at the bottom again in your career. This never-ending roller coaster can create endless stress and pressure for people who hope to win the rat race.

The pressure begins in childhood when parents ask (or tell) their children what they want to "be" when they grow up. It is related to two American middle-class pathologies: conditional love and perfectionism. Too many parents withhold approval and love until their children are "successful." To be successful they must get good grades in school and college and advance steadily in their work. Some controlling parents never give their children the approval they strive for. No matter how much one accomplishes, there is always something more one could do. This is a game no child can win. The only way to keep one's sanity is not to play at all. Realize that you do not need your parents' approval to reach your full potential and be happy.

Perfectionism, the idea that one has to be perfect at everything one does, is a dangerous pathology, born of the low self-esteem caused by conditional love. Perfectionists believe that they will be loved once their work becomes flawless. Perfectionism is really about not loving yourself, putting yourself and other people down for being less than perfect. People treat other people the way they treat themselves. Thus perfectionists are critical of both themselves and others, and find it difficult to love themselves and anyone else. Perfectionists also tend to be very lonely because friendship and love require us to accept people as they are, human frailties and all.

There is a satisfying solution to the problem of careerism, and all it requires is a change in outlook. Rather than focus exclusively on the material (extrinsic) rewards associated with a career, emphasize the internal (intrinsic) rewards that come with enjoyment of the process of work. An important part of the work process is the concept of craft, of doing a job well. Not perfectly—we're not going to fall into that trap—but well. A craft orientation helps build self-esteem because it involves pride in what one does and the way one does it. It can also make work enjoyable because it lends itself to the view of work as fun, as a game whose rules you can make up as you go along.

Take writing, for example. Most writers, including this one, like to write their thoughts down but detest editing or revising what they have written. A speaker I once heard expressed this idea well when he said that he hated writing but loved having written. Then one day I read two books on how to improve one's writing. I found a way to make a game out of rewriting. Most people's writings suffer from unneeded words. Sentences in the passive voice are especially wordy. When I began to revise my work by pretending each removed word was a word "saved" (not wasted), revision became a search for brevity. And it became more fun. I also found I "saved" more words when I set my writing aside for several days after finishing my first draft. Writing has become a game, and a somewhat therapeutic one at that.

Inge Bell (1991:140–41) has beautifully described the idea of craft.

> Craftsmen are people who love their work for its own sake. Their rewards are "intrinsic" rather than "extrinsic," that is, the process of work is directly rewarding to them. They care very little for higher salaries or more prestigious positions. They may even refuse these if it would change the nature of their work. You can find the parallel in your schoolwork. The "intrinsic" reward comes to you when you just plain enjoy an assigned book or find yourself truly fascinated by a research project. The "extrinsic" reward is the grade. The two types of rewards compete for your attention. If you care too much about the grade, you may be too tense to ever feel in-

trinsic pleasure from your studies. If, on the other hand, you love doing a piece of work, it may not matter nearly as much to you how your professor ranks it. Intrinsic rewards are a sort of pay-as-you-go proposition: The fun is in the process. Focusing on extrinsic rewards means focusing only at that point in the very end where you collect your grade, or later, your money or promotion. This empties out the process and concentrates all the meaning at a point outside the process.

Satisfying work and satisfying relationships have in common the need for self-approval.

As important as love and work are in daily life, they cannot be separated from the environment in which they take place. You are much more than a lover and a worker. You are also an educated citizen of a democracy that is experiencing numerous crises. What goes on in this interdependent world eventually affects all of us. It is important to use your sociological imagination to change society for the better.

WORKING FOR SOCIAL CHANGE

There is ample evidence that societal change and self-help can go hand in hand. Working for social change allows one to develop emotional bonds and a sense of community. Emotional ties are important ingredients in individual mental health as well as in effective social movements. Thus, even if you do not become a professional researcher, a wish to improve your mental health and preserve a democratic way of life is an excellent reason to cultivate a sociological imagination. One of the solutions to micro and macro problems may be to have classes in self-esteem and the sociological imagination in secondary schools. Such courses might also cover relationship skills, family planning, drug education, and achieving a sense of spirituality. Thus such courses could not only help to resolve serious social problems but teach students how to improve the quality of their lives.

Working for positive social change involves two elements: (1) a set of goals toward which one strives and (2) a prescribed set of means for reaching those goals. The goals prescribed here are ends that follow logically from the institutional contradictions that cause social problems. That is, if the social structure is the cause of fundamental problems, then only basic changes in that structure will get at the causes of those problems. At first glance, then, these suggestions may seem "radical" and utopian. In view of the complexity of the American crisis, however, these proposals are the ones that follow most logically from our analysis of America's problems and their causes.

1 Reorganize large corporations to meet human needs. Multinational corporations are primary barriers to progressive change. They know no local or national loyalties, and are unconcerned with their role in causing inflation,

This antiwar demonstration in the 1960s outside the doors of the Pentagon illustrates several important aspects of social change. First, progressive change is almost always the result of the actions of groups, not lone individual heroes. Second, most positive political change in American history has been enacted only after protracted struggle on the part of ordinary people exercising their rights under the U.S. Constitution. Third, the myth of individualism which continues to permeate American society is dangerous in an age dominated by mass bureaucracies. Finally, and most important, enough democracy remains in America to effect change if people will only organize and act, yet less than 10 percent of the population ever join progressive social movements. (UPI/Bettmann)

unemployment, pollution, and the perpetuation of gross inequalities—inequalities that are inherently corrupting of democracy. One of the best ways to extend democracy and community responsibility to corporations is to have the workers invest their pension funds in them until they own a majority of the company's stock. This would not only ensure worker ownership and control but strip away the layers of secrecy from which so much corporate scandal grows. Worker-owned companies are much less likely to experience strikes and the problems that accompany worker alienation, especially drug abuse, absenteeism, and sabotage.

2 Reduce the size of the government. The federal government accounts for so much of the gross national product (about one-third) and so many jobs (25 percent of the workforce) that this goal seems like a political and economic impossibility. In other modern democracies government plays a positive role by operating basic utilities and mass transit systems and by regulating business activity. It stimulates the economy in times of recession and cools it off in times of inflation through temporary taxation. For most Americans, the greatest problems represented by government are deficit spending, high taxes, unfair welfare programs for the rich as well as the poor, and gridlock. The system now in place has degenerated into government by special (business) interests, which finance politicians' reelection campaigns and get the legislation they want in return. Overcoming these problems is a complex task, but it is not impossible.

The writers of the U.S. Constitution never dreamed of a class of professional politicians who made officeholding their lifework. The Constitution says nothing about political parties. Our current pathologies suggest the need for (*a*) campaign finance reform (federally financed congressional elections), (*b*) term limitations for senators and representatives, and (*c*) the abolition of subsidies for corporations and for able-bodied adults. Perhaps the best way to reduce the debt and the deficit is to pare down all possible expenditures and to increase government receipts without raising the taxes of working people.

3 Ensure full employment. This goal may require new tax incentives for employee-owned corporations to expand factories and jobs here in the United States. It may also require making government the employer of last resort if the corporate sector does not make enough jobs available. There is no question that government is capable of playing such a role, as Franklin D. Roosevelt's New Deal demonstrated with the Works Progress Administration (WPA), Civilian Conservation Corps (CCC), and similar programs. Moreover, attached to every job ought to be cradle-to-grave benefits: health and dental insurance, life insurance, family leave, and day care for children of employees. Day-care centers go back at least as far as World War II in America, and there is no reason such facilities at job sites could not experience a rebirth. Why not finance these benefits through a combination of government sponsorship, employer contribution, and employee payroll deduction? The vast majority of other industrial democracies already sponsor such programs as paid family leave and national health care. Are Americans any less worthy than citizens of other democracies?

Such programs could also be financed by increases in the taxes paid by those Americans who earn the highest incomes and own the most wealth. The richest 2.5 million Americans now earn more than the poorest 100 million. Clearly this situation is incompatible with democracy in a nation where money buys access and influence. The framers of the Constitution assumed that this would be a middle-class society, and Thomas Jefferson himself warned that if the United States became an urban manufacturing nation, class conflict would follow, for a few people would grow rich while many sank into poverty. "He believed that almost all Americans should continue farming to avert social ills, class distinctions, and social conflict" (Etzkowitz, 1980:3). Jefferson, of course, was writing decades before Karl Marx was born. As the historian Charles A. Beard once noted, one does not have to be a Marxist to know that wealth and power go hand and hand.

How much to limit income and wealth (by inheritance taxes) must be decided by democratic means (perhaps a national referendum or initiative). The late Sidney Lens (1977) believed that at some level, a 100 percent inheritance tax ought to be imposed. Americans have always believed in the unlimited accumulation of wealth. It is part of the American dream, and part of our conception of individualism. Americans have never embraced the idea that a few ought to sacrifice a little for the benefit of all. Would Americans' motivation be stifled if their wealth were limited to $100 million? To $1 billion? For 98 percent of the population, such a limitation would be of no consequence. A national debate on such limits ought to begin soon.

4 Institute a program of social reconstruction. Trillions of dollars' worth of streets, highways, and bridges are in disrepair. Millions of families cannot find housing they can afford. The United States needs better schools and smaller classes, more doctors (and fewer specialists), more nurses and teachers, more computers in schools and in homes, more police and firefighters, more libraries, more drug-treatment facilities (among many other things). A domestic Marshall Plan, similar to the one that rehabilitated European nations after World War II, does not seem unreasonable.

The question is, of course, how to pay for these things. We must reduce spending on weapons systems drastically and convert our economy to meet civilian needs. Many corporations can convert their plants to the manufacture of mass transit systems or prefabricated housing units, or the development of technology.

5 Extend political democracy. Economic democracy is not our only need. Government suffers from concentrations of power. Secretive organizations have led the nation into several wars without submitting the actions to a vote in Congress, as the Constitution requires. This is proof enough of democracy's erosion in America. Many proposals have been offered for extending democracy in America. Michael Lerner (1973) has advocated extensive use of legislative initiatives (proposals for laws or for changes in existing laws that appear on ballots after the proper number of signatures have been collected on petitions; voters then approve or reject the proposals at the next general election). Lerner also advocates more extensive use of the recall, the procedure by which voters can vote a politician out of office.

One of Lerner's more provocative ideas is the use of television to extend democracy. Voters would express their preferences through devices attached to their television sets. They would vote after an electronic "town meeting" at which the issue in question was debated. Representatives would take the results of the vote into consideration in drafting and approving legislation.

Lerner's ideas are not the last word on how to expand democracy in America. The need to do so, however, remains paramount.

6 Tailor our foreign policy to the fact that we live in an interdependent world. Whatever happens elsewhere is a matter of concern here. The United States has political and economic relations and commitments everywhere, so our true interests lie in promoting peace, democracy, and prosperity everywhere.

The United States is only one nation among nearly 150 nations, but we can do more than we are doing now. One valuable policy the United States could develop is to encourage as many Third World nations as possible to coalesce into common-market trading partners. Such arrangements can serve indirectly to promote freedom of travel and other human rights. The arrangement has worked so well in Europe that much of that continent is on the verge of forming a united economic superpower, complete with multiple citizenship privileges, a common currency, and many additional advantages.

In view of the global population and environmental crises, Americans must organize for nonviolent action to oppose corporate and governmental policies that are devastating the environment in their shortsighted concern for profit.

HISTORY MAKING IN A CHANGING AGE

The reforms outlined here are not utopian; they are essential for the existence of a democratic society. If you look at the history of progressive social change in America, you soon discover a central principle. All of the progressive reforms of the nineteenth and twentieth centuries—the abolition of slavery, extension of the right to vote to women, the eight-hour workday, the right to collective bargaining, the Civil Rights acts, the Voting Rights Act, and many other reforms—came only after protracted struggles by people acting in concert. People came together to raise the nation's consciousness by their marches and demonstrations and other persuasive actions. Despite American folklore's emphasis on individual heroes, it is collectivities that produce progressive social change. These movements bring together people who share a genuine concern for one another's well-being and rights. This is what Americans call "teamwork." Collective action, then, is hardly an un-American notion. If you wish to extend democratic life in this society, you must be willing to work for worthy causes—to join and be active in democratic groups and movements. The need to work for social change has rarely been greater, and the number of groups looking for dedicated volunteers and paid employees is astounding. Pick a cause: helping the poor, improving the environment, extending human rights here and overseas, ending hunger and malnutrition, gun control, befriending parentless children, world peace. The list is almost limitless. Such lists appear in nearly every issue of the *UTNE Reader.* Experience in such organizations is invaluable in developing a sociological imagination.

To work for social change is also to stay informed about the issues of the day. One of the assumptions of the framers of the Constitution was that American citizens would take an active interest in public issues, would stay informed and engage in ongoing public debate. Our democracy has degenerated into a place where ten-second sound bites and meaningless political slogans have nearly replaced serious debate on complex issues.

REFERENCES

Bell, Inge. 1991. *This Book Is Not Required.* 2d ed. Fort Bragg, Calif.: Small Press.

Blood, Robert, and Donald Wolfe. 1968. "The Power to Make Decisions." In *Sociological Analysis: An Empirical Approach Through Replication,* ed. Murray Strauss and Joel Nelson, pp. 54–63. New York: Harper & Row.

Bullough, Vern, and Bonnie Bullough. 1977. *Sin, Sickness, and Sanity: A History of Sexual Attitudes.* New York: Garland.

Center, Richard, et al. 1971. "Conjugal Power Structure: A Re-examination." *American Sociological Review* 36 (April): 264–78.

Etzkowitz, Henry, ed. 1980. *Is America Possible?* 2d ed. St. Paul: West.

Farrell, Warren. 1986. *Why Men Are the Way They Are.* New York: McGraw-Hill.

La Bier, Douglas. 1986. *Modern Madness: The Emotional Fallout of Success.* Reading, Mass.: Addison-Wesley.

Lens, Sidney. 1977. *The Promise and Pitfalls of Revolution.* Philadelphia: Pilgrim Press.

Lerner, Michael. 1973. *The New Socialist Revolution.* New York: Delacorte.

Loudin, J. 1982. *The Hoax of Romance.* Englewood Cliffs, N.J.: Prentice-Hall.

McCoby, Michael. 1970. *The Gamesman.* New York: Simon & Schuster.

McKay, Mathew, and Patrick Fanning. 1987. *Self-Esteem.* New York: St. Martin's Press.

Peele, Stanton, and Archie Brodsky. 1978. *Love and Addiction.* New York: Taplinger.

Richman, Judith, et al. 1993. "Workplace Abusive Experiences and Problem Drinking Among Physicians: Broadening the Stress/Alienation Paradigm." Paper presented at the 1993 meeting of the American Sociological Association.

Rubin, Lillian Breslow. 1976. *Worlds of Pain: Life in the Working-Class Family.* New York: Basic Books.

Tannen, Deborah. 1990. *You Just Don't Understand.* New York: Morrow.

Trafford, Abigail. 1984. *Crazy Time.* New York: Bantam.

Webb, M. N. 1992. "Pushing Through to the Top." *Working Woman* 17 (June): 57–60.

EXERCISE 6-1. DEVELOPING SELF-ESTEEM

Building self-esteem is one of the most important things you will ever do for yourself and for those you love. As a beginning, try this exercise. Self-esteem comes in part from confidence that you do some things well. No one does everything well, but this exercise is about finding those things you enjoy doing and feel confident about. Circle those things you believe are your competencies and positive attributes:

1   Your personality. Are you:
   (a) kind, generous, and compassionate?
   (b) a good conversationalist?
   (c) good at making friends?
   (d) good at hosting parties?
2   Your abilities. Are you:
   (a) good at knitting, sewing, or quilting?
   (b) mechanically inclined?
   (c) skilled at woodworking or some other craft?
   (d) a skilled cook?
   (e) able to handle money well, good at saving and investing?
3   Your interests and intellect. Are you:
   (a) musically inclined?
   (b) a good student?
   (c) a good athlete, hunter, angler, or outdoorsperson?
   (d) a gardener?
   (e) good at public speaking?
   (f) a capable teacher?
   (g) a good writer?

Obviously there are many ways to be a competent person. All of them are highly regarded by some people. Deciding which of these activities you feel good about is the beginning of self-esteem.

Other important elements of self-esteem are the ability to overcome the negative messages you give yourself and to handle criticism. The best book I know about these matters is Mathew McKay and Patrick Fanning's *Self-Esteem* (1987). This inexpensive paperback contains valuable insights, interesting discussions, and many exercises designed to deal with negative feelings.

EXERCISE 6-2. HOW TO SELECT A MATE

Many people are confused about what sort of person they'd like for a mate. This confusion frequently stems from previous unsatisfactory relationships. Past dissatisfactions often make people much more aware of what they do not want than of what they do want. People with low self-esteem usually feel they have very little right to ask for anything special in the way of a mate, and frequently settle for anything that comes their way, even if they don't particularly like the person. This is a great mistake; it leads to repression of feelings and a failed relationship down the road.

One way for you to begin to develop these all-important preferences is to recognize your own needs. Try the following exercise. I developed it years ago, and my students still find it valuable and enjoyable.

Take a piece of lined notebook paper and draw a line down the middle of it to create two columns. Label the left-hand column "Physical qualities" and the right-hand column "Personality/values." In the "Physical qualities" column list your decisions about the following attributes and habits:

1   *Height, weight, and hair and eye color.* Think about your preferences here. Are any or all of these things important to you? Do you want your mate to be taller or shorter than you are? Do you strongly prefer that your mate be of the same race or ethnicity?
2   *Habits.*
   (a) Smoking and drinking: Are there any habits that you cannot tolerate? For example, I am allergic to cigarette smoke and alcohol. I cannot tolerate either one of these habits. It is also true that smokers and drinkers tend to socialize with people of similar habits. Thus choosing people with certain habits may also influence the kind of social life you lead.

(b) Other behaviors: Are there additional habits and everyday behaviors you find intolerable, or preferable? Do snoring, loud chewing, casual dress, sniffling, or numerous other habits irritate you? Think of any behaviors that are difficult for you to tolerate and list them. If you are attracted to someone who has any of these habits, it is best to discuss them as early as possible in your relationship.

Now go to the "Personality/values" column. Here address the following issues:

1 Personality traits.
   (a) Interests: It is crucial that couples enjoy doing things together. List a few of your favorite activities you'd like to share with your mate. You might name movies, books, concerts, sporting events, plays, museums, shopping, lectures, conferences, parties, and watching television. How about such outdoor activities as walking, hiking, camping, picnicking, golf, fishing, team sports, exercising? Most people like at least some of these activities.
   (b) Energy level: Are you an energetic person who likes lots of outdoor exercise and recreation? Are you easygoing, preferring to spend your time in such moderate activities as walking and shopping? Compatible energy levels are important if a couple are going to spend any significant amount of time together. Decide where you fit in on this issue and what sort of mate you want.
   (c) Values: Here you must decide how important such things as religion, politics, and child-rearing practices are to you. Can you stand someone who is not religious, or who is very religious? What about political orientation, or the lack of it? What about spending a lot of time (or very little time) with your family, or with your mate's family? How important is it to you to be a member of a close-knit family? Many of these preferences will, of course, emerge from the experiences you and your mate have together. This exercise is about your ideals. They will change in time, but it is important to know what they are now.
   (d) Power. Do you want a relationship that is male-dominated, egalitarian, or female-dominated? What about housework? Many men claim they will gladly share household chores, but frequently do not. How important is this to you? Who would you like to handle the finances—bill paying, saving, and investments? Then there are all those decisions about where you would like to live (house vs. apartment or condo).

All of these preferences can be expressed and learned only with good, clear communication. This is often difficult because men and women express themselves differently. Men tend to believe women want them to take action about a problem. Women complain that men do not listen to them. The two are often like ships that pass in the night when it comes to communicating (Tannen, 1990). If you and your partner have problems perceiving each other's messages, some counseling may be useful.

Remember, you are a human being with the same wants and needs as most other people. You are entitled to get what you want in a relationship. As for your list of ideal attributes, there is probably no person on earth who will match your list completely. In the real world, you will be lucky to find someone with a few of the traits that are most important to you. Your preferences will probably change with age and experience, so this is a good thing. The more flexible you are about all but the most crucial of these matters, the more likely you will be to meet many people who can meet your basic needs. Good luck!

If you would like to learn more about people's mate preferences, try writing a term paper on mate selection among Americans. The social psychology literature is replete with such studies.

SUGGESTED READINGS

Bell, Inge. 1991. *This Book Is Not Required.* Fort Bragg, Calif.: Small Press. This wise and readable book is a first-rate sociological self-help work written with humanistic concern.

Bullough, Vern, and Bonnie Bullough. 1977. *Sin, Sickness, and Sanity: A History of Sexual Attitudes.* New York: Garland. This is a fascinating sociological study of sexual repression in Western civilization and its horrible consequences.

Loudin, J. 1982. *The Hoax of Romance.* Englewood Cliffs, N.J.: Prentice-Hall. This is a beautifully written introduction to the history and pathologies of romantic love in Western culture.

Tannahill, Raye. 1990. *Sex in History.* London: Cardinal. This is an interesting history of sexual behavior in Western societies. Many of the facts detailed here will shock you. During the Middle Ages, for example, there were some 7000 prostitutes in Rome to serve priests.

INDEX